THE
FLOATING ADMIRAL

BY CERTAIN MEMBERS OF
THE DETECTION CLUB

G. K. Chesterton
Canon Victor L. Whitechurch
G. D. H. and M. Cole
Henry Wade
Agatha Christie
John Rhode
Milward Kennedy
Dorothy L. Sayers
Ronald A. Knox
Freeman Wills Crofts
Edgar Jepson
Clemence Dane
Anthony Berkley

HARPER

HARPER

An imprint of HarperCollins*Publishers*
77–85 Fulham Palace Road
Hammersmith, London W6 8JB
www.harpercollins.co.uk

This 80th anniversary edition published in 2011
1

First published in Great Britain by
Hodder & Stoughton 1931

ISBN 978-0-00-741446-8

Printed and bound in Great Britain by
Clays Ltd, St Ives plc

Find out more about HarperCollins and the environment at
www.harpercollins.co.uk/green

FOREWORD

By Simon Brett

PRESIDENT OF THE DETECTION CLUB 2001—

IT is appropriate that the origins of the Detection Club are shrouded in mystery. No official archives for the organisation have ever been kept and so its history has to be pieced together from the memoirs, correspondence, hints and recollections of its members. One reason for this incomplete record may be that the Club originally prided itself on being a kind of secret society, with rituals known only to its initiates. In the days of the internet, however, such a level of security is impossible. Indeed, an extract from the Detection Club's most secret rite, the Initiation of New Members, is readily accessible on Wikipedia.

So the Club's history is, at the best, conjectural. One authority declares that it was founded in 1932 with 26 members, but this assertion is somewhat weakened by the fact that a letter was published in the *Times Literary Supplement* in 1930 and signed by "members of the Detection Club". And the serials *The Scoop* and *Behind the Screen* appeared in *The Listener* respectively in 1930 and 1931. They were written by multiple authors, including Agatha Christie, Dorothy L. Sayers, E. C. Bentley and Anthony Berkeley, under the name of the Detection Club, as was this work, *The Floating Admiral*, whose copyright notice on the first edition reads: "The Detection Club 1931".

So a more likely prehistory of the Club was that round about 1928 Anthony Berkeley Cox (who only used his first two names on his books) and other detective writers started to meet for informal dinners, which then became more established into the rituals of a Club. According to some sources, G. K. Chesterton was appointed the first President—though sometimes referred to as "Leader"—in 1930. Mind you, other authorities say that he didn't take over the Presidential mantle until 1932. Even the Detection Club itself is inconsistent about the date. On its headed notepaper is stated that Chesterton's reign began in 1932, whereas in the List of Members it says 1930. So you can really take your pick.

What is certain, however, is that, on 11 March 1932 the "Constitution and Rules of the Detection Club" were adopted. The opening section of this document reads: "The Detection Club is instituted for the association of writers of detective-novels and for promoting and continuing a mutual interest and fellowship between them." Members had to fulfil "the following condition: That he or she has written at least two detective-novels of admitted merit or (in exceptional cases) one such novel; it being understood that the term 'detective-novel' does not include adventure-stories or 'thrillers' or stories in which the detection is not the main interest, and that it is a demerit in a detective-novel if the author does not 'play fair by the reader'."

In this 1932 Constitution, the Ordinary Meetings of the Club should be "not fewer than four in the year", so things haven't changed that much. In 2010—and for many years before that— the Detection Club met three times.

What has changed is the criterion of admissibility for potential candidates. With the great spread of crime fiction's range, the qualification has been extended way beyond the traditional whodunit (which is just as well, because very few people nowadays write traditional whodunits). The current membership certainly includes writers of "adventure-stories or 'thrillers' or stories in which the detection is not the main interest", as well as practitioners of the historical, legal, forensic, psychopathological and other developing subgenres. Crime fiction is a much broader church now than it was in the 1920s and 1930s, and the Detection Club reflects that.

Some would argue that contemporary mysteries are much more varied and frequently better written than the offerings of that so-called "Golden Age". They are certainly more psychologically credible than many of the works produced at that time. They are also more serious, sometimes even to the point of taking themselves too seriously. In crime fiction, *noir* is the new black.

Most of these differences could be seen as improvements, but the one thing that has been lost with the passage of time is the sense of *fun* that used to be associated with crime fiction. In her introduction to *The Floating Admiral*, Dorothy L. Sayers' description of the collaborative exercise is: "the detection game as played out on paper by certain members of the Detection Club among themselves." And later she writes: "Whether the game thus played for our own amusement will succeed in amusing other people also is for the reader to judge." The fact that the book is being reissued yet again suggests that there are still plenty of readers out there willing to be amused by the game.

A lot of Golden Age crime novels were games. A murder mystery was an intellectual challenge rather on the same level as a crossword—and it's interesting that the two forms of entertainment both developed around the same time. In the days before television, in the days of country house parties, such games were very popular. Collections of crime puzzles—like F. Tennyson Jesse's *The Baffle Book, A Parlour Game of Mystery and Detection*—sold in large numbers. It was indeed the age of the parlour game . . . which hardly exists nowadays. People don't have parlour games. Very few of them even have parlours.

But it is in the spirit of a parlour game that *The Floating Admiral* should be approached. The idea of a serious (should I use that awful word "literary"?) novel written by a relay of authors is incongruous. For a light-hearted work of crime fiction, though, the concept is fun, and I think it's clear that the writers involved in *The Floating Admiral* enjoyed the intellectual challenge that faced them.

I have been involved in a couple of collaborative ventures of this kind and I very quickly discovered that the best job to get is that of the person who starts the story. In the first chapter you can sprinkle clues and inconsistencies with reckless abandon, secure in the knowledge that it won't be you who has to tie up all the loose ends later. As a logical consequence of this, the worst job is writing the final chapter, pulling together all the threads of the story to produce a credible solution to the mystery. The temptation to begin that final chapter with the words "But it was all a dream . . ." is strong.

In *The Floating Admiral* this particular short straw was drawn by Anthony Berkeley, which was probably just as well. The author of *The Poisoned Chocolate Case*, who also, under the pseudonym of Francis Iles, produced the classic thriller *Malice Aforethought*, was equipped both as whodunit plotter and as someone who understood the psychology of the criminal mind. If he couldn't make sense of the ending, nobody could, and I think it's significant that his final chapter is entitled *Clearing Up the Mess*.

Berkeley is one of the contributors to *The Floating Admiral* whose name is still reasonably well known, at least to crime fiction buffs. The same could be said of Monsignor Ronald A. Knox, Freeman Wills Croft and Clemence Dane. Agatha Christie and Dorothy L. Sayers, of course, are big hitters, seemingly destined to endure forever, and G. K. Chesterton is still a well-known literary figure (though the Prologue he wrote to this volume seems to bear no relation to anything in the ensuing novel).

Some of the other contributors' names have dropped off the radar almost completely—except in the consciousness of dedicated collectors—but I was interested to know a little about them, to help me visualise the composition of the Detection Club in its early years. So here are my findings:

Canon Victor L. Whitechurch was, as his title suggests, a clergyman, whose fictional creation Thorpe Hazell was a vegetarian railway detective, intended to be as different as possible from Sherlock Holmes. Whitechurch was one of the first crime writers to submit his manuscripts to Scotland Yard to check he'd got his police procedural details right (an effort that many contemporary practitioners of the genre still don't bother to make).

G. D. H. (George Howard Douglas) and M. (Margaret) Cole were a husband and wife team of crime writers. Both left-wing intellectuals, in 1931 G. D. H. formed the Society for Socialist Inquiry and Propaganda, later to be renamed the Socialist League. Amongst the undergraduates he taught at Oxford was the future Prime Minister, Harold Wilson.

Henry Wade was the pseudonym of Henry Lancelot Aubrey-Fletcher, 6th Baronet, who was awarded both the D.S.O. and the Croix de Guerre for his bravery in the First World War. As well as writing twenty crime novels, he was High Sheriff of Buckinghamshire.

John Rhode was one of the pseudonyms of Cecil John Charles Street. Also writing as Miles Burton and Cecil Waye, in his lifetime he published over 140 books.

Milward Kennedy was the pseudonym of Milward Rodon Kennedy Burge, an Oxford-educated career civil servant, who specialised in police procedurals. He also wrote books under the androgynous name Evelyn Elder.

Edgar Jepson had an enormously varied literary career. As well as crime novels and popular romances, he wrote children's stories and is probably best remembered now for his fantasy fiction. His son and daughter were both published authors and his granddaughter is the writer Fay Weldon.

So just a few snapshots of the 1931 Detection Club members who collaborated on *The Floating Admiral*. I find it intriguing to imagine the dinners they must have shared when they cooked up the ideas for this relay novel. Also the conversations . . . I'm sure, like contemporary members of the Detection Club, though they talked a bit about the craft of crime writing, it was when they got on to other topics that they became more energised. I can visualise religious discussions between the Catholic convert Ronald Knox, the Anglican canon Victor Whiteside and the Christian humanist Dorothy L. Sayers. I wonder how the idealistic Socialism of G. D. H. and M. Cole went down with the aristocratic Henry Wade. And, writing all those books, John Rhode must have had difficulty finding time to attend the dinners.

But enough nostalgia. One thing I am sure of, though . . . The dinners of the embryonic organisation, during which the plot of *The Floating Admiral* was hatched, would have been conducted in just the same spirit of good humour and congeniality which, I am glad to say, still characterises today's Detection Club.

What can be wrong, after all, with an exclusive organisation of some sixty members which exists, in the words of Dorothy L. Sayers, "chiefly for the purpose of eating dinners together at suitable intervals and of talking illimitable shop"?

CONTENTS

CONTENTS

INTRODUCTION

By Dorothy L. Sayers

THE FLOATING ADMIRAL

WHEN members of the official police force are invited to express an opinion about the great detectives of fiction, they usually say with a kindly smile: "Well, of course, it's not the same for them as it is for us. The author knows beforehand who did the job, and the great detective has only to pick up the clues that are laid down for him. It's wonderful," they indulgently add, "the clever ideas these authors hit upon, but we don't think they would work very well in real life."

There is probably much truth in these observations, and they are, in any case, difficult to confute. If Mr. John Rhode, for example, could be induced to commit a real murder by one of the ingeniously simple methods he so easily invents in fiction, and if Mr. Freeman Wills Crofts, say, would undertake to pursue him, Bradshaw in hand, from Stranraer to Saint Juan-les-Pins, then, indeed, we might put the matter to the test. But writers of detective fiction are, as a rule, not bloodthirsty people. They avoid physical violence, for two reasons: first, because their murderous feelings are so efficiently blown-off in print as to have little energy left for boiling up in action, and secondly, because they are so accustomed to the idea that murders are made to be detected that they feel a wholesome reluctance to put their criminal theories into practice. While, as for doing real detecting, the fact is that few of them have the time for it, being engaged in earning their bread and butter like reasonable citizens, unblessed with the ample leisure of a Wimsey or a Father Brown.

But the next best thing to a genuine contest is a good game, and *The Floating Admiral* is the detection game as played out on paper by certain members of the Detection Club among themselves. And here it may be asked: What is the Detection Club?

It is a private association of writers of detective fiction in Great Britain, existing chiefly for the purpose of eating dinners together at suitable intervals and of talking illimitable shop. It owes no allegiance to any publisher, nor, though willing to turn an honest penny by offering the present venture to the public, is it primarily concerned with making money. It is not a committee of judges for recommending its own or other people's books, and indeed has no object but to amuse itself. Its membership is confined to those who have written genuine detective stories (not adventure tales or "thrillers") and election is secured by a vote of the club on recommendation by two or more members, and involves the undertaking of an oath.

While wild horses would not drag from me any revelation of the solemn ritual of the Detection Club, a word as to the nature of the oath is, perhaps, permissible. Put briefly, it amounts to this: that the author pledges himself to play the game with the public and with his fellow-authors. His detectives must detect by their wits, without the help of accident or coincidence; he must not invent impossible death-rays and poisons to produce solutions which no living person could expect; he must write as good English as he can. He must preserve inviolable secrecy concerning his fellow-members' forthcoming plots and titles, and he must give any assistance in his power to members who need advice on technical points. If there is any serious aim behind the avowedly frivolous organisation of the Detection Club, it is to keep the detective story up to the highest standard that its nature permits, and to free it from the bad legacy of sensationalism, clap-trap and jargon with which it was unhappily burdened in the past.

Now, a word about the conditions under which *The Floating Admiral* was written. Here, the problem was made to approach as closely as possible to a problem of real detection. Except in the case of Mr. Chesterton's picturesque Prologue, which was written last, each contributor tackled the mystery presented to him in the preceding chapters without having the slightest idea what solution or solutions the previous authors had in mind. Two rules only were imposed. Each writer must construct his instalment with a definite solution in view—that is, he must not introduce new complications merely "to make it more difficult." He must be ready, if called upon, to explain his own clues coherently and plausibly; and to make sure that he was playing fair in this respect, each writer was bound to deliver, together with the manuscript of his own chapter, his own proposed solution of the mystery. These solutions are printed at the end of the book for the benefit of the curious reader.

Secondly, each writer was bound to deal faithfully with *all* the difficulties left for his consideration by his predecessors. If Elma's attitude towards love and marriage appeared to fluctuate strangely, or if the boat was put into the boat-house wrong end first, those facts must form part of his solution. He must not dismiss them as caprice or accident, or present an explanation inconsistent with them. Naturally, as the clues became in process of time more numerous, the suggested solutions grew more complicated and precise, while the general outlines of the plot gradually hardened and fixed themselves. But it is entertaining and instructive to note the surprising number of different interpretations which may be devised to account for the simplest actions. Where one writer may have laid down a clue, thinking that it could point only in one obvious direction, succeeding writers have managed to make it point in a direction exactly opposite. And it is here, perhaps, that the game approximates most closely to real life. We judge one another by our outward actions, but in the motive underlying those actions our judgment may be widely at fault. Preoccupied by our own private interpretation of the matter, we can see only the one possible motive behind the action, so that our solution may be quite plausible, quite coherent, and quite wrong. And here, possibly, we detective-writers may have succeeded in wholesomely surprising and confounding ourselves and one another. We are only too much accustomed to let the great detective say airily: "Cannot you see, my dear Watson, that these facts admit of only one interpretation?" After our experience in the matter of *The Floating Admiral*, our great detectives may have to learn to express themselves more guardedly.

Whether the game thus played for our own amusement will succeed in amusing other people also is for the reader to judge. We can only assure him that the game was played honestly according to the rules, and with all the energy and enthusiasm which the players knew how to put into it. Speaking for myself, I may say that the helpless bewilderment into which I was plunged on receipt of Mr. Milward Kennedy's little bunch of brain-teasers was, apparently, fully equalled by the hideous sensation of bafflement which overcame Father Ronald Knox when, having, as I fondly imagined, cleared up much that was obscure, I handed the problem on to him. That Mr. Anthony Berkeley should so cheerfully have confounded our politics and frustrated our knavish tricks in the final solution, I must attribute partly to his native ingenuity and partly to the energetic interference of the other three intervening solvers, who discovered so many facts and motives that we earlier gropers in the dark knew nothing about. But none of us, I think, will bear any malice against our fellow-authors, any more than against the vagaries of the River Whyn, which, powerfully guided by Mr. Henry Wade and Mr. John Rhode, twin luminaries of its tidal waters, bore so peacefully between its flowery banks the body of the Floating Admiral.

PROLOGUE

By G. K. Chesterton

"THE THREE PIPE DREAMS"

THREE glimpses through the rolling smoke of opium, three stories that still hover about a squalid opium joint in Hong Kong, might very well at this distance of time be dismissed as pipe dreams. Yet they really happened; they were stages in the great misfortune of a man's life; although many who played their parts in the drama would have forgotten it by the morning. A large paper-lantern coarsely scrawled with a glaring crimson dragon hung over the black and almost subterranean entrance of the den; the moon was up and the little street was almost deserted.

We all talk of the mystery of Asia; and there is a sense in which we are all wrong. Asia has been hardened by the ages; it is old, so that its bones stick out; and in one sense there is less disguise and mystification about it than there is about the more living and moving problems of the West. The dope-peddlers and opium hags and harlots who made the dingy life of that place were fixed and recognised in their functions, in something almost like a social hierarchy; sometimes their vice was official and almost religious, as in the dancing-girls of the temples. But the English naval officer who strode at that instant past that door, and had occasion to pause there, was in reality much more of a mystery; for he was a mystery even to himself. There were

6

bound up in his character, both national and individual, the most complex and contradictory things; codes and compromises about codes, and a conscience strangely fitful and illogical; sentimental instincts that recoiled from sentiment and religious feelings that had outlived religion; a patriotism that prided itself on being merely practical and professional; all the tangled traditions of a great Pagan and a great Christian past; the mystery of the West. It grew more and more mysterious, because he himself never thought about it.

Indeed there is only one part of it that anybody need think about for the purposes of this tale. Like every man of his type, he had a perfectly sincere hatred of individual oppression; which would not have saved him from taking part in impersonal or collective oppression, if the responsibility were spread to all his civilisation or his country or his class. He was the Captain of a battleship lying at that moment in the harbour of Hong Kong. He would have shelled Hong Kong to pieces and killed half the people in it, even if it had been in that shameful war by which Great Britain forced opium upon China. But when he happened to see one individual Chinese girl being dragged across the road by a greasy, yellow ruffian, and flung head-foremost into the opium-den, something sprang up quite spontaneously within him; an "age" that is never really past; and certain romances that were not really burned by the Barber; something that does still deserve the glorious insult of being called quixotic. With two or three battering blows he sent the Chinaman spinning across the road, where he collapsed in a distant gutter. But the girl had already been flung down the steps of the dark entry, and he precipitated himself after her with the purely instinctive impetuosity of a charging bull. There was very little in his mind at that moment except rage and a very vague intention of delivering the captive from so uninviting a dungeon. But even over such a simple mood a wave of unconscious warning seemed to pass; the blood-red dragon-lantern seemed to leer down at him; and he had some such blind sensation as might have overwhelmed St. George if, charging with a victorious lance, he had found himself swallowed by the dragon.

And yet the next scene revealed, in a rift of that vision-ary vapour, is not any such scene of doom or punishment as some sensationalists might legitimately expect. It will not be necessary to gratify the refined modern taste with scenes of torture; nor to avoid the vulgarity of a happy ending by killing the principal character in the first chap-ter. Nevertheless, the scene revealed was perhaps, in its ultimate effects, almost more tragic than a scene of death. The most tragic thing about it was that it was rather comic. The gleam of the tawdry lanterns in the dope-den revealed nothing but a huddle of drugged coolies, with faces like yellow stone, the sailors from a ship that had put into Hong Kong that morning, flying the Stars and Stripes; and the final feature of a tall English naval officer, wear-ing the uniform of the Captain of a British ship, behaving in a peculiar way and apparently under rather peculiar influences. It was believed by some that what he was per-forming was a horn-pipe, but that it was mingled with motions designed only to preserve equilibrium.

The crew looking on was American; that is to say, some of them were Swedish, several Polish, several more Slavs of nameless nationality, and a large number of brown Las-cars from the ends of the earth. But they all saw something that they very much wanted to see and had never seen before. They saw an English gentleman unbend. He unbent with luxuriant slowness and then suddenly bent double again and slid to the floor with a bang. He was understood to say:

"Dam' bad whisky but dam' good. WhadImeansay is," he explained with laborious logic, "whisky dam' bad, but dam' bad whisky dam' good thing."

"He's had more than whisky," said one of the Swedish sailors in Swedish American.

"He's had everything there is to have, I should think," replied a Pole with a refined accent.

And then a little swarthy Jew, who was born in Budapest but had lived in Whitechapel, struck up in piping tones a song he had heard there: "Every nice girl loves a sailor." And in his song there was a sneer that was some day to be seen on the face of Trotsky, and to change the world.

The dawn gives us the third glimpse of the harbour of Hong Kong, where the battleship flying the Stars and Stripes lay with the other battleship flying the Union Jack; and on the latter ship there was turmoil and blank dismay. The First and Second Officers looked at each other with growing alertness and alarm, and one of them looked at a watch.

"Can you suggest anything, Mr. Lutterell?" said one of them, with a sharp voice but a very vague eye.

"I think we shall have to send somebody ashore to find out," replied Mr. Lutterell.

At this point a third officer appeared hauling forward a heavy and reluctant seaman; who was supposed to have some information to give, but seemed to have some difficulty in giving it.

"Well, you see, sir, he's been found," he said at last. "The Captain's been found."

Something in his tone moved the First Officer to sudden horror.

"What do you mean by found?" he cried. "You talk as if he was dead!"

"Well, I don't think he's dead," said the sailor with irritating slowness. "But he looked dead-like."

"I'm afraid, sir," said the Second Officer in a low voice, "that they're just bringing him in. I hope they'll be quick and keep it as quiet as they can."

Under these circumstances did the First Officer look up and behold his respected Captain returning to his beloved ship. He was being carried like a sack by two dirty-looking coolies, and the officers hastily closed round him and carried him to his cabin. Then Mr. Lutterell turned sharply and sent for the ship's doctor.

"Hold these men for the moment," he said, pointing to the coolies; "we've got to know about this. Now then, Doctor, what's the matter with him?"

The doctor was a hard-headed, hatchet-faced man, having the not very popular character of a candid friend; and on this occasion he was very candid indeed.

"I can see and smell for myself," he said, "before I begin the examination. He's had opium and whisky as well as Heaven knows what else. I should say he's a bag of poisons."

"Any wounds at all?" asked the frowning Lutterell.

"I should say he's knocked himself out," said the candid doctor. "Most likely knocked himself out of the Service."

"You have no right to say that," said the First Officer severely. "That is for the authorities."

"Yes," said the other doggedly. "Authorities of a Court Martial, I should say. No; there are no wounds."

Thus do the first three stages of the story reach their conclusion; and it must be admitted with regret that so far there is no moral to the story.

CHAPTER I

By Canon Victor L. Whitechurch

CORPSE AHOY!

EVERYONE in Lingham knew old Neddy Ware, though he was not a native of the village, having only resided there for the last ten years; which, in the eyes of the older inhabitants who had spent the whole of their lives in that quiet spot, constituted him still a "stranger."

Not that they really knew very much about him, for the old man was of a retiring disposition and had few cronies. What they did know was that he was a retired petty officer of the Royal Navy, subsisting on his pension, that he was whole-heartedly devoted to the Waltonian craft, spending most of his time fishing in the River Whyn, and that, though he was of a peaceful disposition generally, he had a vocabulary of awful and blood-curdling swear-words if anyone upset him by interfering with his sport.

If you, being a fellow-fisherman, took up your position on the bank of the River Whyn in a spot which Neddy Ware considered to be too near his, he would let drive at you with alarming emphasis; if boys—his pet aversion—annoyed him in any way by chattering around him, his language became totally unfit for juvenile ears. Once young Harry Ayres, the village champion where fisticuffs were concerned, had the temerity to throw a stone at the old man's float; he slunk back home afterwards, white in face and utterly cowed with the torrent of Neddy Ware's lurid remarks.

He lived in a small cottage standing quite by itself on the outskirts of the village, and he lived there alone. Mrs. Lambert, a widow, went to his cottage for a couple of hours every morning to tidy up and cook his midday meal. For the rest, Neddy Ware managed quite well.

He came out of his cottage one August morning as the church clock, some half a mile distant, was striking four. Those who knew his habits would have seen nothing unusual in his rising so early. The fisherman knows the value of those first morning hours; besides which, the little River Whyn, which was the scene of his favourite occupation, was tidal for some five or six miles from the sea. For those five or six miles it meandered, first through a low valley, flanked by the open downs on one side and by wooded heights on the other, and then made its way, for the last four miles, through a flat, low-lying country till it finally entered the Channel at Whynmouth. Everyone knows Whynmouth as a favourite South Coast holiday resort, possessing a small harbour at the mouth of its river.

Twice a day the tide flowed up the Whyn, more or less rapidly according to whether it was "spring" or "neap." And this fact had an important bearing on the times which were favourable for angling. On this particular morning Neddy Ware had planned to be on the river bank a little while after the incoming tide had begun to flow up the stream.

Behold him, then, as he came out of his cottage, halfway up the wooded slopes of "Lingham Hangar," crossed the high road, and made his way down to the level of the river. He was fairly on in years, but carried those years well, so much so that there was only just a sprinkling of grey in his coal-black hair. A sturdy-looking man, clean-shaven, but with a curious, old-fashioned twist of hair allowed to grow long on either side of his head just in front of his ears; brown, weatherbeaten, lined face, humorous mouth and keen, grey eyes. Dressed in an old navy blue serge suit, and wearing—as he invariably did—a black bowler hat. Carrying rods, landing net, and a capacious basket containing all kinds of the impedimenta of his craft.

He reached the grassy bank of the river, put his things on the ground, and very slowly filled a blackened clay pipe with twist tobacco—which he rubbed in his hands first—and proceeded to light it, glancing up and down the river as he did so.

Where he was standing the river took a curve, and he was on the outer side of this curve, on the right bank. Away to the left the stream bent itself between the heights on the one side and open meadows on the other. To the right, bending away from him, was the flat country, the river's edges bordered with tall-growing reeds. From this direction the tide was flowing towards him, swirling round the bend.

His first task was to haul in three or four eel lines he had thrown out the evening before, the ends being tied to the gnarled roots of a small tree growing on the bank. Two of the lines brought to land a couple of fair-sized eels, and, very dexterously, he detached the slippery, twisting fish from the hooks, washing the slime off afterwards. Then, slowly, he commenced putting one of his rods together, arranging his tackle, baiting with worms, and casting into the stream. For some little time he watched the float bobbing about in the swirl of the eddies, now and again striking when it suddenly disappeared beneath the surface, once landing a fish.

He glanced around. Suddenly his float lost interest. He

was gazing down-stream, as far as he could see around the bend. Slowly a small rowing-boat was coming up-stream. But there was something peculiar about her. No oars were in evidence. She appeared to be drifting.

The old sailor was quick to recognise the little craft.

"Ah," he muttered, "that's the Vicar's boat."

Lingham Vicarage stood, with its adjacent church, quite apart from the village proper, about half a mile down the river. The grounds ran down to the water's edge, where there was a rough landing-stage. The Vicar, he knew, kept his boat at this stage, moored by her painter to a convenient post. There was a little creek running into the grounds, with a wooden boat-house, but, in the summer months, especially when the Vicar's two boys were home from school, the boat was generally kept on the river itself.

As it came nearer, Ware laid down his rod. He could see now that there was someone in the boat—not seated, but, apparently, lying in the bottom of her, astern.

The boat was only about fifty yards away now. The swirl of the tide was bringing her round the outer side of the bend in the river, but Neddy Ware, who knew every current, saw that she would pass beyond his reach. With the quick action of the sailor he did not waste an instant. Diving into his basket he produced one of the coiled up eel lines with its heavy, lead plummet. And then stood in readiness, uncoiling the line and throwing the slack on the grass.

On came the boat, about a dozen yards from the bank. Skilfully he threw the plummet into her bows, and then started walking along the bank up-stream, gently but steadily pulling on the line till, at length, he brought her close up to the bank and laid hold of the painter at her bows. The end of the painter was dragging in the water. As he pulled it out he glanced at it. It had been cut.

He made it fast to a tree-root. The boat swung round, stern up-stream, alongside the bank. And Ware got into her. The next moment he was on his knees, bending over the man who lay in the stern.

He lay there on his back, his knees slightly hunched up, his arms at his sides, quite still. A man of about sixty, with iron-grey hair, moustache and close-cropped, pointed beard, dark eyes open with fixed stare. He was clad in evening dress clothes and a brown overcoat, the latter open at the front and exposing a white shirt-front stained with blood.

Sitting on one of the seats, Ware made a swift examination of the boat.

A pair of oars lay in her, the metal rowlocks were unshipped. Apparently the dead man was hatless—no—there *was* a hat in the boat, lying in the bows; a round, black, clerical hat, such as Mr. Mount, the Vicar, usually wore.

Neddy Ware, having looked around, got out of the boat and glanced at his watch. Ten minutes to five. Then, leaving the little craft moored to the bank, he hurried off as fast as he could go, gained the high road, which was some hundred yards away from the river, and started in the direction of the village.

Police Constable Hempstead, just on the point of turning into bed after having been on duty all night, looked out of the window in answer to Ware's knock at the door.

"What is it, Mr. Ware?" he asked.

"Something pretty bad, I'm afraid."

Hempstead, wide awake now, slipped on his clothes again, came down and opened the door. Ware told him what had happened.

"I must get the Inspector out from Whynmouth—and a doctor," said the constable, "I'll phone to the station there."

He came out again in two or three minutes.

"All right," he said. "They'll run over in a car at once. Now you come along with me and show me that boat and what's in it. You haven't been messing about with any-thing—moving the body and so on, I hope?"

"I shouldn't be such a fool," replied Ware.

"That's all right. You haven't seen anyone else?"

"No one."

The policeman went on asking questions from time to time as they hurried along. He was a smart man, this young constable, eager for his stripes, and wanted to make the most of the opportunity. As soon as they reached the river bank he took a glance at the boat and its contents, and exclaimed:

"*Hullo!* Don't you know who that is, Mr. Ware?"

"Never saw him before that I know of. Who is he?"

"Why, it's Admiral Penistone. He lives at Rundel Croft —that big house the other side of the river just opposite the Vicarage. Leastways, he's been in residence there about a month. He only bought it last June. A new-comer."

"Oh! Admiral Penistone, is he?" said Neddy Ware.

"That's the man, right enough. But, look here: are you sure this is the Vicarage boat?"

"Certain."

"Queer, eh? That seems to mean something happened *this* side of the river, for of course there's no bridge till you get to Fernton—three miles lower down. Ah, and the parson's hat, eh? Let's see; what time did you first see the boat coming along?"

"A little after half-past four, I should say."

Hempstead had his note-book out and was making pencilled jottings in it. Then he said:

"Look here, Mr. Ware, I want you, if you will, to go back to the road and stop Inspector Rudge when he comes along in his car."

"Very well," replied Ware; "nothing more I can do?"

"Not yet, at any rate."

Hempstead was an astute man. He waited until Neddy Ware was out of the way before he began a little examination on his own account. He knew very well that his superior officer would take the case fully in hand, but he was anxious to see what he could, without disturbing anything, in the meantime.

As he got into the boat, he noticed a folded newspaper, half sticking out of the dead man's overcoat pocket. He took it out, gingerly, looked at it, and replaced it.

"Ah," he murmured, "the *Evening Gazette*, last night's late London edition. He wouldn't get that here. The nearest place where it's sold is Whynmouth."

He would very much have liked to examine the contents of all the pockets of the dead man's clothes, but felt he had better not. So he got out of the boat, sat down on the bank, and waited.

After a bit the sound of a car running along the main road was heard, and in a minute or two, four men came across the meadow; Neddy Ware, a police inspector in uniform, and two men in plain clothes, one of them a doctor, the other a detective-sergeant.

Inspector Rudge was a tall, thin man, with sallow, clean-shaven face. He came up to Hempstead.

"You haven't moved anything?" he asked curtly.

"No, sir."

Rudge turned to the doctor.

"I won't do anything, Doctor Grice, till you have made your examination."

Doctor Grice got into the boat and proceeded to examine the body. It was only a few minutes before he said:

"Stabbed to the heart, Inspector, with some narrow-bladed instrument—a thin knife or dagger. Death must have been instantaneous. There'll have to be a post-mortem, of course."

"How long has he been dead?"

"Some hours. He probably died before midnight."

"Nothing more?"

"Not at present, Inspector."

"Very well. I'll have a look now."

He turned the body over, shifting it slightly.

"No sign of blood under him," he said, "or anywhere else in the boat that I can see. Let's have a look in his pockets—ah, it wasn't robbery. Gold watch and chain—wallet full of notes—they were not after that. Evening paper here—last night's date. That must be noted. Now—we've got to be as quick as possible. Tell me, Hempstead, what do you know about him?"

"He's Admiral Penistone, sir. Retired. A new-comer hereabouts. Bought Rundel Croft, a big house on the other side of the river, a few months ago. Took up residence there lately. I believe he has a niece living with him. But it's not in my district, sir."

"I know."

The Inspector turned to Ware.

"You say the boat belongs to the Vicar here?"

"Yes."

"How long would it take for the tide to bring it up from his place?"

"Forty to forty-five minutes," replied Ware promptly, "with the tide as it is to-day."

"I see. Now, the question is how are we to move him? We might pull the boat back against the tide. Won't do, though. Those oars must be tested for finger-prints before they are handled. Let's see—Vicarage on the telephone, Hempstead?"

"Yes, sir."

"All right. I'll go there now. I want to see the Vicar. We'll phone to Whynmouth for an ambulance. Have to run him to Rundel Croft round by Fernton Bridge. You remain here, Hempstead, and if anyone comes along don't let 'em touch anything. I shall want you, Sergeant—we'll have to put you across the river from the Vicarage if we can get a boat there; I want you to mount guard over the Admiral's boat and boat-house. Perhaps you won't mind coming too, Mr. Ware. You may be useful. There! We'll get a move on. Come along, Doctor."

In a very short time the Inspector was driving the car down the short bit of road leading from the highway to the Vicarage. The front door of the latter faced the river, a lawn stretching down to the bank. Opposite, about a hundred yards from the bank, stood a large, red-brick, Tudor mansion, with a broad sweep of lawn in front and a boat-house.

The Inspector, the Vicar's hat in his hand, got out of the car and rang the bell; the others followed. It was a few minutes before the maid, who evidently had only just come down, opened the door and said her master was not up yet.

"Will you kindly tell him that Inspector Rudge wants to see him at once. Say I'm sorry to disturb him, but it's most important."

"I'll tell him, sir. Won't you come in?"

"Thank you, no. I'll wait here."

"Hullo, I say, are you a policeman?"

He turned. Two boys had come across the lawn, aged, respectively, about sixteen and fourteen, dressed in flannel trousers and shirts open at the neck, and carrying bathing towels. They were regarding him eagerly.

"Yes," he said, "I am."

"Good egg!" exclaimed the elder, "just what we want,

isn't he, Alec? Look here; some blighter has taken our boat —cut the painter. Perhaps you've heard about it, though? Is that what you've come about?"

The Inspector smiled grimly.

"Yes—that's what I've come about, young gentlemen," he replied, dryly, "but you needn't worry about your boat. It's been found."

"Hooray!" exclaimed the other boy. "Got the beggar who took it?"

"Not yet," said Rudge, with another grim little smile, "that may not be so easy. Have you got another boat handy?" he asked.

"Only our old punt—she's in the boat-house."

"Well, do you two young gentlemen think you could manage to put my detective-sergeant here across the water in her? He wants to pay a call at Rundel Croft."

"Rather!" Peter Mount looked with boyish admiration at the sergeant. "Is there going to be a man-hunt? Cheerio! We'll help you. But you don't suspect old Admiral Peni-stone of sneaking our boat, do you? He crossed back in his own last night. He'd been dining here, you know."

"Oh, had he!" said the Inspector. "No, we don't suspect him. Now—will you do what I asked?"

"Come on," said Alec to Sergeant Appleton, "the tide's running pretty strong, but we'll put you across all right."

They went down to the boat-house with the sergeant.

"Good morning, Inspector. Good morning, Doctor Grice—ah—it's you, Ware, I see. What's the meaning of this early morning deputation?"

The Vicar had come out of the house; a man of about fifty, of medium height, sturdily built, with clear-cut features and hair a little grey. He asked the question of the Inspector, who replied:

"I'll explain directly, Mr. Mount. Is this your hat?"

The Vicar took it and looked at it.

"Yes; certainly it is."

"Then would you mind telling me if you remember when you had it last?"

"That is quite simple. To be absolutely accurate, at twenty minutes past ten last evening."

"And where?"

"You are very mysterious, Inspector. But I'll tell you. My neighbour who lives opposite was dining with us last evening, with his niece. They left just about ten. I went down to the river to see them off, and put my hat on. After the Admiral had crossed the stream in his boat with his niece I sat down in that little summer-house and smoked a pipe. I took off my hat and laid it on the seat beside me—and, absent-mindedly, I forgot to put it on again when I returned to the house. It was then that I set my watch by the clock in the hall—twenty minutes past ten. But will you tell me why you ask me this—and what you have all come about?"

"I will, sir. This hat was found in your boat early this morning. Your boat was drifting with the tide up-stream. And in her was the dead body of your opposite neighbour, Admiral Penistone—*murdered*, Mr. Mount."

CHAPTER II

By G. D. H. and M. Cole

BREAKING THE NEWS

"MURDERED! Good God!" the Vicar said—and it was well known, the Inspector reflected, that the Vicar of Lingham had a ridiculously exaggerated respect for the Third Commandment. He had stepped back a pace at the shock of the news, and some of the colour was fading from his cheeks. "But—*murdered.* . . . How—what do you mean, Inspector?"

"I mean," said Rudge, "that Admiral Penistone was stabbed to the heart some time before midnight last night—and his body placed in your boat."

"But what—why . . . ? How could he have been?"

"And your hat," the Inspector remorselessly amplified, "was lying in the boat beside him. So you see," he added, "that the first thing I had to do was to make enquiries at your house."

The Vicar turned on his heel abruptly. "Come into my study," he said. "We can talk better there—I don't suppose you want my sons, at present?" The Inspector shook his head, and followed him into a quiet, brown room with wide sash windows, the very model of what a clerical study, owned by a none too tidy cleric, should be. As he led the way in, the Vicar stumbled over something, and with a little gasp caught hold of the table for support. "You— you must excuse me," he muttered, as he motioned the

Inspector to a chair and sank into one himself. "This is—
a very great shock. Now, will you tell me what I can do
for you?"

Rudge scanned him a minute before replying. Undoubtedly he had received a very great shock. He was pale; his
hands were none too steady; and his breath was coming
and going quickly. Whether the cause was merely the
sudden impact of violent death on a sheltered clerical life,
or whether there was some graver reason, the Inspector
did not know enough to decide. At any rate, there was no
sense in causing further alarm at the moment. So when
he spoke it was in a gentle reassuring tone.

"What I want to find out immediately, Mr. Mount, is
exactly what happened last night, as far as you know it.
Admiral Penistone, you say, came over to dine with his
niece—what is the lady's name, by the way?"

"Fitzgerald—Miss Elma Fitzgerald. She is his sister's
daughter, I understand."

"About what age?"

"Oh—I should say a year or two over thirty."

"Thank you. They arrived—when?"

"Just before seven-thirty. In their boat."

"And left?"

"Slightly after ten. I can't fix it to the minute, I'm
afraid; but they were just taking their leave when the
church clock struck, and Admiral Penistone said, 'Hurry
up, I want to get back before midnight'—or something of
that sort; and within a very few minutes they were gone."

"And you saw them off?"

"Yes. I went down to the landing-stage with them, and
Peter—that's my eldest son—helped them to start. It's
sometimes a little awkward getting off, if the current is
running strongly."

"Did you actually see them land?"

"Yes. It wasn't dark. I watched them take the boat into the Admiral's boat-house, and then, a little later, I saw them come out of the boat-house, and go up to the house."

"I should have thought those trees at the back of the boat-house would have screened them from you," said the Inspector, who had made good use of his eyes. "Or do you mean they were crossing the lawn?"

The Vicar looked at him with respect. "No, they were in the trees," he said. "But Miss Fitzgerald had on a white dress, and I saw it showing through them."

"But Admiral Penistone hadn't a white dress?"

"No. . . . I suppose," the Vicar reflected, "that now you mention it I couldn't say I saw the Admiral leave the boat-house—but seeing his niece I naturally concluded he was with her."

"Very naturally," Rudge concurred soothingly. "And you yourself stayed out smoking until——?"

"Twenty past ten."

"And then?"

"I locked the house up and went to bed."

"And you heard nothing more of your neighbour?"

"Nothing," said the Vicar. "Nothing at all," he repeated more loudly.

"What about your sons? Or your servants? Would they have heard anything?"

"I don't think so. They had all gone to bed when I came in."

"Thank you. Now, Mr. Mount, can you tell me this? Did Admiral Penistone seem in his usual spirits during the evening?"

The question appeared to distress the Vicar. "I—I don't think I can really answer that," he said. "You see, I haven't known the Admiral at all long. He has only recently come to the neighbourhood. . . . I really hardly know him."

"But still," Rudge persisted, "you might have noticed if he seemed distressed, or worried in any way. Did he?" And, seeing the Vicar still hesitated, he pressed his point. "If you did notice anything, Mr. Mount, I really think you should tell me. It's of the highest importance that we should find out everything we can about the poor gentleman's state of mind at the time—and I assure you I know how to be discreet."

"Well," said the Vicar, fidgeting a little. "Well . . . it's nothing, probably. But I should say—yes—that the Admiral was perhaps a little worried. He was not as—as amiable as usual. And he was generally a very pleasant man —not at all snappish."

"He was snappish with Miss Fitzgerald, perhaps?" the Inspector suggested quickly; and the Vicar blinked.

"Oh, no . . . hardly . . . I shouldn't say that at all."

"But he acted as though there was something on his mind. . . . I suppose you've no idea what it was?"

"I think—I don't know—it may have been his niece's marriage. He said something about it. Nothing much."

"Oh, she's getting married, is she? Who to?"

"Somebody called Holland, Arthur Holland. From London, I think. I don't know him."

"And Admiral Penistone didn't approve?"

"I don't mean that. I mean, I don't know. He didn't say. Only he seemed as though something might have gone a little wrong. Perhaps it was to do with her settlements; she has a good deal of money, as I understand, and the Admiral is—was her trustee. But I really don't know anything about it."

"I see. Had you, yourself, known Admiral Penistone long?"

"Only since he came here, about a month ago. I called on him, you know; and we got acquainted."

"And you saw each other fairly often?"

"Oh, two or three times in the week, perhaps. Not more."

"Ever hear him speak of any enemies—anyone who'd have a reason for killing him?"

"Oh, no, no!" The Vicar looked shocked, but hastened to add, "Of course, I really know nothing of his life before he came here."

"Had he many friends? In the neighbourhood? Or outside? Where did he live before?"

"Somewhere in the West, I believe. I don't remember his ever telling me the district. I don't think he knew many people about here well. Sir Wilfrid Denny, over at West End, saw most of him, I fancy. I believe he had old friends down to meet him, sometimes."

"Ever meet any of them yourself?"

"Oh, no," said the Vicar.

"I see. Well, I think I'd better be getting over to his place now," the Inspector said. "I'm very much obliged to you, Mr. Mount. I'll want to have a word with your sons and your servants some time, just in case any of them noticed anything that might help us. But that can wait. By the way," he turned at the door to add, "can you tell me what sort of a young lady Miss Fitzgerald is? Liable to—to be very upset, I mean?"

The Vicar smiled a little, almost in spite of himself. "I shouldn't think so," he said. "I don't think Miss Fitzgerald is at all the fainting type."

"Very devoted to her uncle, eh?"

"I couldn't say, particularly. About as much as most nieces are to their uncles, I imagine. Perhaps she is rather a reserved young woman—has interests of her own. But this is just gossip—you can see for yourself what you think, Inspector."

"That's true enough. Well, I'll be going," the Inspector said, and noted the expression of relief which overspread the Vicar's face. "I know we aren't popular visitors," he thought to himself, "at the best of times. But need he show *quite* so plainly how glad he is to get rid of me? I wonder if there could be any other reason—if he knows anything more than he's said. But—the Vicar of Lingham, and a most respectable Vicar, from all I've ever heard of him! I must say it doesn't sound likely." And, so thinking, he made his way back to the car, and drove rapidly the three miles or so which he had to cover to reach the house a hundred yards away.

It was close on eight o'clock by the time he reached his destination; but Rundel Croft obviously did not keep early hours. One or two of the windows facing him still had their blinds down; and the hall, when he was admitted to it, was obviously undergoing its matutinal clean-up. A rather down-at-heels butler, of the type which seems to have become a butler because its wife is a good cook and itself has no special ability of any kind, opened the door to him and blinked uneasily in his face. Rudge asked for Miss Fitzgerald, and was told that she was not yet about. Apparently she always breakfasted in bed. Rudge then asked for Admiral Peniston.

"He's in his room, still," the butler said, looking faintly hostile, as though he did not approve of early morning visitors.

"No, he isn't," Rudge said sharply. "He's had an accident." The butler goggled at him. "Look here—what's your name?"

"Emery."

"Look here, Emery, I'm Inspector Rudge from Whynmouth, and I must see Miss Fitzgerald at once. Admiral Peniston has met with a very serious accident—in fact, he's dead. Will you find Miss Fitzgerald's maid, if she has one, and tell her that I want to speak to Miss Fitzgerald as soon as she can possibly come down. And come back here when you've done it. I want a word with you."

With no more than an inarticulate noise the butler shuffled off, and it was ten minutes or so before he returned, with the news that Miss Fitzgerald would be down in a quarter of an hour. The Inspector took him aside into a square, rather beautiful morning-room, and began questioning him about his master's movements of the night before. But he got very little help from his interview. It seemed to him that the man must be either phenomenally stupid or else dazed with shock at his master's death; and yet the latter did not seem to be the case. Beyond a muttering or two of "Dear, dear!" and the like, he hardly appeared to have taken in the news; and the Inspector felt some surprise that a retired naval officer should keep so incompetent-looking a servant. Yet the house appeared well cleaned, if it did rouse itself somewhat late in the day.

Admiral Penistone, the Inspector learned, had last been seen by his staff at about a quarter past seven on the previous evening, when he and his niece had gone down to the boat-house to row themselves over to the Vicarage. (He never allowed anyone to disturb him in the morning until he rang, which accounted for his absence being unknown.) As he was going to the boat-house, he had told Emery that he need not wait up, but was to lock the front of the house and go to bed, leaving the french window of the drawing-room, which led to the lawn and the river, unbolted. "I was to lock it," Emery said, "but Admiral Penistone always had his own key."

"Stop a moment. Was this window bolted when you came down this morning, or not?"

"No," Emery said; but added that that didn't mean anything. Half the time the Admiral didn't bolt it. It was locked, and nobody was likely to come burgling from the riverside.

Then he hadn't seen the Admiral again? No. Or Miss Fitzgerald? Yes, so to speak. He meant that, as he and his wife were going up to bed, a bit after ten, might have been quarter-past, they'd seen Miss Fitzgerald coming up the path from the boat-house. At least, they'd seen her dress; they couldn't see her properly in the dark. The Admiral wasn't with her then; but they supposed he was behind, locking up the boat-house. No, he didn't know if the boat-house was locked now; he supposed it was, but it wasn't his work to go down to the boat-house. No, he couldn't say they'd actually seen Miss Fitzgerald come in; she might have, or she might have stopped on the lawn. He and his wife weren't particularly noticing; they were going to bed.

And that was all Emery had to say. Questioned about his late master's mood of the previous evening, he seemed to have no idea, and simply stared with a moon-faced imbecility. He "supposed he was much as usual." The Admiral was occasionally "short" with his servants (the Inspector reflected that it would take a saint not to be short with Emery at least a dozen times a day); but beyond that his butler had nothing to say. Masters, apparently, were phenomena that were occasionally short, like pastry; but one accepted the fact, and did not conjecture about the cause. At least, not if one were as limp and uninterested as Emery appeared. No, his wife and he had only been a month with the Admiral; they had applied for the post from an advertisement; they were last with a lady and gentleman in Hove, for a year and a half. At this point, somewhat to Rudge's relief, a much more intelligent-looking maidservant appeared, and announced that Miss Fitzgerald was awaiting him in the dining-room.

"She's ugly!" was the Inspector's immediate reaction on first beholding the niece of the late Admiral Penistone. And then: "No, I'm not so sure that she would be, in some lights. But she'd take a good bit of making-up, I shouldn't wonder. And, jiminy! isn't she sulky-looking!"

Miss Elma Fitzgerald was very pale. But it was not the pallor of fear for a possible accident to her uncle, but that peculiar to a very thick, opaque skin. She was big and heavily-made, with long limbs and broad shoulders, and would have been better suited, obviously, by long trailing draperies than by the tweed skirt and jumper which she had rather carelessly put on. She had largish, strongly-marked, but roughly-designed features, with a wide jaw and full chin, and dark brows nearly meeting in her white face. Her hair was dark and coarse, done in flat plaits around her ears, and under her eyes, which were so little open that the Inspector could not at first glance determine their colour, were lines and dark pouches. She was, to him, distinctly unattractive; and "a year or two over thirty" was, he thought, a generous description. Yet she was certainly a woman of personality, and in a kinder light and with artificial aids to lighten her skin and hide the disfiguring lines, she might even have been attractive.

"Yes?" she said in a voice that contrived to have a rasp and a drawl simultaneously. "What do you want?" At any rate, the Inspector thought, she was not going to waste his time.

"I am sorry to have to tell you, Miss Fitzgerald," said he, "that Admiral Penistone has met with a serious accident."

"Is he dead?" The tone was so matter-of-fact that the Inspector jumped slightly.

"I am afraid he is. But did you—were you expecting——?"

"Oh, no." Still she had not raised her eyes. "But that's the way the police always break things to one, don't they? What happened?"

"I'm sorry to say," said the Inspector, "that the Admiral was murdered."

"*Murdered?*" At that the eyes did open wide for a moment. They were grey, very dark grey. They would have been fine eyes, Rudge noted, if the lashes had been longer. "But—*why?*"

As that was exactly what the Inspector wanted to know himself, he was momentarily brought to a stop.

"His body was found," he said, "at half-past four this morning, drifting in a boat up-stream and stabbed to the heart." Miss Fitzgerald merely bowed her head in acquiescence, and seemed waiting for him to continue. "Damn her!" the Inspector thought. "Hasn't she got *any* natural feelings? You'd think I'd told her there was a cat on the lawn!" Aloud he said: "I'm afraid this must come as a good deal of a shock to you, madam."

"You need not consider my feelings, Inspector," said Elma Fitzgerald, with a glance which said, more plainly than words: "And it is a gross impertinence on your part to make any enquiries into them!" "I suppose you have some idea why—this happened? Or who did it?"

"I am afraid I don't see it very clearly yet," the Inspector said. "I wondered—if you could . . ."

"I can't," said Miss Fitzgerald with decision. "I haven't any idea"—she spoke slowly—"why anyone—anyone at all—should want to kill my uncle. I suppose——" But the sentence stopped there. Whatever it was she supposed, the Inspector, wait as he might, was not to be privy to it. "What do you want me to tell you?" she continued at length. ("I wish you'd be quick and go about your business," her voice conveyed.)

"Just this, madam," the Inspector said. "When did you last see Admiral Penistone?"

"Last night. When we came back from dining at the Vicarage."

"What time would that be?" The Inspector believed in getting his information confirmed from as many sources as possible.

"Oh . . . a little after ten, I think. It struck ten just before we left."

"And you rowed across, and came up to the house with the Admiral?"

"No, he didn't come up to the house when I did. He was locking the boat-house, and he said he thought he'd like a cigar before he went to bed. So I said good night to him, and came straight up to the house."

"Was there anyone about when you came in?"

"No; but Emery and his wife had only just gone to bed, I think. I saw the lights going on and off as I came up. They must have been shutting up the house."

"And then—what did you do?"

"I came straight up, and went to bed myself."

"You didn't hear Admiral Penistone come in?"

"No. But I wasn't listening particularly. He often stays up quite late, walking about," said Miss Fitzgerald.

"I gather," said the Inspector, "that Admiral Penistone, last night, appeared rather worried and distressed?"

"I don't think so. . . . No. Why should he have been?"

"You hadn't had a—a disagreement with him at all?"

"You mean," said Miss Fitzgerald with disconcerting penetration, "about my marriage. That—is—pure—gossip." There was a considerable amount of contempt in her tone. "My uncle was not in the least opposed to my marriage. He was a little worried, I believe, about the best way of arranging the money side of it—but that was only a

question which would settle itself, in time. That was all."
But there must be a little more to it, the Inspector swiftly
reflected, or she wouldn't have tumbled so quick to what
I was talking about.

"Then you can't suggest at all what was worrying him?"

"I don't think for a moment there was anything," said
Miss Fitzgerald; and made a slight movement that at least
suggested a gesture of dismissal.

"I see. Well . . ." The Inspector would have liked to
continue the interview, but did not see, at the moment,
exactly what other information he could well demand.
And it was perhaps hardly in the best of taste to sit there
pestering a lady in her first grief—if she was grieved. There
was a sudden twitch of a strong, rather large hand, that
suggested more emotion than appeared on the surface, at
any rate. "Just one more thing, Miss Fitzgerald, and then
I need not trouble you further. Can you give me the name
of Admiral Penistone's lawyers?"

"Dakers and Dakers. They live somewhere in Lincoln's
Inn, I think."

"Thank you. And if I could see Admiral Penistone's
papers now—and the servants——"

"I think all his papers are in the study. Emery will show
you." Miss Fitzgerald leaned across and touched the bell.
"Inspector," she said, a little suddenly, "will you tell me
—what happens? Will they be bringing him—here?" It
was the first trace of real emotion her voice had shown, and
Rudge hastened to assure her that the body would be taken
to the mortuary, and that every effort would be made to
spare her as much as possible.

"Thank you," she said, returning to indifference again;
and at that moment Emery shuffled in. "Emery, take the
Inspector to the Admiral's study, and let him see anything
he wants to. And you'd better none of you go out of the

house. The Inspector may want to speak to you." She leaned
back in her chair, and made no movement, as Rudge, looking, he hoped, not as puzzled as he felt, followed Emery
out of the room.

The Admiral's study was a large and pleasant room on
the first floor, looking out upon the lawn and the river. It
was in fairly good order, though it had obviously not been
cleaned this morning, and there were a few papers, dating
probably from the previous evening, lying untidily upon
the desk. Rudge took in the appearance of the room with a
practised eye, and reflected that it ought not to take long
to make it yield up any secrets it possessed. Then he dismissed the hovering Emery. "And you're not to let anybody into the house for the present, please, without asking me about it," were his final instructions. Emery, with
a muttered "Very good," shuffled off again.

The desk and a small filing cabinet which stood beside
it were the only likely receptacles for papers in the room.
The filing cabinet, when opened, disclosed nothing but
newspaper cuttings neatly sorted. The desk was locked, but
Rudge had prudently possessed himself of the dead man's
keys, and he very soon had it open. The first thing which
he found was a pistol, perfectly clean and fully loaded,
lying all by itself in a little drawer. He formed his mouth
into the shape of a soundless whistle, and proceeded to un-
earth writing-paper and envelopes, a drawer full of pipes,
another with a few letters of recent date, another with
bank-books, stub-ends of cheque-books, income-tax forms
and other financial paraphernalia, and a fifth which contained only a large legal envelope inscribed Elma Fitzgerald. In view of what the Vicar had said, the Inspector
conjectured that the contents of this envelope might possibly have some bearing upon his case, and he settled himself
down to study them as a preliminary. The first item was

the "Last Will and Testament of John Martin Fitzgerald,"
bulky and wordy beyond even the normal run of such
documents; and the Inspector, whose mastery of legal jargon was not as thorough as he could have wished, found
some trouble in disentangling its provisions. He had succeeded in making out that John Martin Fitzgerald was the
Admiral's brother-in-law, and that his will devised his
property, whatever that might be, in equal proportions to
his son Walter Everett Fitzgerald, "if he should be found
to be alive at the date of my death," and his daughter
Elma Fitzgerald; and had noted that if the son turned out
to be dead ("I suppose he must have disappeared or something. It's a funny way to put it anyhow.") Elma Fitzgerald would get all the property on her marriage—when
his attention was arrested by what sounded like an alterca-
tion below-stairs. For a moment or two he listened, and
judged that, in spite of his orders, some visitor must be
trying to force an entrance into the house. And as he
strongly mistrusted Emery's power to oppose even a determined fly, he went down into the hall to see what it was
all about, and found, as he had anticipated, a pink and
perplexed butler feebly flapping at an enraged visitor who
had already penetrated as far as the foot of the stairs.

"—the Inspector *said*——" he was bleating.

"To hell with the Inspector!" the intruder retorted; and,
glancing up, found himself looking straight into the eyes
of the said Inspector—a contingency which disconcerted
him not at all.

Nor need it have done so. Whoever he was, the intruder
was easily capable of dealing with a dozen inspectors. He
must have been six foot three at the very least, with the
build and gait of an athlete, and an athlete, moreover, who
specialised in events requiring exceptional strength. Above
a pair of magnificently broad shoulders was set a hand-

some head with sunburned face and neck, a square chin, and short aquiline nose, brown hair cropped so close that it could hardly indulge its natural curls, and big, fiery, hazel eyes, which glared up at Rudge with all the righteous indignation of a supporter of Law and Justice resenting the interference of Law with his own avocations.

"I told Mr. Holland," Emery bleated, "that you'd said nobody was to be let in without orders."

"And I told him," Mr. Holland remarked, "that I was coming in."

"You're Mr. Holland?" the Inspector said. "Mr. Arthur Holland?" Holland nodded. "And you want to see——?"

"I've come to see Miss Fitzgerald," Arthur Holland said. "And let me tell you I'm in a hurry, whoever you are. Here, Emery, go and tell Miss Fitzgerald I'm here, and be quick about it, will you?"

"Half a moment, sir," the Inspector said, while a maid-servant came out of one of the rooms opening into the hall, and began to whisper to the butler. "If you'll excuse me, I want a word or two with you myself, first. Did this man tell you that Admiral Penistone has——?"

"Been killed? Yes," the young man said. "Is that any reason why I shouldn't see Miss Fitzgerald? She'll need someone——"

"Beg pardon, sir." Emery approached deferentially. "But Miss Fitzgerald's away."

"*Away!*" The exclamation burst from both men simultaneously.

"Yes, sir. She's just had her bag packed, and driven off in her car, Merton says." He indicated the maidservant in the hall. "Not ten minutes ago, sir."

"Whew!" With an internal whistle the Inspector brooded on this new development.

CHAPTER III

By Henry Wade

BRIGHT THOUGHTS ON TIDES

STILL frowning with annoyance at the escape of this important witness, Inspector Rudge turned to his companion.

"If you'll kindly step into the study, sir," he said, "there are some questions that I'd like to ask you."

"They'll have to wait," said Holland curtly, turning towards the front door. "I'm going to find Miss Fitzgerald."

"No, sir!" There was a ring of authority in the Inspector's voice that brought even the masterful Holland up with a round turn. Rudge was not going to lose two witnesses before he had done with them.

"I must ask you to attend to me first, sir, please. I shall not detain you longer than I can help."

With a wry smile, Arthur Holland followed the Inspector into the study and, declining a chair, leant his back against the tall mantelpiece.

"Well, what is it?" he asked. "Fire away."

Rudge took out his note-book and made a show of preparing to take down vital information. He had often found this effective with recalcitrant witnesses.

"Your full name, sir, please?"

"Arthur Holland."

"Age?"

"Thirty-three."

"Address?"

"Lord Marshall Hotel, Whynmouth."

Rudge looked up.

"That's not your permanent address, sir?"

"I hope not."

"Then may I have it, sir, please?"

"I haven't got one."

The Inspector's eyebrows lifted, and he opened his mouth as if to argue the point but, changing his mind, licked his pencil and wrote down, audibly:

"No permanent address."

After a moment's thought he continued:

"Occupation?"

"I'm a trader."

Rudge looked slightly puzzled.

"Commercial traveller, sir?"

"Good God, no! I trade in raw materials—rubber, jute, ivory—that sort of thing."

"In London, sir?"

Holland writhed with impatience.

"They don't grow in London, man. I'm in England now, fixing up markets."

"Ah!" The Inspector felt as if he were getting nearer the bone. "Then will you tell me, sir, in what part of the world you get your raw material for the London market?"

"I didn't say the London market. I said I was in London to fix up markets—London's only a centre, the markets may be in any part of the world."

The policeman's irritatingly stupid questions were drawing more information out of Arthur Holland than he had intended to give.

"Quite, sir; but you haven't answered my question. In what part of the world do you yourself get the material for which you are trying to find a market?"

"Oh, wherever I think the going's good at the moment," replied Holland airily. "Burma, Kenya, S.A., India—I move about."

Holland hesitated.

"It won't be very difficult for me to find out, sir," said Rudge quietly. "Better for you to tell me."

The reply came slowly—almost unwillingly:

"China."

"I see, sir. And no particular or permanent address in China?"

"No."

Inspector Rudge whisked over a page and started afresh.

"Now about last night, sir. Were you at the Lord Marshall last night?"

"Yes, I was."

"You arrived at . . . ?"

"I got to Whynmouth just before nine."

"Ah; by the express?"

"Yes."

"From London?"

"Yes."

"And you spent the evening . . . where?"

"In Whynmouth."

"You didn't come out here to see your young lady?"

"I knew she was dining out. I stayed in Whynmouth."

"Very patient of you, sir. You remained in the hotel?"

"I had a stroll by the sea after dinner. I went to bed early."

"Perhaps there would be someone who would be able to confirm what you say about your movements, sir?"

The Inspector's voice was casual—too casual. Holland's eyes narrowed.

"Are you suspecting me of killing the Admiral?" he asked harshly.

"Oh, dear, no; oh, dear, no. Why, I didn't even know of your existence till an hour or so ago. Funny, isn't it? No; that's just routine. We like to know—and if possible to confirm—the whereabouts of everyone in any way connected with the deceased at the time of the crime. I just thought it possible you might know of someone who could confirm your statement."

"How can anyone prove whether I was in bed or not? I happen to make a practice of sleeping alone. Funny, isn't it?" quoted Holland with a sneer.

"Ah, then you know the crime was committed after you went to bed?"

Holland stared.

"How the devil should I? I've only just heard of it."

"Quite, sir; quite. Like me only just hearing of you. Now about Miss Fitzgerald. Have you any idea where she's gone?"

"Not the slightest."

"But when you were dashing off to find her just now, you must have had some idea of where to look."

"She might have gone to London."

"And you might be able to find her in London?"

"I might."

"Then perhaps it would be as well if you did, and asked her to return here without delay."

Holland nodded.

"I'll tell her, but she's likely to please herself about that."

"It'll be wise if she pleases herself by coming back, sir. You'll keep in touch with us, in any case, won't you, sir?"

Holland halted, with his hand on the door.

"Does that mean that I'm to be under observation or whatever you call it?"

"I shan't put a man on to watch you, sir, but I'd like you to keep in touch."

With a grunt Miss Fitzgerald's "young man" swung open the door and strode out of the room. There was a smile on Inspector Rudge's face as he pressed the bell.

"I'd like to see Miss Fitzgerald's maid—Merton, I think you said her name was—please, Emery."

A minute later Merton was sitting on the edge of a chair, nervously eyeing the formidable Police Inspector. She was a fresh-looking English girl of about twenty-six, attractive without being actually pretty, and evidently intelligent. Inspector Rudge decided at once to put her at her ease— one of his favourite alternatives of examination.

" 'Merton' they call you?" he said with a friendly smile. "Sounds a bit formal to me. I expect you've got another name, eh?"

"Jennie's my Christian name, sir."

"Ah, that's better. Well, Jennie, this is a sad affair and I don't want to upset you more than I can help, but I must just ask you a few questions about your employers. You see, I don't know anything of them; not been here long, have they?"

"No, sir; only about a month."

"Were you with them before they came here?"

"Oh, no; I come from Whynmouth myself. I've only been here three weeks."

"Ah, so Miss Fitzgerald didn't bring a maid with her when she came?"

"Oh, yes, she did—a French one—Mademoiselle Blanc she called herself, but Miss Fitzgerald called her Célie. She didn't stay long—told the other girls the place was like a mortuary—'dead-house' she called it—I don't know whether she meant Rundel Croft or Whynmouth, but I suppose she thought it was dull. Anyway she packed up and went off without waiting for her month, nor yet her wages, so the girls say. Miss Fitzgerald had to go to Marlow's Agency for another maid in a hurry and as they hadn't got one but they knew I'd been in a maid's situation but I'm living with mother now—she's not well—they asked me, and I consented to oblige."

The last sentence, though rather involved, had the merit of explaining the situation. Inspector Rudge nodded.

"I see; so you don't really know Miss Fitzgerald very well."

"Not so very, but I'm not blind."

"I'm sure not. What did you see?"

"Just that they didn't look much like an uncle and niece to me."

"Oh, they didn't? Why not?"

"The way she spoke to him—sharp and sarcastic—more like a wife, I should say. Not that I mean there was anything *wrong*."

"But he was old enough to be her uncle—or her father, wasn't he?"

"Oh, yes—if you think that matters."

"Did they seem fond of each other?"

"Not so as you'd notice it."

"Rather the reverse in fact?"

"Well, of course, I really couldn't say. It's not my place to be with them—only with her."

Jennie evidently felt that she had said too much already.

"Well, about her then. You knew that she was engaged to this Mr. Holland, of course?"

"So she told me."

"Did she seem to be in love with him?"

"I'm sure I couldn't say."

"You didn't see them together much?"

"Not so much. But I never saw them kissing or holding hands."

"Ah!" Here evidently was significance—a criterion.

"Now tell me, Jennie, did Miss Fitzgerald care about her appearance?"

Jennie stared.

"Funny your asking that, sir. It always puzzled me. Sometimes she didn't and sometimes she did. She'd be downright plain some days—like she was this morning—and then she'd take and do herself up till she looked real handsome."

"And when did she do that? When her young man was coming?"

"I never could make out when she did or why she did —but it wasn't for him. Last night she was lovely—took over an hour to dress, when she usually flung her things off and on in five minutes. That white dress she wore was her favourite—it was chiffon with an overcoat of cream lace; she always wore a coloured flower—artificial—with it."

"Ah! I'd like to have a look at that dress sometime," said Rudge. "I've heard it mentioned more than once."

"Well now, that's another funny thing," said Jennie, who was now fully at her ease—as Rudge had intended. "She's taken it with her! She only told me to pack sleeping things and a change of underclothes and stockings, but she must have packed that herself after I'd done."

"But didn't you take it away—to brush, or whatever you do to it—when you called her this morning?" asked the Inspector, fumbling with half-guessed mysteries.

"Well now, there you are again! I didn't call her before you came—she likes to sleep late. But when I went to tell her you were here I went to pick up her dress and shoes and things to take away, but she snapped at me fierce and told me to go away, she wanted to get up. Of course, I went, but when she'd come down to see you, I went back to get them—and they were gone!"

"Gone! All the clothes she wore last night?"

"The dress and shoes and stockings were."

"Didn't you look for them?"

"Of course I did. They weren't anywhere."

"So that's why you think she took them with her?"

"Well, she must have. Where else could they be?"

Inspector Rudge looked thoughtfully at the girl, then nodded his head and drew out the notebook which had not previously appeared at this interview.

"I see, Jennie; thank you. I won't keep you longer now. Don't tell anyone else about that dress and things, but have a good hunt and, if you find them, let me know."

When the girl had gone, Inspector Rudge sat back in his chair and pondered what he had just heard. The maid's judgment as to the relations existing between Elma Fitzgerald and her uncle, and again between her and her *fiancé*, might be at fault; the question of Miss Fitzgerald's spasmodic attention to her appearance was at present beyond him; but surely the disappearance of the dress and shoes which she had been wearing at the time of the tragedy— or at any rate on the evening of the tragedy—was significant? Could she be in some way connected with her uncle's death? She had appeared neither surprised nor distressed when she heard of it, but if she had been guilty—or even cognisant of it—would she not have feigned both? However, it was too early yet to indulge in surmise—let alone theories; there were many facts to be collected first.

To begin with, the newspaper. How had it come into the dead man's pocket? Rudge happened to know that the late London edition of the *Evening Gazette* did not reach Whynmouth till 8.50—the express by which, incidentally, Arthur Holland had arrived. No doubt a copy would be delivered at Rundel Croft, but that could not be till about 9 p.m. and the Admiral had left the house at 7.15 for his dinner at the Vicarage. Unless he had got a copy from the

Vicarage, that seemed to imply that Penistone had returned to Rundel Croft after leaving the Vicarage at 10 p.m.—but then why was the paper in his overcoat pocket? Had he gone back to fetch it in order to read it out of doors—surely that was inconceivable? Or had he, on his way back to Rundel Croft, met someone who gave him the paper—not the delivery boy, it was too late for that. Someone, perhaps, who had brought the paper out with him—had brought it, perhaps, from London—Arthur Holland, for instance? Holland, who had spent the evening by the seashore and then gone early to bed—by himself. But here again was surmise—facts were what he wanted. Rudge rang the bell.

"Emery, did your master take in the late London *Evening Gazette?*"

"Yes, sir. Tolwhistle's boy brings it out of an evening—gets here about nine."

"Did it get here last night?"

"Yes, sir," said Emery, a faint look of surprise on his stodgy face.

"Where did you put it?"

"In the hall, sir."

"Is it still there?"

"I couldn't say."

"Go and have a look, and if it's not there, find out whether it's been tidied away."

Looking more surprised than ever, Emery slouched out of the door. Rudge thought it would probably be ten minutes at least before the tortoise-like butler returned, so he reached for the telephone which stood upon the writing-table and put a call through to Tolwhistle's, the Whynmouth stationer. The number was engaged, and while he waited Rudge let his mind drift back to the missing dress. He remembered that when he sent Emery off to ask Miss

Fitzgerald to come and see him it was ten minutes before the butler returned and then it was with the information that Miss Fitzgerald would be down in *a quarter of an hour*. There was, in fact, an interval of twenty-five minutes between his despatching his message and the arrival of Miss Fitzgerald. Did her appearance—slovenly in the extreme—justify or explain such a long delay? Was it possible that the mysterious "niece" had spent part of the time in hiding the clothes she had . . . ?

The telephone bell trilled.

"Tolwhistle's? I want to speak to Mr. Tolwhistle, please. That you, Mr. Tolwhistle? Inspector Rudge here. I want some information; quite confidential. Sounds trivial, but isn't. Do you supply the Reverend Mount, Vicar of Lingham, with newspapers? You do. Does he have a late London *Evening Gazette*? Left it off at the end of last year? Said what? Oh, spoilt the morning's—yes, I see. Any chance of anyone else supplying him? No, you'd have heard of it, of course. Thank you, Mr. Tolwhistle. Keep my questions to yourself. I'll explain them some day."

That settled the question of whether the Admiral had got the paper from the Vicarage; there remained the two alternatives of his having come back to the house, fetched his own paper, and gone out again, or having met someone outside who had for some reason given him the paper.

Impatient at the long absence of Emery, Rudge went to look for him. There was no sign of the butler, but Police Constable Hempstead was standing in the hall.

"I came to report that the body has been taken to the undertaker's, sir. I formally handed it over and obtained a receipt."

The Inspector blinked. Here was efficiency carried to full stretch.

"Right," he said. "This house isn't in your district, I think you said?"

"No, sir, but the corpse was found in it."

"And you think it your duty to see that its presence is accounted for?"

"That's for you to say, sir."

Rudge grinned. He knew that this keen-eyed young constable was itching to be "in" the investigation.

"All right," he said. "Here's a job for you; go down to the boat-house and find out from Sergeant Appleton whether he's found anything significant. No. I'll come with you. If there's anything, I shall want to see it for myself and we mustn't keep our detective-sergeant there all day."

And so, forgetting all about the newspaper, Inspector Rudge accompanied P.C. Hempstead across the park to the boat-house. As he went, he asked his subordinate whether anything particular had struck him about the case.

"One or two things, sir. In the first place, the body's clothes were almost dry—the back *quite* dry. But there was a heavy dew last night. If he had been lying about in grass, or even in the boat, since midnight (Doctor Grice fixed the time of death, you remember, sir, as before midnight) wouldn't the clothes have been wet?"

Inspector Rudge eyed his companion with interest.

"From which you infer . . . ?" he asked.

"That the Admiral was killed indoors and kept indoors —or at any rate under cover—for some time after he was killed."

The Inspector was silent for so long that Hempstead began to fear that he had exceeded his duty. Just as they reached the boat-house, however, Rudge said:

"That's a neat point; we'll talk about it later. Ah, Appleton, sorry to keep you waiting. Found anything?"

Detective-Sergeant Appleton was a square, solemn-looking man, valuable as a detective rather for his persistence in following up small clues than for any brilliance in deducing theories from them.

"Only two suggestive points, sir. This boat's very clean and rather wet inside—looks as if it might have been swabbed out recently. That's one; the other is that its bow's facing inwards. The Vicar's sons tell me that the Admiral always used to go in stern first, so as to be facing the right way when the boat went out again."

"Ah, Navy trick, eh? That's worth noting. Nothing else? No blood, signs of struggle, footmarks, finger-prints?"

"No to the first two, sir. There are one or two good footmarks I've covered over with boards and there look to be plenty of finger-prints all over the boat and sculls."

"We'll have to examine them later. Any theories, Appleton?"

"None, sir."

Inspector Rudge sat down on the bank and motioned to his subordinates to join him.

"Light up," he said, pulling a pipe out of his pocket. "Think better smoking, and we must think now. The Vicar's hat, in the first place; why was it in the boat?"

"Put there by the guilty party to throw suspicion on the Vicar," hazarded Sergeant Appleton.

"Improve on that, Hempstead?"

"The other alternative is that the Vicar left it there himself, sir, and forgot he had."

"He stated positively that he had his hat on when he saw the Admiral off after dinner last night and that he left it on the seat in the summer-house."

"But supposing he went out in the boat after that, sir?"

"Ah, you mean . . . well, never mind what you mean. Now, why was the painter cut?"

"Someone was in a hurry," said Appleton.

"Someone wanted to suggest that the boat was stolen," murmured Hempstead.

"And the rowlocks were unshipped," the Inspector added his quota of surmise, "either because the body was dumped into the Vicar's boat from another and the boat then cut adrift, or . . . to suggest that explanation, eh, Hempstead?"

"Possibly, sir."

"Now, can anyone explain why the body was found where it was and when it was?" asked the Inspector, adding to himself, "and if it was."

Sergeant Appleton brightened.

"Yes, sir," he said. "I thought that out while I was waiting. If the murder was committed at midnight, as Doctor Grice says, and the boat cut adrift then, it would have gone right out to sea, because the tide was at full ebb then. My theory is that the murder was committed several miles up-stream and that before the boat reached Whynmouth the tide turned and it floated back to where it was found."

"What time did the tide turn?"

"According to Mr. Ware, sir," said Hempstead, "it turned about 3.45 a.m."

"Well, let's work this out. He told us, you remember, Hempstead, that it would have taken forty to forty-five minutes for the boat to get from the Vicarage to the spot where he was when it reached him; what time was that?"

"Just after 4.30 a.m., sir."

"That means it left—or passed—the Vicarage at about 3.50 a.m.—only five minutes after the tide turned?"

"That's right, sir."

"Then that means that if it was set adrift from here or from the Vicarage it must have been only just before 3.45 a.m.—otherwise it couldn't have got back to where Ware found it by the time it did. But it's nearly light by 3.45— they wouldn't have left it as late as that. It looks as if Appleton's theory was the right one."

Sergeant Appleton beamed, but P.C. Hempstead looked mulish. Rudge noticed the look.

"Out with it, Hempstead," he said. "You've got a theory, I can see."

"Well, sir, if I might make the suggestion, you've over-looked slack tide. For an hour or so before the turn the tide's so slack that it's barely running. It's possible that a boat might fetch up against the bank for quite a time. My theory, as you know, sir, is that the body wasn't in the boat long enough for the dew to make the clothes wet. I think it was set adrift from here about 2.30 or 3 a.m. If the person who did it was a stranger to the place he might not think of the river being tidal—he'd expect the boat to float straight out to sea. But what happened was that it floated a few hundred yards, and then, as the tide slackened, drifted into the bank; at 3.45, when the tide turned, it drifted off again and so floated up on the flow till it reached the spot where Neddy Ware found it at half past four."

CHAPTER IV

By Agatha Christie

MAINLY CONVERSATION

"THAT'S a pretty good theory too," said Rudge.

He always believed in being diplomatic with his in-
feriors. In this instance, nothing in his face showed which
of the two theories struck him as being the right one.

He nodded his head once or twice and then rose to his
feet. He looked behind him at the trees near the boat-
house.

"There's one thing that strikes me," he said. "I wonder
if there's anything in it?"

Appleton and Hempstead looked at him enquiringly.

"In my conversation with the Vicar, he mentioned that
he had seen Miss Fitzgerald's white dress through the
trees."

"As she was going up to the house, sir—yes, I remember his saying that. Anything fishy about that, do you
think, sir?"

"No, I imagine it's perfectly possible. Miss Fitzgerald
was wearing a white chiffon dress with a cream lace coat.
If the Vicar saw the dress, then clearly she was not wearing any coat or cloak over it. After all, why should she?
It was quite a warm night."

"Yes, sir."

Appleton looked puzzled.

"On the other hand, the Admiral, when he was found, was wearing a thick brown overcoat. Anything strike you as odd about that?"

"Well—yes, I suppose it is a little queer—that the lady shouldn't have had anything warmer in the way of a wrap than a lace coat, and that the Admiral—yes, sir, I take your meaning."

"I'm going to ask you, Sergeant, to take a boat across to the Vicarage and ask there if the Admiral was wearing a coat last night."

"Right, sir."

When the sergeant had departed, the Inspector turned to Hempstead.

"Now," he said with a twinkle; "I'm going to ask you a question."

"Yes, sir?"

"Who is the biggest talker in Whynmouth?"

P.C. Hempstead grinned in spite of himself.

"Mrs. Davis, sir, who keeps the Lord Marshall. Nobody else can get a word in edgeways when she's about."

"One of that kind, is she?"

"Yes, indeed, sir."

"Well, that will just suit me. The Admiral was a new-comer to the place. There's always talk about a new-comer. For ninety-nine false rumours, there will be one true thing that somebody has noticed and observed. Attention has been focussed on Rundel Croft. I want to know just what has transpired in village gossip."

"Then it's Mrs. Davis you want, sir."

"I want to go over to West End too, and see Sir Wilfrid Denny. He seems to be the only person in the neighbourhood who knows anything about the murdered man. He might possibly know whether the Admiral had any enemies."

"You think he was in hiding, sir?"

"Not exactly in hiding. He came here openly, under his own name. It's not an unusual thing for a retired naval man to do. But the loaded revolver in the desk tells a tale. That's *not* so usual. I could do with knowing a little more about Admiral Penistone's career. Ah! here comes the sergeant back again."

The sergeant, however, did not return alone. With him were the two boys from the Vicarage. Their eager, boyish faces were alight with curiosity.

"I say, Inspector," cried Peter, "can't we help in any way? Haven't you got a job for us of any kind? Fancy old Penistone, of all people, to get murdered!"

"Why do you say 'of all people,' young gentleman?" enquired the Inspector.

"Oh! I don't know." The boy flushed. "He was so very —well, correct and nautical. All present and shipshape! Sort of old fellow who'd look at you if you forgot to call him 'sir' even once."

"A martinet and a disciplinarian, eh?"

"I suppose that's what I mean. Years behind the times."

"I don't think he was a bad old geezer," said Alec tolerantly.

The Inspector turned to Appleton.

"What about the coat?"

"The Admiral, sir, was *not* wearing a coat when he came to dinner last night."

"Rather not," said Peter. "Just nip across the river and there you are. Why should he wear a coat? The Fitzgerald hadn't got one either."

"Wasn't she *sweet*?" minced Alec. "All in white like a blushing bride. And old as the hills really."

"Well," said Rudge. "I must be getting along."

"Oh, but, Inspector, what about *us*?"

Rudge smiled indulgently.

"Suppose you two young gentlemen have a look for the

weapon," he suggested. "It wasn't in the wound. Somewhere along the river bank maybe. . . ."

He retreated, smiling to himself.

"That'll keep 'em busy," he said to himself. "And do no harm either. They might even come across it—stranger things have happened."

As he got into his car and drove in the direction of Whynmouth, his brain worked busily. The evening paper was now accounted for. The Admiral must have returned to the house some time between ten o'clock and midnight, donned an overcoat and slipped the evening paper into his overcoat pocket. Then he had gone out again—where?

Had he taken the boat? Had he gone either up-stream or down-stream to keep some appointment? Had he walked to some house near by?

As yet, the whole thing was a mystery.

On arrival at Whynmouth, Rudge pulled up opposite the Lord Marshall Hotel.

The Lord Marshall prided itself on its old-world air. The hall was dark and narrow and an intending visitor was bewildered by finding no one to whom to apply. Usually, deceived by the general dimness, application was made to a guest who repulsed the new-comer frostily. On the walls were sporting prints of a humorous nature and several glass cases containing fish.

Rudge knew his way about the Lord Marshall well enough. He crossed the passage and tapped at a door marked "Private." The high-pitched voice of Mrs. Davis bid him enter.

At sight of him the lady took a deep breath and began without wasting a minute:

"Inspector Rudge, isn't it? And it's well I know you by sight, as indeed for the matter of that I know everybody in these parts. And not only by sight, too, for we've passed a remark now and again though I dare say you don't re-

member. But there, as I always say, to be well known to
the police isn't what you might call a compliment and I'm
just as well pleased that we haven't, as you might say,
really met before. And I can tell you this, Inspector Rudge,
you couldn't have done a wiser thing than come straight
to me this morning! Seeing that you're a new-comer in the
place—only been here two years, haven't you, or is it
three?—I declare time does run away. That's what I'm
always saying. No sooner is one meal over than it's time for
another. And dinner I will have served to time. These new-
fangled people arriving in cars, eight o'clock, nine o'clock,
even, and wanting dinner. Cold supper, I can manage, I
says, but dinner is served at seven o'clock, and then everyone's free to walk about and very pleasant it is around the
harbour on a summer evening, and so the young people
think—and even the older ones!"

Feeling the need of refilling her lungs, Mrs. Davis paused
for an infinitesimal moment. She was a jolly, good-
humoured-looking woman of fifty, dressed in black silk.
She wore a gold locket and several rings.

Without allowing Rudge a chance to speak, she swept
straight on:

"You needn't tell me what you've come about. It's
Admiral Penistone. Got the news half an hour ago, I did.
And 'Well,' I said, 'we're here to-day and gone to-morrow.'
But not gone this way, most of us—or so I devoutly hope.
Stabbed to the heart with a narrow instrument, that's right,
isn't it? And depend upon it, that's a stiletto, that's what I
said! One of those nasty, murdering Eyetalian stilettos.
Wops they call them in New York—the Eyetalians, I mean,
not the stilettos. And you mark my words, you'll find out
that whoever murdered the Admiral had been in Italy.
Naturally it couldn't have been an Eyetalian—he'd have
been noticed. Used to sell ice cream, they did, in my young
day. But now they have Walls and those others and much

more wholesome stuff, I dare say. No—we don't have many
foreigners in Whynmouth—except of course Americans—
and they're not really what you'd call foreigners—just a
kind of queer English, that's how *I* look upon them! And
the stories those boatmen tell them—why you'd think
they'd be afraid of a judgment—and the poor innocents
lapping it up—but there, I'm getting away from the subject. And a sad subject it is." She shook her head, but with
no overdone air of melancholy. "Not that you can say the
Admiral was one of us yet. Why, he'd only passed through
Whynmouth half a dozen times. Barely knew him by sight,
we did. And his niece! A most peculiar young lady, if you
ask *me*, Mr. Rudge! Very odd things I've heard about *her*.
Her young gentleman's actually stopping in the house now.
Came down last evening by the 8.30. And if you ask me,
I say 'No.' "

"Eh!" said Rudge, completely bewildered by this sudden
dramatic stop interrupting the flow of speech.

"I say 'No,' " repeated Mrs. Davis, nodding her head
very violently.

"No to what?" asked the Inspector, still puzzled.

"I say, if you ask me if he's the murderer, I say 'No!' "

"Oh! I see, but I never suggested anything of the kind."

"Not in words, but it's what it comes to. Cut the cackle
and come to the horses, as Mr. Davis used to say. I'm never
one for beating about the bush."

"What I was going to ask you was——"

Mrs. Davis interrupted serenely.

"I know, I know, Mr. Rudge. Whether Mr. Holland
went out or not last night, I cannot tell you. Bit of a rush
we had with the charabancs, and you can't notice everything. What I mean to say is, you can't be in two places at
once. And what with the gas being poor and one thing
and another, I'm putting in the electricity this year. Old-
world is old-world, but some things people won't stand.

Hot water system last year and electricity this. But there, I'm wandering off the point again. I was just going to say —what was I going to say?"

The Inspector assured her that he had no idea.

"Admiral Penistone was a friend of Sir Wilfrid Denny, was he not?" he asked.

"Now there's a nice gentleman for you—Sir Wilfrid Denny. Always a cheery word and a joke. A shame he should be so hard up, poor gentleman. Oh! yes, he and the Admiral were acquainted. They do say that's why the Admiral came down here to live. But I don't know about that. There's those who say that Sir Wilfrid was none too pleased when he heard his friend was coming down here to live. But there, people will say anything, won't they? I'm never one to say a word myself. Too much harm done by gossiping. Keep a still tongue in your head and you can't go far wrong. That's my motto. And one thing I will say is a wicked shame. To take the Vicar's boat to do their dirty work in. Trying to drag him into it, poor gentleman. As if he hadn't had trouble enough in his life."

"Had a bit of trouble, has he?"

"Well, it's a long time ago now. Six and four the little boys were, and how she could do it! Depend upon it, a woman who leaves her husband and her children—well, there's not much to be said for her—not when it's a good Christian husband like the Vicar. (There's some I could name as *deserve* to be left.) Leaving her little children, that's what I can't get over. And a pretty gentle lady too, by all accounts. I never saw her myself. It happened before Mr. Mount came here. And who it was she went off with, I've forgotten. But a very handsome gentleman, I've always heard. Those handsome ones have a way with them, there's no denying it. Well, well, I wonder what's become of her? Dear, dear, life's a sad mix-up. And if I haven't gone right away from the subject again! Talking about

Mr. Holland we were—and he's a handsome fellow if you like. And yet they say Miss Fitzgerald doesn't seem to think so, for all they're engaged to be married."

"So that's what they say?"

Mrs. Davis nodded very significantly.

"And what the Admiral wanted to see Mr. Holland about, I've no idea," she went on. "But it's crossed my mind that maybe the young lady wanted the engagement off, and sent her uncle to do the dirty work for her. Though why it couldn't have waited till the morning . . . I dare say that's exactly what the Admiral thought, and why he changed his mind and said he had a train to catch."

Inspector Rudge made a valiant effort and interpreted this cryptic pronouncement.

"Do you mean," he said, "that Admiral Penistone called here last night?"

"Why, of course he did. Asked the Boots for Mr. Holland. And then, just as the man was going off, called him back again, hemmed and hawed and looked at his watch, and said he had a train to catch, there wouldn't be time for him to see Mr. Holland."

"What time was this?"

"I couldn't say exactly. It was after eleven o'clock. I was in bed, and glad to be there. Such a day as we'd had. Really, these charabancs—they do take it out of one! There were a lot of people about still. These warm nights you can't get the people to bed."

"A train to catch," mused the Inspector.

"That would be the 11.25 I expect," said Mrs. Davis. "The up train for London. Six in the morning it gets there. But he didn't go by it. What I mean is, he couldn't have gone by it, because if he had, he wouldn't have been lying murdered in the Vicar's boat."

And she looked at Inspector Rudge triumphantly.

CHAPTER V

By John Rhode

INSPECTOR RUDGE BEGINS TO FORM
A THEORY

INSPECTOR RUDGE assumed an expression of profound admiration. "My word, Mrs. Davis, it takes a woman like you to put two and two together like that!" he exclaimed. "Of course the Admiral could not have caught the train, now I come to think of it!"

Mrs. Davis chuckled good-humouredly. "There, now you're laughing at me," she said. "I don't know how it is, but most of my visitors always seem to find a joke in something or other I say to them. Perhaps it's just as well, it keeps them cheerful and contented, and what I always say is: make your visitors happy as long as you're sure they have got enough money to pay their bills. Not that they often manage to hoodwink me——"

"I'm sure they don't," interrupted the Inspector politely. "It would take a clever man to do that, I'm certain. By the way, how was it you knew all about the murder of Admiral Penistone before I got here?"

"It isn't always those that get about the most that hears the most," replied Mrs. Davis roguishly. "Here am I, not been outside the house this blessed morning, and I warrant I know more about it than anybody else in Whynmouth, barring the police, of course, Inspector. You see, it's this

way: you came in by the hotel entrance, and you wouldn't
have noticed it. But if you go up the side street there's another door that leads into the Shades. It's put there, apart
from the house, so that it won't interfere with the hotel
visitors. They get their drinks in the smoking-room, and
pay more for them, too. It's the outside customers that use
the Shades, fishermen and the like of that, such as the gentlemen who use the smoking-room wouldn't care to asso-
ciate with. Not that there's anything amiss with them, bar
that they're a bit free with their language sometimes.
They're polite enough to me when I go in there in the
mornings at opening time to see that all's right and comfortable."

"Ah, so you heard about the murder in the Shades this
morning, did you, Mrs. Davis?" suggested the Inspector.

"Why! that's just what I was going to tell you about!"
exclaimed Mrs. Davis, in a slightly hurt tone. "But you
gentlemen in the police are all the same. You're so short
with your questions that a body can hardly get a word in
edgeways. As I was going to say, I was in there this morning when Billy the barman was taking down the shutters,
and as soon as he unlocked the door in walked a couple of
chaps with ambulance badges on. I asked them if there
had been an accident, and they told me how Mr. Ware of
Lingham had found the Admiral's body in the Vicar's boat,
which was floating about, with no one in sight."

At this moment, as though in answer to Inspector
Rudge's inward prayer, an agitated-looking cook appeared
from the back regions and muttered something in Mrs.
Davis's ear. "Why, there now! if it hadn't altogether
slipped my memory," she exclaimed. "I've been so interested hearing you talk, Inspector, that I've never ordered
the joint for lunch. You'll excuse me if I run off and see to
it, won't you, Mr. Rudge?"

The Inspector waited till Mrs. Davis had disappeared, then, when he was satisfied that she was out of hearing, rang a bell marked "Porter." In a few minutes a bald-headed individual hustled into the entrance hall, still struggling with the short jacket which he had hastily thrust on over his rolled-up shirt sleeves. From his appearance he seemed to have been interrupted in the act of stoking the central heating system. He looked at Inspector Rudge enquiringly. "Yessir," he remarked.

"I'm Inspector Rudge, and I came here to make certain enquiries. You knew Admiral Peniston, I believe?"

The man scratched his head. "Well, sir, I can't rightly say as I knew him," he replied. "I've only seen him once in my life, and that was last night. Came in here, he did, and asked for Mr. Holland."

The Inspector nodded. "So I believe. Now, I'm particularly anxious to know how he was looking then. Did he seem worried, or anxious, or anything like that?"

"I couldn't very well say, sir. You see, it was gone eleven, and I was just going to shut up the house. Mrs. Davis is always telling me to be careful of the gas, and there was only one light burning. The Admiral came just inside the door, and stood where you might be standing now, sir. 'Is Mr. Holland in?' he asks, sharp like. And almost before I had time to say he was in bed, he said that it didn't matter and that he couldn't wait, as he had a train to catch. He wasn't here no more than a few seconds, sir. He seemed in a hurry, but I couldn't properly see his face. I wouldn't have known who it was if he hadn't told me."

Again the Inspector nodded. "You'd recognise him again if you saw him, I suppose?" he asked.

"Well, sir, I might and I mightn't. I never got a proper sight of him, as you might say."

"Oh, well, it doesn't matter," said the Inspector carelessly. "Was Mr. Holland in when Admiral Penistone called?"

"I'm pretty sure he was, sir, leastways, his boots was outside his door. I saw them when I went up to bed soon after. And he didn't come in later, I know that for a fact."

"How can you be sure of that?"

"Why, sir, because I locked the door as I always do round about half-past eleven. If anybody wants to get in after that, they presses the bell, which rings in my room, and I comes down and lets them in. And the bell didn't ring last night, sir."

"I see. And when is the door opened again?"

"I unbolts it first thing, when I comes down in the morning, sir, round about six, that is."

"What do you do after you unlock the door?"

"Why, sir, I lights the kitchen fire and puts on the kettle for a cup of tea."

"Did you happen to see Mr. Holland this morning?"

"I was in the hall when he went out after breakfast, sir. About nine o'clock that would have been. And he hasn't come back since, at least not that I know of."

The sound of Mrs. Davis's voice, rapidly growing in intensity as she returned from the back regions, caused Rudge to beat a hasty retreat. He slipped out of the hotel, and began to walk towards the police station, reviewing the scraps of information which he had picked up at the Lord Marshall, and congratulating himself upon having had the idea of interviewing Mrs. Davis. Gossip though she might be, her freely-expressed opinions of people were based upon a certain native shrewdness. The Inspector felt that he had already gained a valuable side-light upon Sir Wilfrid Denny, and that even the revelation of that curious episode in the Vicar's past might prove instructive. As to Holland, Mrs. Davis's conviction that he was not the

murderer was certainly well-grounded if he had spent the
night in the hotel.

But of course, the most interesting thing he had learnt
was the alleged visit of Admiral Peniston shortly after
eleven last night. Unfortunately it was impossible to decide whether the caller had been the Admiral or not. The
porter's identification of him was obviously worthless. He
did not know the Admiral by sight, he could not even
undertake to recognise the caller again. Where, in fact,
had been the Admiral? He had last been seen shortly after
ten, by the boat-house. That would have given him an
hour to get to Whynmouth. Hardly time to have walked
the distance, and yet he was hardly likely to have taken
the car out. Had he done so, somebody would have been
sure to have heard him. Could he have come down in his
boat? Possibly, if the tide had been flowing the right way.

Inspector Rudge frowned. He was no seaman, and he
had begun to regard the vagaries of this infernal River
Whyn as a personal affront to him. His idea of a self-
respecting river was a placid stream which knew its own
mind and flowed always in the same direction, like, say, the
Thames at Maidenhead. But the Whyn was mad, subject,
like a lunatic, to the influence of the moon, and changing
the direction of its flow in obedience to some law which
was past the Inspector's comprehension. He decided that
he would have to consult some expert on that point. For
the present, he imagined that if the tide had been flowing
down the river, there was no reason why the Admiral
should not have called at the Lord Marshall at the time
stated.

But on the other hand, his behaviour there had been
quite contrary to what the Inspector had gathered of his
character. He seemed to have been of a peremptory and
determined nature. Rudge could not have imagined him

walking into the place, with the intention of seeing Holland, and then suddenly changing his mind on the score that he had barely time to catch his train. It would have been more like him to have stamped about the hall till Holland had been dragged from his bed.

Unless—yes—that was a possibility. Suppose his visit to the hotel had been merely to assure himself that Holland had arrived? From the fact that the porter had offered to go and see if he was in, he would have known that he was staying in the house. Perhaps, having ascertained this, his object had been accomplished, and the excuse about the train had been trumped up on the spur of the moment, to account for his exit. He might not have wanted to see Holland just then.

On the other hand, if the visitor had not been the Admiral, why had he given his name? To make it appear that the Admiral had been in Whynmouth at that particular time? This opened up a wide field for speculation, in which one central fact was apparent. The visitor must have known something of Admiral Penistone's movements that evening. And therefore every effort must be made to trace him.

And what about Holland himself? The Inspector was not at all satisfied on the subject of that impulsive gentleman. Mrs. Davis may have been right in her conjecture that Miss Fitzgerald was not eager to marry him, but he was by no means certain that she was equally right in her opinion that he was not the murderer. There was no means of verifying his statement that he had spent the night in the hotel. He could easily have slipped out during the confusion that appeared to have reigned before eleven, and returned just after six in the morning, when the door was unlocked and the porter was busy with the kitchen fire. Had he done so, and met the Admiral in Whynmouth or elsewhere? The more he considered the matter, the wider the field of speculation seemed to extend before Rudge's vision.

His original intention had been to drive out and see Sir Wilfrid Denny at West End, after he had finished with Mrs. Davis. But the possible light which that loquacious lady had thrown upon the Admiral's movements decided him to defer the visit. He had formed the rudiments of a theory as to the time and place of the murder, but the possibility of this theory depended upon the tides in the River Whyn, and upon this subject he must seek expert advice. Why not have another chat with Neddy Ware? He knew the tides as no one else did, his hobby had rendered a study of them absolutely necessary to him. And besides, there was always the chance that he might have observed some detail which he had not recollected in the first excitement of his discovery.

Inspector Rudge turned his car towards Lingham once more, and very soon reached Ware's cottage. The old man was at home, smoking his pipe contemplatively after his midday meal. He greeted the Inspector hospitably, and the two sat down in a room decorated with models of ships and faded photographs of the vessels in which Ware had served.

"You want to know about the tides in the river?" he replied, in answer to the Inspector's explanation of the cause of his visit. "Why, they're simple enough, so long as you remember that it's high water, Full and Change, at Whynmouth at seven o'clock."

Rudge laughed. "I haven't a doubt it's simple enough to you," he said. "Personally, I haven't the foggiest idea what you're talking about. What on earth do you mean by high water, Full and Change?"

"Why, merely that it's high water at Whynmouth at seven o'clock nearabouts, on the days when the moon is full or new," replied Ware. "Now, take this morning's tide, for instance. To-day's Wednesday, the 10th. It was new moon on Monday, that's to say it was high water at Whynmouth at seven on Monday evening. It would be about eight yesterday evening and half-past this morning. You can allow six hours between high and low water, making it low water at half-past two this morning. The tide up here begins to flow half to three-quarters of an hour after low water at Whynmouth, or say soon after three. And that's when I went out fishing."

"After three!" exclaimed Rudge. "But I thought you said the church clock struck four not long before you saw the boat?"

"The clock!" replied Ware, in a voice of supreme contempt. "You don't expect the tide to fall in with the children's games you play with the clock in summer, do you? You play a game of make-believe with the time, just because you haven't the courage to face the prospects of getting up an hour earlier than usual. It may be all very well for landsmen, but it won't do for sailors. To them, time's time, and you can't alter it."

"I see. Then, by summer-time the tide began to flow this morning up here, soon after four. From what you tell me, then, I gather that it began to ebb about ten last night?"

"That's right, ten or a little before," agreed Ware. "As I say, the moon was new two days ago, which means that it was pretty well the top of the springs last night. I reckon the ebb must have run down the river nigh on three knots for the first couple of hours or so. After that it would have slacked off a bit, as it always does."

"So that a man leaving here between ten and eleven would have had no difficulty in getting to Whynmouth by boat?" suggested Inspector Rudge.

"He'd have drifted there and likely enough gone straight

out to sea," replied Ware. "That is, if he didn't use his oars. If he did, he could have got to Whynmouth in under the hour, easy."

The old sailor had glanced shrewdly at the Inspector as he spoke. Rudge saw what was in his mind, and smiled. "You can guess what I'm getting at," he said. "I thought it possible that Admiral Penistone might have taken his boat down to Whynmouth last night. But if he did, the boat cannot have come back by itself. Somebody must have rowed it back and put it into the boat-house."

He paused, half expecting some comment from Ware, but the old man merely nodded, and continued puffing at his pipe in silence. Rudge tried a new tack. "Why was the painter of the Vicar's boat cut, and not untied, Ware?" he asked abruptly.

Ware smiled. "Because it couldn't have been anything else, as the Vicar's boys could tell you, if you asked them," he replied. "It's no business of mine, this murder, but naturally my mind's been on it all the morning."

"I'd very much like to hear the conclusions you've come to," said Inspector Rudge quietly. "Why do you say that the painter of the Vicar's boat couldn't have been untied, for instance?"

"I haven't come to any conclusions," replied Ware impassively. "That is, I don't know who killed the Admiral, if that's what you mean. But it isn't difficult to understand how the boats came to be found as they were."

"Not for you, perhaps," remarked the Inspector, "but it would be a great help to me if you'd explain."

"Aye, that I will. Now take the Vicar's boat first. She's not kept in the boat-house while the boys are at home, but out in the stream, tied to a post. Sometimes the lads remember to take the oars and crutches out of her when they come ashore, mostly they don't. I've seen them left in her dozens of times.

"Now, suppose they'd been out in her yesterday evening, and tied her up when the tide was high, or well up, as it would have been any time between seven and ten. You'll find, in any tidal river, that the greater part of the rise happens during the first three hours of the flood, and the greater part of the fall during the first three hours of the ebb. Right. They come in when the tide's well up, and what do they do? One of them stands up in the bow, and makes the painter fast to the post. They're both well-grown lads, and they'd naturally make fast about four or five feet above the water. Then they'd pole the stern round, till it touched the bank and they could jump ashore. Maybe they were afraid of being late for dinner, and forgot the oars and crutches in their hurry."

Inspector Rudge nodded. This did not seem to take him any further than he had got already.

"Now, take the Admiral's boat," continued Ware. "From what I hear, she was seen either in, or alongside, the Rundel Croft boat-house soon after ten. Now this I'm pretty sure of. If anybody took her out between ten and one this morning, they didn't row far up the river. You don't make much headway with a heavy boat like that against a three-knot tide. You take it from me, if she went out at all, she went down-stream, and not up.

"After one this morning—I'm talking in shore time now, not real time—things would be different. There'd be only a gentle stream running down till four, perhaps a knot at the most. Anyone could row against that; it wouldn't take them more than a couple of hours to come up from Whynmouth, say, taking it easy. That's clear enough, isn't it?"

"Perfectly clear," replied Rudge. "It comes to this. If

the Admiral was murdered in his own boat, it must have been somewhere below Rundel Croft, anywhere as far down as Whynmouth, in fact?"

"That's right. Now I suppose whoever murdered him brought the boat back with the body in it. Suppose they got back round about slack water. The chap, whoever he was, sees the Vicar's boat moored to the post in the stream, and hits upon the idea of putting the body in it. He goes alongside, lifts the body in, and then what does he do next? How is he going to cast off the Vicar's boat? Tell me that?"

"I don't exactly see the difficulty," replied the Inspector. "It wasn't made fast with a chain and padlock."

"You didn't see what I was getting at just now," said Ware, with a touch of impatience. "Why, when he got back, it was dead low water, and the river had fallen three or four feet since the boat had been made fast. Don't you see? Unless he was a very tall man, he wouldn't be able to reach the knot unless he swarmed up the post. There was only one thing for him to do, and that was to cut the painter. And there's one thing about that you may not have noticed. That painter is a nearly new piece of inch-and-a-half manilla."

"I noticed that it looked fairly new. But I can't see for the moment what that's got to do with it."

"Ever tried to cut new manilla with an ordinary pocket knife? No, I suppose not. But you can take it from me that you'd find it a pretty tough job. And when you'd finished you'd have left a frayed edge. But this rope was cut clean through, like as though it had been cut with one stroke of a very sharp knife. Anyway, cut it was, and the boat left to drift."

Ware tapped out his pipe, and began slowly to refill it. He drew from his pocket the end of a cake of tobacco, which he shaved carefully into the palm of his hand. "This knife is pretty sharp," he remarked. "I keep it so on purpose to cut up my baccy. But I wouldn't reckon to cut through that painter with it at one stroke. No, it was a sharper and stronger knife than this that did the job, I'll be bound."

While he proceeded to fill and light his pipe, Inspector Rudge's thoughts were busy. The possibility that Admiral Penistone had taken his boat out again and rowed down the river seemed to be greatly strengthened. In that case, he had probably been murdered somewhere near Whynmouth, and his body had reached the spot where it was found much as Ware had supposed. But was there any way of verifying this?

In the first place, what time had he started? The doctor had given it as his opinion that he had been killed before midnight. Again, if he had indeed been the visitor to the Lord Marshall, he had reached Whynmouth soon after eleven. His departure from Rundel Croft could not have been very long deferred; his impatience to leave the Vicarage seemed to point to a desire to start as soon as possible. His excuse to his niece for not going up to the house with her, that he wished to smoke a cigar before going in, was probably mainly to get her out of the way. He had probably intended to start as soon as she was out of sight and hearing.

But if he had done so, how was it that the Vicar, who was in the summer-house till twenty minutes past ten, had not seen him? Suddenly Rudge remembered the Vicar's evident confusion when he had heard of the murder. Was it possible that he had actually seen the Admiral's departure on this mysterious journey, and had his own very good reasons for not disclosing the fact? It was at least possible.

The Inspector's reflections were interrupted by a remark

from Ware, who had at last succeeded in getting his pipe to draw satisfactorily. "Queer thing that I don't seem to recognise Admiral Penistone," he said. "There was only one of that name in the Navy List when I was serving, and I saw him more than once."

"Did you? When was that?" asked Rudge eagerly.

"Why, on the China Station, twenty years ago and more. I was in the *Rutlandshire* then, one of the three-funnelled County class cruisers, she was, and the very devil to roll in a seaway. I remember once being caught in the edge of a typhoon, and she pretty nigh carried everything away, alow and aloft. That's her, over there."

He pointed with the stem of his pipe to one of the photographs that adorned the room. "Her sister ship was on the same station with us. *Huntingdonshire*, she was called, and you couldn't tell t'other from which, except by the bands on their funnels. Our six-inch guns for'ard was a bit higher above the deck, that was all. *Huntingdonshire's* skipper was a man called Penistone, and a better officer you couldn't meet. The *Huntingdonshires* swore by him. She was always a happy ship, all on board properly looked after. And smart too. Captain Penistone had been a gunnery expert before he was promoted, and he kept it up on his own ship. When he commanded her, *Huntingdonshire* had the best gunnery record in the Navy."

"Was this the same man whose body you saw in the Vicar's boat this morning?" asked Rudge.

"Well, if it was, he's changed a lot since I knew him. Not that the body I saw wasn't about the same height, and all that. But, if it was the same face, it has changed a lot in the last twenty years. It was the expression I go by mostly. The Captain Penistone I knew was a jovial sort of chap, with a cheery word for everybody, no matter whether he was just a stoker or the Admiral himself. And

the chap I saw this morning, looked, with all due respect
to him, an ill-tempered sort of devil."

"I fancy he was, from what I've heard of him," replied
Rudge. "Well, Ware, I'm much obliged to you for what
you've told me. By the way, you'll have to give evidence
at the inquest, you know. You'll get a summons to attend
in due course. And I'll drop in for another yarn sometime,
if I may?"

"Aye, you're always welcome," said Ware cordially.
"And if you're a fisherman, I'll take you to a spot where
there's some fine sport to be had. It's private by rights,
like all the fishing here, but no one minds about me."

Inspector Rudge left the old man's cottage, and started
up his car. It was time to pay his deferred visit to Sir
Wilfrid Denny. As he drove towards West End, his
thoughts were busy with the problem of how to discover
whether or not Admiral Penistone had rowed down-stream
the previous night. If he had he was not likely to have
been observed. The river ran out of sight of the road for
the greater part of its course. Only at one point, Fernton
Bridge, was it visible. There were certainly a few cottages
close to its banks, but their inhabitants were pretty certain
to have been in bed by ten o'clock. There was, therefore,
only the faint possibility that someone had crossed Fernton Bridge at the moment that the Admiral had passed
beneath it.

The fact that his journey was not likely to have been
observed had another bearing on the matter. His murderer
must either have known of his intention, or must have
seen him by chance, either at Fernton Bridge or in Whynmouth. But if he had met him by chance, how did he
happen to be provided with a suitable weapon? People
didn't as a rule carry about with them daggers capable of
inflicting such a wound. No, the casual meeting did not

seem to fit in, somehow. The crime must have been premeditated. But until he could learn more of the Admiral's associates it was impossible to guess who could have known of his plans. There was always the likelihood, of course, that the murderer had arranged the rendezvous.

As he crossed Fernton Bridge, Rudge stopped the car and looked over the parapet on either side. He found that he could see a few hundred yards, both up- and downstream, before bends hid the river in either direction. On a clear night a boat would show up against the water for some distance. Having satisfied himself of this he continued his journey.

West End was a suburb of Whynmouth on the harbour side of the river, and consisted mainly of red-brick villas, each standing in its square of garden. But one older stonebuilt house remained hidden from its neighbours and the railway to the north by a high shrubbery. This, as Rudge had ascertained, was called Mardale, and was the residence of Sir Wilfrid Denny. The drive gate was open, and he drove in, to be struck at once by the neglected and overgrown appearance of the lawn that sloped down to the river, and the state of dilapidation into which the house had been allowed to fall. He remembered Mrs. Davis's hint as to Sir Wilfrid's lack of means, which had apparently been fully justified.

There seemed to be nobody about as he rang the bell, but, after a long wait, an elderly and rather forbidding-looking dame appeared, and looked enquiringly at him.

"Is Sir Wilfrid Denny at home?" he asked.

"No, he ain't," replied the woman. "'E was called to London hunexpectedly, and left by the first train this morning."

CHAPTER VI

By Milward Kennedy

INSPECTOR RUDGE THINKS BETTER OF IT

A TACTFUL question or two elicited the facts that the "call" had been a telephonic one, and that it was not Sir Wilfrid's habit to go often or regularly or, above all, early to London. He was not, it seemed, a city magnate, but a retired civil servant—"one of those conciliar officers," the woman explained. The Inspector began to understand the untidiness of the drive; for whilst your Business Man usually acquires his knighthood at the height of his prosperity and retires to affluence, your civil servant finds that a title is small compensation for the difference between salary and pension.

The news of Sir Wilfrid's absence was disconcerting, but on the whole, and after a couple of seconds of quick thinking, not altogether unwelcome. Inspector Rudge was subconsciously aware that his enquiries were becoming unduly dispersed and that none of them by itself had so far earned the description of "thorough." As he thanked the woman, gave her a polite message for Sir Wilfrid asking him to get in touch with the police on his return, started up the car and drove back towards Lingham, his subconscious feelings took definite shape in his conscience, so definite that just before he reached the fork of the road he pulled in close to the hedge, stopped the car, lit his pipe, took out his notebook, and meditated.

He had been dashing about to and fro—from the Vicarage to Rundel Croft, from Rundel Croft to Whynmouth, from the Lord Marshall Hotel to Ware's cottage, from the cottage back to West End, and now he was going—well, where was he going now? Of course, he had wasted very little time, for the distances were all of them small; incidentally he wondered whether a little while ago he had been quite safe to assume that the Admiral could hardly have reached the Lord Marshall on foot by eleven o'clock, for now that he came to consider it the distance from Rundel Croft could not be much over two and a half miles at the outside. However, that was by the way; what the Inspector wanted at the moment was to plan out his campaign.

What had he learnt, in the first place, at Rundel Croft? By Jove, he had forgotten all about that newspaper. If Emery had discovered the "regular" copy still in the hall, might not the explanation of the copy in the dead man's pocket be that he had indeed gone into Whynmouth? Well, it was idle to speculate; there, obviously, was one loose thread to be picked up. For the rest, his enquiries had been directed to two distinct purposes—to find out something about the people involved, their history and characteristics and so on, and on the other hand, to discover what had happened after the dinner at the Vicarage on the previous evening. The more he considered it, the more annoyed he felt at Miss Fitzgerald's flight—he hoped to goodness that was too strong a word; and he wondered, doubtfully, whether he had not been a bit too generous in the liberty he had allowed to Holland. Still, neither of them, perhaps—unless his impressions were all wrong—was the best source for information about the Admiral. But what else had he to go upon? Practically nothing but the gossip of the Vicarage, the servants, old Ware and Mrs. Davis, none of whom could boast more than a month's acquaintance with the dead man. The Vicar had suggested that the Admiral usually was genial enough; his sons had implied rather the opposite. And old Ware—well, what reliance could be placed on his opinion? A petty officer could hardly have been intimate with the captain of a cruiser; and besides, twenty years was long enough to dim the vividness of his recollection. Of course, Sir Wilfrid Denny might have been able to help, but it was rather a leap in the dark. He might have known the Admiral no longer than had the Vicar; and if he had seen more of him in the past month it might simply be that the ex-gunnery expert had no particular penchant for clergymen; that would not be an unprecedented trait in a retired Admiral.

No, Rudge told himself, he must clearly get to work on less haphazard lines; there would be records at the Admiralty, there were the solicitors, there would be "references" given to the house-agents when the lease of Rundel Croft was signed. And the thought of the solicitors reminded him of the will. He had not finished his study of it; its provisions might be of first-rate importance, as a guide to motive. He did not even know whether it was a copy of a proved will, though that obviously would make a vital difference.

There seemed to be plenty of enquiries to set on foot, and the first essentials seemed to be a telephone and a staff; it was not much use leaving both the sergeant and the constable to spend their day at the boat-house while he himself tried to be everywhere at once and to do three jobs at the same time. Still, he would not be in too much of a hurry; he was enjoying his pipe and he wanted to look all round the problem. What about last night's events? By Jove, there was a point which he seemed to have missed. Where was the key of the french window? Was the Admiral the only one who had a private key, or did his niece possess one also?

Rudge puffed away at his pipe and flicked over the pages of his notebook. The maid—yes, Jennie Merton: nice little thing, and quite intelligent. She had given him a pretty clear picture of Elma Fitzgerald and her uncle and the household as a whole. Had she, though? Had he not been a shade too ready to take her opinion as reliable? She had been there just three weeks; and yet when she had told him that Elma and the Admiral were "sharp" with one another, and that Elma and Holland did not "hold hands" much and that she could not understand the whys and wherefores of Elma's variability in getting herself up and putting on her best clothes—well, had not he been a bit too ready to think that there was something mysterious, almost sinister, in all of this? More likely the other maid, the one who had been so bored that she had left after a week of Rundel Croft, could have told him the inner history of the Admiral's household: perhaps they were used to a gayer life. . . . Anyhow, she must have been pretty thoroughly bored if she had chucked her wages in order to get away. He pulled himself up sharply; here he was, on the brink of labelling the vanished maid as a foreign adventuress—and all on the strength of a few words of Jennie Merton's.

And when he came to think about it, there was something, well, a little confusing about Jennie's account of the morning, and the disappearance of that white evening dress. Emery, apparently, had found Jennie, and Jennie had gone to wake up her mistress and to tell her she was wanted (the whole process taking no less than ten minutes). Then Jennie was told to clear out at once, as her mistress wished to get up. But at some stage she was told to pack a few things for the night. And when she started on the packing—and that, presumably, was while her mistress was being interviewed downstairs—the white frock had vanished and was nowhere to be found. Yet Jennie blandly assumed that the frock was *afterwards* packed in the bag by her mistress, as if that explained everything. It certainly seemed to suggest that her wits were not so wonderfully sharp after all. And what was more, he would have another word or two with her on the subject.

There was certainly a good job of work to be done at Rundel Croft. That was not to say there was nothing to do at the Vicarage. If the two boys had found no trace of the weapon, a proper search might need to be organised. And then the Vicar's hat: on the one hand he had been so quick to remember where he had absent-mindedly left it, which seemed a bit inconsistent; and on the other he had shown no perturbation when the subject was mentioned—at any rate infinitely less than at other points in the interview.

Inspector Rudge knocked out his pipe and started up the car. He was for Rundel Croft, and as he turned into the drive he found yet another reason for his decision— the traces in the boat and boat-house. He left the car in front of the house and hurried round and down in search of his two subordinates. They greeted him in a manner which suggested that they were bursting with news.

"Well, Sergeant?" he asked. "Anything important? Found the weapon?"

"No, sir, but——"

"What, then? The footprints?"

"Er—no, sir."

"H'm. Well, we'll hear about it in a minute."

Then he realised that he was being rather needlessly abrupt and that Sergeant Appleton in particular was now wearing a distinctly sullen expression.

"Sorry," he said with a pleasant smile. "The point is that we've a lot to get through and I want to get started at once on the jobs that are going to take the most time. Just set the wheels moving, you know. So if you haven't actually caught the murderer, or as good as done so——"

"Not quite that, sir," the sergeant answered, his good humour restored.

"Then you, Sergeant, come up to the house with me. Hempstead, you'll stay on here. We'll be down again as soon as we can. Keep an eye on the opposite bank too."

The two men hurried back to the house, and the Inspector led the way straight to the french window which was foremost in his thoughts; one thing was certain, the key was not on the outside. They hurried round to the front door and rang the bell; after an interval of at least three minutes, during which the Inspector fumed impatiently, Emery opened it and admitted them with the same air of incompetent reluctance which had been the Inspector's first impression of him.

"I want another word with you, Emery," he began, sternly.

"Here it is," said Emery.

"Here what is?" The man really seemed to be half-witted as well as painfully slow.

"*Evening Gazette*," Emery explained, turning and pointing to a side table in the hall.

"The regular copy? The one which is delivered about nine? Where was it?"

"There."

"But you told me you weren't sure. If it was lying there all the time——"

"No more I was," Emery asserted, in weak indignation, "and the minute I went to see and my back was turned, you skipped off."

The Inspector snorted; he was unable to deny that the man had some reason on his side, but people who were as slow as the butler must expect all kinds of criticism.

"Had it been read?" was his next question. He saw at once that it was not calculated to produce a helpful answer, so he hastily amended it and extracted from Emery the opinion that the paper had not been touched since first it had been laid by him on the table.

The Inspector nodded; then picked up the paper and requested the butler to lead the way to the study. The sergeant was distinctly puzzled, particularly at the appropriation of the *Evening Gazette*, but followed in silence, and closed the study door behind the little procession.

"Now, Emery," the Inspector resumed, with difficulty restraining a tendency to shout, "I want to know about the keys of the french window—the one you shut but did not bolt. First of all, were all the other doors locked and bolted when you went to bed last night? They were, eh? So that this was the only way by which the Admiral and Miss Fitzgerald could get in. I see. And now this window—how many keys are there?"

"I've got my key here on my ring," the butler replied and quite briskly produced a fat bunch, selected the key and proffered it for inspection. The other took it, satisfied himself that it was the right key by unlocking the window, and handed back the bunch. He had wondered how the butler managed to remember not to leave the key in the lock inside; the bunch explained it.

"Right," he said. "How many others are there?"

"Only the one that I know of. The one the Admiral had himself."

"Sure of that?"

"It's the only one I ever heard of."

"Miss Fitzgerald hasn't got one?"

"No."

"How d'you know?"

"Well, once or twice of an evening she's borrowed the key from the Admiral."

"Oh, does she often go out in the evening?" The Inspector could not resist this deviation from the main channel of his questions.

"Now and again. With Mr. Holland," the butler told him, with an approach to a smirk.

"Walking out, eh?" Rudge suggested vulgarly; and the smirk became an accomplished fact. Rudge made a mental comparison of this with Jennie Merton's opinion; then, as if determined to keep Emery in his place, he asked sharply: "What's happened to the second key—the Admiral's?"

"Well, I—I really couldn't say."

"Where did the Admiral keep it? On a ring with other keys like you do, or separately?"

"By itself," Emery told him. "It used to lie on his table in the pen tray. It had a label."

The Inspector strode sharply across the room.

"Well, it's not there now," he announced. Several bright ideas sprang into his mind. The Admiral must have given the key to his niece when she walked up to the house ahead of him. She must either have come in and locked the door behind her—and so locked her uncle out: in which case how did he get the overcoat? Or else she must have left the window open, probably with the key in the lock and her uncle must have come in, locking the door and pocketing the key—but there had been no odd key in his pockets, certainly none with a label.

Sergeant Appleton coughed.

"Maybe this is it, sir," he said and held out a key to which was attached a small metal label with the word

"Window" engraved on it. He added, in answer to the Inspector's rather angry questioning look, "We were going to tell you, sir, by the boat-house."

"That's all for the present," the Inspector said to Emery. "I may want you again later, so you'll keep handy, see? Is there another telephone? Then this is an extension, I suppose?" (He pointed to one on a table at the far end of the study.) "Just switch it through to here. And another thing: I shall want to see the maid—Merton—again in a few minutes."

"Well, she's gone out," the butler told him, with perhaps a tinge of malicious satisfaction.

"But I told you, didn't I——" the other began, angrily.

"It's her mother. She's queer."

The Inspector snorted again, and the butler hastily withdrew. It was useless to find fault with the poor creature; he could no more stop Jennie Merton going out than Mr. Holland coming in, as Rudge observed to the sergeant.

"No harm done," he added, in reference to the key; the sergeant rightly took this to be a veiled apology. "Where did you find it?"

"In the boat—the Admiral's boat."

"You haven't been messing about——"

"Oh no, sir. Not that there's any danger. Apart from the oars and rowlocks, she's as neat as a new pin."

"H'm. What about the key for finger-prints?"

But it was easy to see that the rough surface of the label would not "take" a finger-print.

"Someone took trouble with the boat," said Rudge thoughtfully, "so I wonder how the key came to be left there."

"I don't think the state of the boat means much—necessarily," the sergeant suggested. "I had a word with the Vicar's boys. They say that Admiral Penistone always gave her a mop over, like, last thing after he'd finished with her for the day."

The Inspector considered this. It seemed to fit in with the description of the Admiral as a precise martinet; and it might help to explain why, after hustling away from the Vicarage—directly after ten, because he must be in by midnight!—he had dawdled behind at the boat-house. But it was far from conclusive.

"Well, fire ahead," he urged the sergeant.

"It just caught my eye, the edge of the label affair. Just sticking out from under the bottom boards of the boat. As if it had been dropped and had slipped down inside."

"We'd better try it, just to make sure."

He fitted it into the key-hole, and locked and unlocked the window.

"That's it all right," he agreed and stood silent for a few moments, tapping the key against the palm of his left hand and staring absent-mindedly about the room. Suddenly he emerged from his brown study and walked across to the mantelpiece. He took down a large, framed photograph of a naval officer in full-dress uniform.

"That's him all right, isn't it? Admiral Penistone?"

"Yes," said Sergeant Appleton in some surprise; he was enlightened about the conversation with old Ware.

"It doesn't sound likely to me that he's not the real Admiral Penistone," was his comment. "If he isn't, he's pinched the whole outfit," and he pointed to an engraved cup which also stood on the mantelpiece. A further scrutiny, moreover, revealed a "group" of naval officers in the centre of which was a younger but unmistakably a likeness of the dead man. The names of the group were neatly printed below the photograph; and in the centre was the name of Captain Penistone.

"I don't think there's more than a shade of doubt,"

the Inspector agreed. "But we can't afford to take chances. That's one job I've got for you—to ring up the Admiralty."

As he spoke, he took down a copy of *Who's Who* from a shelf full of reference books.

"Here we are," he said. "H'm. No address given, I see— just the outline of his career in the service. Gunnery, yes. China Squadron. Seems to have been a bit of a star-turn. Funny that he should have retired so young—I thought the axe was a modern invention. Anyway you ring up the Admiralty. If he's the right man, they can probably tell you a bit more about him, or suggest how we can find out. Go ahead, Sergeant, get on to the Admiralty."

Sergeant Appleton took off the receiver. The line was dead; the lamentable Emery obviously had failed to switch the telephone through. The sergeant set off to remedy matters, and took the opportunity to give the butler a piece of his mind.

He returned to find the Inspector seated at the writing-desk, deep in a fresh attempt to translate legal language into common sense. It was not really as difficult as he had fancied, on his previous and hurried inspection of the will. The estate of Admiral Penistone's brother-in-law apparently was divided equally (apart from one or two small legacies) between Elma Fitzgerald and her brother. Until her brother's death was established, she and her uncle were trustees for his share, the interest upon which, less a consideration to both of them, was to be put to the capital; on his death, the money went absolutely to her. As for her share, she did not receive the principal until she married, and until then her uncle and Mr. Edwin Dakers, of Dakers and Dakers, were trustees. The only remarkable clause was a provision that if she married without the written approval of her uncle, she retained only a life interest in her share, the money on her death going to a series of charities. The Inspector was rather gratified to find that, as he had suspected, there was no question of the Admiral having been her sole trustee; his recollection of the law was that such a situation was hardly possible. The document of course was a copy; Dakers and Dakers probably would know if it was a copy of a proved will, and it might be necessary, for formal purposes, to inspect the original at Somerset House. The sergeant could talk to Mr. Edwin Dakers. . . .

But the sergeant did not seem to be getting on with his telephoning, the fact of the matter being that he was far from certain how exactly one "rang up the Admiralty" and for whom one asked when one was in touch with that august department. The local exchange had not been particularly bright either, but was supposed to be making enquiries. The Inspector frowned, and glanced restlessly at the *Evening Gazette* which he had thrown down on the desk. He must have a careful look through the copy in the dead man's pocket. The way it was folded might be suggestive, or there might be a marked paragraph. The Admiral would surely not have bought an extra one, knowing that his own would be lying in the hall, unless there had been something of special importance in it. The "news" did not look anything out of the usual: a "London Flat Tragedy" occupied most of the front page, together with an account of fresh trouble in Manchuria (Moscow, as usual, was said to be giving liberal help to the latest unpronounceable War Lord) and a picture of the bridesmaids at a wedding at St. Margaret's.

The telephone bell rang. The sergeant, still apprehensive, took up the receiver. His expression changed rapidly to one of surprise.

"Who? Yes. Hold on and I'll fetch—oh, very well. Who?

Oh, yes, yes, just wait——" he beckoned frantically to the Inspector, who came quickly across the room.

"Who is it?"

"Miss—yes—I'm listening—Miss Fitzgerald."

"Give it to me," the Inspector demanded. "Come on, man." The sergeant was scribbling illegible notes on the pad before him. At length and rather doubtfully he handed over the instrument. "Miss Fitzgerald? This is Inspector Rudge. I'm glad you've rung up. I want to ask you——"

"Sorry," he heard in Elma Fitzgerald's flattest tones, "I can't wait now. I've sent you a message. And by the way, I'm *not* Miss Fitzgerald."

There was a click as she rang off. The Inspector swore, and joggled the lever furiously up and down.

"Trace that call, please," he demanded of the exchange, and explained who he was.

"It's all right, sir," said the sergeant. "She was speaking from the Carlton, in London. She said so herself, and besides I heard the hotel exchange say so when the call came through."

"What was the message? Wouldn't wait to speak to me, eh?"

"She said she understood you wanted to get in touch with her, and with Mr. Holland. So you'd be interested to know that they were both staying at the Carlton and would be there for the next day or two, and then they would come back. She'd be out dancing to-night but would always be glad to see you by appointment. But would you remember to ask for Mrs. Holland, as she was married by special license to-day."

The Inspector digested—or began to digest—this news in silence. If Elma and Holland were man and wife, it made it difficult to . . . And then the will. If the Admiral

was dead, the clause about his consent to his niece's marriage presumably fell to the ground . . . Elma's message
certainly gave him something to think about.

"Well, Sergeant," he decided, "we'd better get on with
it. Hurry up that call to the Admiralty, and after that I
want you to get hold of Mr. Edwin Dakers," and he rapidly fired off a series of instructions, including one that
he was to be told when Jennie Merton came back. "I'm
going down to the boat-house," he ended and departed via
the french window.

He found Hempstead patiently on guard.

"Any news?" he asked him.

"No, sir. No one been here."

"No fresh discoveries?"

"No, sir. The sergeant told you about the key?"

"Yes. Good work. Anything happened opposite?"

"No, sir. The young gentlemen have been looking everywhere for the knife, but I don't think they've found anything. They said they were going to have a bathe now."

The sun was getting hot, and there was a note of envy
in the constable's tones.

"Seen the Vicar?"

"Yes, sir. He's been watering the garden."

"What, this morning? In the sun?"

"Yes, sir, with a hose. Worth watching, it was. He
watered pretty well everything in sight—even the flowers
now and again. But I shouldn't say he's done them much
harm. I reckon he doesn't know an awful lot about gar-
dening, and that's just what Bob Hawkins, who goes in
twice a week, says."

The Inspector surveyed the boat-house and its contents.

"We'll make casts of those footprints if we can," he said,
"though they don't *look* very distinctive. And I think
we'll take out the oars and rowlocks. We can't keep this

place under observation for ever and if there *are* any finger-prints that'll tell us anything, we don't want them mucked up."

He stepped into the boat and began cautiously to hand out the articles in question to Hempstead. Whilst he was so doing, the sound of voices on the opposite bank made him turn, rocking the boat rather perilously. The two boys, clad in bathing dresses, with towels in their hands, were coming down the rough, red-brick path from the summer-house. A sudden thought struck the Inspector.

"Hullo!" he called, as they reached the Vicarage landing-steps. "I wonder whether you'd let me have the loan of your old punt for a while? It would save me going round by road every time."

"Rather!" the elder of the two answered.

"If you could bring her across and swim back," Rudge suggested.

"That's the idea," the boy answered with a grin.

By the time the paraphernalia from the boat had been landed safely, the punt had arrived; the Inspector moored it to a ring in the Rundel Croft landing-stage.

"How many times a day do you bathe?" he asked pleasantly. "Or has the search made you so hot?"

"It's all part of the search," the younger replied, perhaps detecting a note of criticism in the question.

"We're going to try diving for the weapon," the other added.

"Good," said Rudge, "though I'm afraid that what with the mud and the tide, and not knowing quite how big the weapon is likely to be, it won't be easy. I'd hoped you'd find it on the bank somewhere, but it seems you've drawn a blank."

"All we've found is the Admiral's favourite pipe," said Peter.

"Indeed! And where did you find that?"

"In father's study. He must have left it behind last night. He was smoking it after dinner."

"Sure it's his?"

"Oh, yes. You'll see why when you see it. A dirty old meerschaum shaped like a nigger's head."

"You haven't got it here, then?" As he asked, he realised that the question was a foolish one.

"It's up at the house." Alec nobly refrained from a sarcastic comment, and stepped to the end of the punt, preparatory to diving into the river.

"I say, Alec, don't you think we ought to tell him——?" his brother checked him.

"Tell him what? Oh, that. You are a fool, Peter. No, it's got nothing to do with it."

"What's that?" the Inspector enquired.

"Oh, nothing," was the airy answer. "Something we lost, not something we found."

"Better tell me, then," Rudge suggested. "Police job to find things, you know."

"Then you can do the diving instead of us," Alec suggested, brightly. "Still, as Peter's said so much, I'd better tell you. But it's got nothing to do with your business. At least, I don't see why it should have. It's just that we—or at least Peter—left a knife in the summer-house yesterday afternoon, or he says he did, and it's not there now."

"Is that so?" Hempstead too pricked up his ears. "What sort of a knife? A pocket-knife, I suppose."

"Well, no. It was a large-sized Norwegian knife. We'd used it to point a stake—you want a sharp knife for that. Anyway, it's lost; and the chances are that Peter never left it in the summer-house at all. He's as bad as father for not knowing where he's put things."

And he plunged into the river, promptly followed by

Peter, the Inspector getting somewhat splashed in consequence. But he was content to get this fresh news at the
cost of a few drops of water, and with a smile on his face
he watched the two lads swim across, scramble out on to the
far bank and begin to dive valorously in search of the
unknown weapon.

The smile slowly faded; evidence—or call it information
—seemed to be piling up. He thought of the proverb about
the difficulty of seeing the wood for the trees.

"Interesting, sir, wasn't it?" Hempstead's voice broke in
on his thoughts. "Things begin to take shape, as you
might say."

The latter phrase was as much a question as the former.

"Maybe," the Inspector answered him, slowly, "but
there are plenty of puzzles yet. One thing, Hempstead,
is that overcoat. Suppose the Admiral went out in his boat:
well, I grant you he might take an overcoat with him, but
it would need to be a very cold night before you or I'd
put on a thick overcoat to row in. Other things apart, you
want your arms free, don't you?"

The constable produced a throaty noise meant to convey
assent without definitely committing him to it.

"And another thing," Rudge went on, "is that evening
paper. Oh, lots of puzzles there are about that, as well
as the cross-word. But the biggest is 'where did he get it?'
It must have come by the eight-thirty last night—there's
no getting away from that."

There was a pause; and then he added slowly and almost breathlessly, "Unless it came down by road."

And then he turned to Hempstead, just sharply enough
to catch him smothering a yawn. He remembered that the
unfortunate constable had been on night duty. That in
turn suggested two things to him—first that he must get
the oars and rowlocks up to the station, and that Hemp-

stead could see to that and have himself "relieved" at the same time; and secondly——

"You didn't notice anything particular in the way of cars in the neighbourhood, round about half-past ten, say, last night, did you, Hempstead?"

The constable considered the point.

"Well, now you come to mention it, sir," he said at length, "there was a car stopped in Lingham just about a quarter to eleven or thereabouts. I noticed it stop by the lamp in the Square. Closed car, it was, with a woman in it."

"Alone?"

"That I couldn't say. I only know there was a woman because I saw her lean out of the window and speak to the chauffeur, or whoever was driving."

"Would you know her again?"

"Can't say I should, sir. And I didn't notice the number of the car much, either—you see there was no occasion, then. I just happened to notice the car. It didn't stop above a couple of minutes and then drove on. Along the Whynmouth road."

"And that, of course," said Inspector Rudge, "would take it past the Vicarage."

CHAPTER VII

By Dorothy L. Sayers

SHOCKS FOR THE INSPECTOR

THE Inspector ruminated for a few moments upon the fascinating possibilities suggested by this piece of information, and then, dismissing Hempstead with the advice to get a good meal and turn in, he walked slowly back towards the house.

"Yes, sonny, what is it?"

This was to Peter Mount, who had suddenly appeared at his elbow.

"A note for you from father," said the boy. "I came across with it."

"About the funeral, I expect," said Rudge to himself. But the note ran:

DEAR INSPECTOR RUDGE,

I am anxious to run up to London this afternoon on an urgent matter connected with my clerical duties. I hope that there will be no objection to my doing so. I should not think of absenting myself if the case were not of great importance, since I know that you would prefer to have all your witnesses on the spot. However, I trust that I shall not be detained very long, and I shall, of course, make a point of being back in time to attend the inquest which, as I am informed by Mr. Skipworth,

*will take place the day after to-morrow. I will keep you
informed as to my movements, should you require to get
in touch with me at any time, and should I be detained
overnight, shall be staying at the Charing Cross Hotel.*

*Apologising for any inconvenience this request may
cause you,*

Yours very truly,
PHILIP MOUNT.

"Good lord! Another of them," was the Inspector's mental comment. He stood for a few moments undecided,
the note open in his hand.

He had to make up his mind. If he forbade the Vicar
to go—well, he could scarcely do that without committing
himself to an accusation, for which step he was certainly
not prepared. He could *ask* the Vicar not to go—but behind the courtesy of the expression the note seemed to
carry a suggestion of mild determination. He had nothing
definite against the Vicar, except that his hat and his coat
had been found in a curious place, and that he was a bad
gardener. He turned to Peter.

"I think I'd like to see your Dad if he can spare a few
moments."

"Right you are."

"How did you get across, by the way?"

"Your new policeman brought the punt over for me—
but he isn't very good at it."

Rudge noted with satisfaction that Hempstead's deputy
had arrived. That meant that he himself would be free to
leave Rundel Croft if he wanted to. He spoke a word or
two to the new arrival—a very stout man called Bancock
—stepped into the punt and was poled across by Peter. On
the way up to the Vicarage he noticed the drenched area
round the summer-house. The hose had caught a clump

of begonias at the edge of a garden-bed. One or two of
the plants had been actually broken by the force of the
stream, and on others the water-drops were standing like
miniature burning-glasses under the bright sun. The Vicar
would probably wonder, next day, why their foliage
should be speckled with white heat-blisters.

The Vicar was in his study. He greeted Rudge cordially,
but his face looked a little drawn. No doubt he had received a severe shock, thought Rudge. It was a strong face,
though, and handsome in its rather set, ecclesiastical way.
It looked honest, but you could never tell. According to
local report the Vicar was a ritualist, and ritualists had odd
ideas about the truth. They would, for instance, subscribe
to the Thirty-nine Articles and then unblushingly invent
ingenious ways to get round them. Rudge was rather well
up in the different varieties of parsons, for his brother-
in-law was people's warden at St. Saviour's, Whynmouth.

"Well, Inspector, I hope you haven't come to tell me
that I mustn't go to town."

"Well, no, sir—not exactly. I shouldn't like to go so
far as that, though I don't say but what I hadn't rather
you stayed here. Still, as I understand you to say the business is urgent——"

He paused, to give the Vicar time to explain what the
business was, but Mr. Mount merely said:

"Oh, yes; it is very important. If it would have waited
a couple of days I should have tried to put it off, but I fear
that is quite impossible."

"I see, sir." Rudge could not for the life of him see what
clerical business could be so urgent as that, unless it was
a summons from the Archbishop of Canterbury or an important conference, and if it were, why should not the
Vicar say so? Mr. Mount's face displayed, however, only
the bland severity of one about to read the First Lesson.

"I take it that will be all right then, Inspector?"

"Oh, yes, sir. Provided, as you say, you keep in touch with us. And I'm very much obliged to you for letting me know of your intentions. It isn't everybody would be so considerate."

"We both have our duty to do," replied the Vicar. "Besides," he added, with a slight twinkle, "if I had gone off without letting you know, you might have imagined I was running away from you, and that would never do."

Rudge laughed dutifully.

"There's just one or two things I was going to ask you, sir," he said, "and I'm glad to have this opportunity. About the late Admiral Penistone. Should you say he was a quick walker?"

"No," said the Vicar. "Admiral Penistone never cared to walk much, owing to a wound he got in his foot during the War. A piece of shrapnel, I understand. He was not actually lame, but it tired him to walk very far or very fast. He always preferred to take the car or go by the river if possible."

The Inspector nodded. This upset his recent calculations and left him where he was before. He went on to the next point.

"Do you sleep on the river side of the house, sir?"

"No. My sons and the servants sleep on that side, but my bedroom window is at the other side, overlooking the lane. Sometimes I get called up in the night to visit the sick or dying, and it is more convenient for them to be able to knock me up without disturbing the household. There is a side-door, you see, which opens on to the lane, with a bell which rings in my bedroom."

"I see. Does your window command the high road?"

"Yes, in a sense. I mean, I can see the road, but it is, of course, a couple of hundred yards from the house."

"Quite so. I suppose you did not happen to see a closed car pass along last night in the direction of Whynmouth?"

"That is rather a vague question. At what time do you mean?"

"At about a quarter to eleven. I thought perhaps you might have seen it when you were undressing."

The Vicar shook his head.

"No," he said at once, "I am afraid I cannot help you. I came straight upstairs at ten-twenty, undressed and went to bed. I do not think I looked out of the window at all. But in any case, at the time you mention, I should be either in the bathroom along the passage, or" (he twinkled again) "saying my prayers."

"Just so," said Rudge, embarrassed as every true Englishman is at the mention of private devotions. "Well, it was just a chance, sir, but a very slight one. I couldn't really have expected you to notice. You'll be good enough to ring me up when you get to town, sir?"

"I certainly will," said the Vicar. "And thank you very much for your permission to elope. I promise you that I will not break my parole."

"I'm quite sure of that, sir," replied Rudge, with conviction, and took his leave.

He strolled slowly back through the Vicarage garden, his heavy boots squeaking loudly on the gravel in the hot hush of the August morning. Peter was still idling about the boat-house. Rudge looked at the post in the stream, with the end of rope still fastened to it by a couple of half-hitches. He wondered whether he had assumed too hastily that the body had been dumped into the Vicar's boat from another boat. He ought at least to take the precaution of examining the bank for footprints.

Search, however, revealed nothing very helpful. The grass edge was crumpled and broken in places, as it would naturally be if the Vicar's family were accustomed to board the boat from that point, but the grass itself was too short and dry to show definite footprints, and anything below high-water mark would naturally have been obliterated when the tide came up that morning.

Rudge sat down on the bank and stared at the river. The tide was just running down to the slack, and the ripples went clucking and clapping against the sides of the punt and the boat-house. On the other side lay the Admiral's boat, shivering slightly as the wash of the stream lifted her stern and dimmed the outlines of her mirrored shape in among the brown shadows. Between bank and bank the sun blazed full on the water. Rudge found the tune running in his head:—

"*Ol' man River, dat ol' man River.*
He must know sumfin', he don' say nuffin'——"

That reminded him that he had promised to get his landlady Paul Robeson's record of "Swing low, sweet chariot." And his wireless needed a new accumulator. Curse the river, with its perpetual chuckle and its imbecile tidal vagaries. He knew the Ouse at Huntingdon—slow, solitary, regulated by pumps and weirs, and little used for boating because of its derelict and weed-grown locks. He had seen rivers in Scotland, tumbling and brawling and full of stones, useful for nothing but for fishing in—if you liked that kind of thing. He had even taken a holiday trip to Ireland and seen the majestic Shannon harnessed and set to churning out electricity. But this river was a secretive beast and no good to anybody. What was the sense of a river with three feet between its high and low tide twice a day?

He looked at the mooring-post again ("Swing low, sweet chario-ot") and measured with his eye the distance be-

tween the hitch of rope and the level of the river. Nearly
eight feet. Neddy was right. Anybody on the river waiting to loose the boat at low tide would have to cut the
painter. The boat would swing very low indeed ("coming
for to carry me home"), and the painter would need to
be a long one, if the boat was to ride in the water. Suddenly he got up, started out of his drowsy ruminations.

"I say, sonny," he said aloud.

Peter emerged from the boat-house.

"How long should you say your painter was?"

"It's about three fathoms—eighteen feet, you know.
It has to be pretty long, you see, to allow for the fall
of the tide."

"Yes, I thought it would be." Rudge measured with his
eye the end of rope as it trailed in the stream, then tried
to remember the look of the end left on the Vicar's boat.
Five feet or so at the most, he thought. But he couldn't
be sure. Probably it was quite all right, but, just as a matter of routine, it wouldn't be a bad idea to fit the two cut
ends together. He stared at the post again. He could see
clearly in his mind's eye the Vicar's boat with the new
manilla cut through and Neddy Ware demonstrating on
his plug of tobacco the sharpness of the knife that had
made the cut. The sun on the river was dazzling. Gazing
at the post, Rudge's eyes swam with water. But it seemed
to him that that end was cut less cleanly than the other.

"What is it?" asked Peter, staring first at the post and
then at the Inspector.

"Nothing much," said Rudge, "just a little job I thought
of, which I shall have to see to presently. I'll go across now,
I think, if you are not wanting the punt."

He poled himself across without disaster, and found
P.C. Bancock stolidly reading a newspaper on the farther
bank. Telling him to keep an eye on the house and to take

any telephone messages, Rudge hurriedly climbed into the police car and drove round across Fernton Bridge to Lingham. The Vicar's boat was there, having been carefully loaded on to a farm cart and locked up in the "Dance Hall" of the local pub, where also lay, in charge of the local undertaker, the body of Admiral Penistone. On consideration Rudge had thought this the best arrangement, since the inquest would have to be held at Lingham, and it seemed better to leave the body there for the present, bringing it back, if necessary, to Rundel Croft for the funeral.

But the body did not interest Rudge for the moment. The boat with its painter was his object. On entering the "Dance Hall" Rudge found the police photographer in possession. He appeared to have reaped a rich crop of finger-prints, and was now methodically exposing plates upon them. Rudge nodded to him to carry on, and then pulling out a folding tape-measure from his pocket he stretched it carefully along the painter. The precise measurement came out at four feet nine inches, from the cut end to the ring on the boat's nose.

He came out again, drove back, cursing the silly necessity of having to go three miles out of his way on every journey and, returning to Rundel Croft, got out the punt once more. Poling across to the mooring-post, he took his measurements.

From the bottom of the hitch to the end of the rope was eight feet, and, allowing for the rope used in surrounding the post and making the hitches, and for the spare end, you got another three feet. That brought the whole length of rope on the post to eleven feet. Add four feet nine inches, and you got a total of fifteen feet nine inches only. Two feet three inches of rope still remained unaccounted for.

Rudge, clinging affectionately with one arm to the post while he made his measurements, and digging his toes well in to prevent the punt from drifting off and leaving him like a monkey on a stick, shook his head at this. Then he took the cut end of the painter in his hand and considered it attentively. He had been right. This was no clean cut like the other. A sharp knife had been used, but the rope had parted gradually, the strands loosening out under the strain and one final strand having ravelled out beyond the rest.

He was left with his new puzzle. Why should anybody need a bit of rope only a couple of feet long? It could hardly have been used to tie anything up, for the thickness of the rope meant that nearly the whole of this length would be taken up in making the knot. Well—it was one more riddle.

He pushed off from the post and took up the punt-pole once more. That piece of rope ought to be found if possible. But probably it had merely been thrown into the river, and if so, it would have gone out to sea by this time. Or (since the ridiculous Whyn flowed both ways) it might have gone up-stream after the Admiral. That did not seem to be a very promising line of research.

No message of any kind had been received at the house during his absence, and not quite knowing what to do, he wandered into the Admiral's study. There he found the sergeant, who, after considerable back-chat with the local exchange, had succeeded in getting through to the Admiralty and was trying to explain to a languid voice at the other end what department he wanted and whom he wished to speak to. The Inspector took over the instrument.

"This is the Whynmouth police," he said, in a peremptory tone calculated to convey that, though the Navy might be the Senior Service, the Law was more important still. "We want information about the career of Admiral Penistone, retired, late of the Chinese Squadron, and now living at Lingham. Will you kindly put me on to the proper person at once. The matter is urgent."

"Oh!" said the voice. "What do you want to know about him? I could look up his record for you, of course, I——"

"I don't want that," said the Inspector. "I want to speak confidentially to somebody in authority—and the quicker the better."

"Oh!" said the voice again. "Well, I don't know. You see, everybody's out at lunch, I think. One o'clock, you know. Look here. I think you'd better ring up again in an hour or two and ask for Extension fifty-five—they'll probably be able to tell you something there, don't you know. I'll send them a chit about it."

"Thank you." The Inspector slammed the receiver down and, after allowing the statutory thirty seconds, took it off again.

"Number please," said the exchange.

"Look here, miss," said Rudge. "Have you got a London telephone directory? You have. Good. Would you look up the number of Messrs. Dakers and Dakers for me? They're solicitors in—wait a moment—in Lincoln's Inn. Yes, I'll spell that. That's right, Dakers and Dakers. It's rather urgent."

"I'll r-r-ring you," said the exchange.

The remarks of the young man at the Admiralty had reminded Rudge that he had been on the job since six o'clock and had had no breakfast. He rang the bell and asked Emery if he could be given something to eat.

"Well," said the retainer, dubiously, "I don't know, I suppose so." He pondered, and then added: "Me and Mrs.

Emery was just sitting down to gammon rashers. I dare say you could have a gammon rasher if you fancied it."

The idea seemed good to the Inspector. He replied that he should fancy it very much indeed.

"Well, I'll tell her," said Emery. He went out, and returned again in a few minutes.

"I suppose you would be wanting something to drink," he suggested, reluctantly.

"Anything that's going," said Rudge, pleasantly.

"Well, I dare say you could have a glass of beer," said Emery. "Me and Mrs. Emery was just sitting down to a glass. Mrs. Emery felt she needed a drop of something to raise her spirits."

The Inspector readily accepted the offer of beer. Emery shambled slowly away, returning presently to enquire:

"If I was to bring it in on a tray, would that do for you? We ain't never been accustomed to have the police about the place."

The Inspector signified that whatever was most convenient to Mr. and Mrs. Emery would suit him. The man retired again, and after a considerable time returned to announce in a mournful tone:

"Mrs. Emery says you can have a gammon rasher if you want it. She says she hasn't made no sweet to-day, on account of being low in her spirits, but perhaps a piece of the Stilton would do for you."

The Inspector replied that it would do admirably, and at that moment the telephone rang. On answering it Rudge found that he was through to Mr. Dakers's office. Mr. Edwin Dakers and Mr. Trubody were both out. Could the speaker do anything?

The Inspector explained that he wanted to speak urgently to Mr. Edwin Dakers on business connected with

Admiral Penistone. No, he was not speaking for the Admiral. The Admiral, in fact, was dead.

"Indeed? Mr. Dakers will be very sorry to hear that."

"In fact," said the Inspector, "he has died under very mysterious circumstances. I represent the police."

"Indeed? Mr. Dakers will be greatly distressed. If you will give me your number, I will ask him to ring you as soon as he comes in."

The Inspector thanked the speaker and then remembered that Sergeant Appleton was still somewhere about, and unfed. He rang the bell again. Emery shuffled in and began at once with a reproachful expression.

"Now it ain't no good you ringing. Nobody can't hurry a gammon rasher. They wants a good deal of cooking if they ain't to give you bile."

"Quite so," said Rudge, "but I was thinking about my sergeant. Do you think you could manage a meal for him too?"

"The sergeant," said Emery, "is taking a bite in the kitchen along of me and Mrs. Emery. No offence, I hope."

"Certainly not, no," said Rudge, "I'm very glad he should." Emery withdrew again, while the Inspector pondered on Sergeant Appleton's superior enterprise and resourcefulness.

The gammon rasher—cut thick and well fried up— was brought in by Mrs. Emery, a little bird-like woman with snapping eyes and a masterfulness of manner which explained to some extent her husband's crushed and wilted appearance. A single glance at the perfectly-cooked rasher with its accompanying green peas and chips explained another riddle. Evidently, Emery's feeble-mindedness was the price the Admiral paid for Mrs. Emery's culinary skill.

Rudge expressed his appreciation.

"And how I could bring myself to do it I'm sure I don't

know," said Mrs. Emery, "with the poor master gone so sudden and Miss Elma away and the whole place in a up-roar. Even the very smell of the meat seems almost 'eart-less, as you might say. But there! that Emery is a man and man must 'ave 'is meat, if the 'ole world was to be swal-lowed up in Noah's flood."

"True," said the Inspector, "we are a callous sex, I'm afraid, Mrs. Emery. It's a great upset to you naturally. And with Miss Fitzgerald going away unexpectedly it's all left on your shoulders."

"Ah!" said Mrs. Emery. "And when isn't it left on my shoulders, I should like to know? A lot Miss Elma troubled herself about the house. Might be a man for all the help she was. Now the poor Admiral, he liked to have things pleas-ant about him, and for all he was sharp in his ways, it was a pleasure to serve him. Many's the time I've had to speak sharp to Emery, for I could see as his shiftless ways was a hard trial to the master—but there! Emery's but a poor creature, though he is my husband. The Admiral, he gave him notice to leave at the end of the month but there! I didn't pay no attention. I just cooked him a nice dinner, such as he had a fancy for, and he said to me, 'Mrs. Emery, tell that blistering swab of a husband of yours that he can stay on and here's half a guinea for you to buy a bit o' ribbon.' He was a good master, and I'd say so if I was on my death-bed."

"I'm sure of it," said Rudge, sympathetically. He felt that he had unaccountably neglected Mrs. Emery. If you want the truth about a man's character, he had always maintained, ask the servants. He now had two testimonies in the Admiral's favour and he felt they were to be relied upon. Neddy Ware had echoed the opinion of the Ad-miral's own crew—and a crew is seldom mistaken about its captain. And Mrs. Emery's evidence agreed with theirs.

"I suppose," he said, "that Admiral Penistone was a bit short-tempered at times, eh?"

"I don't think none the worse of him for that," retorted Mrs. Emery. "I'd rather a man was short-tempered than poor-spirited any day. And the master had a lot to put up with. What with Miss Elma treating him so bad, and his worries and one thing and another——"

"What worries were those?"

"Well, now, Inspector, I don't know as I could rightly say what worries. But I did hear as he hadn't been treated proper by the Admiralty when he was a young man, and he never rightly got over it. Something to do with foreign parts, it was, and he'd say that he'd get himself set right yet, if it took him a lifetime. But Miss Elma, she hadn't no more sympathy with him than a man hasn't when you're fratcheted to death with babies." Without pausing to explain this obscure comparison, Mrs. Emery went on still more rapidly. "She wouldn't listen to a word, Miss Elma wouldn't, just sat there looking as sulky as a cow and wouldn't so much as put her hand to a duster or put up a vase of flowers to make the place look homelike. And sorry I'm sure I am for Mr. Holland, and him such a nice gentleman, if he marries our young lady, though what he could see in her I don't know. It's a miracle to me, with all these decent, sensible girls about that a man will always pick on the wrong sort, and as to being good-looking, I never could see it."

"Well," said Rudge, "it's past praying for now. They were married this morning."

"Well, I never," said Mrs. Emery. "*That's* what your sergeant was looking so sly about! 'There's a surprise in store for you, ma'am,' he says, 'but I'll not tell you,' he says, 'for you'll be hearing it soon enough.' Fancy! But if that isn't just like Miss Elma, before her poor uncle's cold as you might say, the 'eartless 'ussy! And surprised I am at Mr. Holland doing such a thing, but there! Anything she said he followed like a lamb with a blue ribbon round its neck, but them big fellows is often the meekest when it comes to a woman."

"You think Mr. Holland is very fond of Miss Fitzgerald, then?" suggested Rudge. Would he ever get to the bottom of the relations between this pair? No two people seemed to agree about them.

"Fond he was," said Mrs. Emery, "and is, I've no doubt, though how long it lasts is another matter. She took it cool enough, but that's her way. Herself and her fancies, that's all that young lady ever was in love with, if you ask me, and he'll soon find it out. Things look different when you're married. Artful she was, too, leading him on and putting him off as the fancy took her. But as to caring for him, no, and the master knew that as well as anybody. If he'd been alive they wouldn't have got married so easy, and that's a fact, but to go right off and join their 'ands over his dead body, as you might say, is what I shouldn't hardly have thought Mr. Holland capable of."

"H'm!" said the Inspector. He was trying to remember how long it took to get a special license. He seemed to remember dimly that it required at least a day's notice. "Maybe they had planned to get married to-day in any case."

"Then they ought to have altered their plan," replied Mrs. Emery. "Disgusting, I call it. But I shouldn't wonder if they had, come to think of it. Maybe that's what Mr. Holland was so anxious to see the Admiral about last night."

"Oh, yes. He rang up from Whynmouth, didn't he?"

"He did. I took the message myself. Wanted to see the master very urgent. I said as him and Miss Elma was over at the Vicarage and wouldn't be back till late—for I expected they'd stop to eleven o'clock or such, playing cards or something of that. The Vicar don't mind playing cards for all he's such a man for services and saints' days, but that's only to be expected, for fancy dress and candles is not what you could call religion, don't you think so yourself? Well, I said to him, they won't be back till eleven, I said, saying what I thought right at the time, which I couldn't be expected to know they would be early that night of all nights. One can but act for the best. So I said, why not go over to the Vicarage, but Mr. Holland says, 'no, he'll leave it and perhaps he might come up later.'"

"And did he?"

"Not that I know of, but there, I'm a sound sleeper, thank God, and need to be, the work there is in this house. Emery, he's supposed to do the cleaning, but half the time I has to do it after him, and as for Jennie, she's a good girl but run off her feet by Miss Elma as won't do step or stitch for herself. Cooking is what I was engaged to do and with Miss Elma breakfasting in bed and getting up at all hours, I've only got one pair of hands."

"Quite so," said Rudge, "and very capable ones I'm sure they are, Mrs. Emery."

"I'm sure I said when I come here as I ought to have a kitchen-maid under me, with all these brick floors. That's the worst of these old-fashioned houses. But I've no complaint of the Admiral, for a rich man he was not, not but what she might have done something to help him if she had liked, for she's got plenty, so I'm told. And what she did with her allowance it's difficult to say, not that it's any of my business, for it's not, but nobody can't help their thoughts. And spend it on dress she did not, nobody could say that against her, barring an evening frock now and again, or a handsome coat. But them's not the things as

takes the money, as you'll know well enough if you're a
married man. It's the shoes and gloves and bags and stockings and jumpers. And I'm sure Miss Elma bothered as little
about them as a young lady could do. That French maid
she had, she used to complain dreadful of the shabby way
Miss Elma went about."

"Ah, yes—the French girl. What was she like?"

"Girl?" said Mrs. Emery. "They calls 'em all girls nowadays. But if ever she sees forty again, I'll be surprised. A
nice little thing enough, to speak to, and spoke English
beautiful. But I don't like a maid as is too intimate with
her mistress. I've seen Miss Elma catch that woman's eye
sometimes, when the master happened to be a bit put out
and looks pass between them which did not ought to pass
between persons in their stations of life. Let servants stick
together and masters stick together—that's my motto, but
for young ladies to be taking their maids into their confidences about the master of the house is unbecoming, to
my way of thinking. It's my belief there was some trouble
about it, or why did Ma'amselle go off so quick without
her wages? There's the front door bell, who'll that be, I
wonder? I hope Emery is answering it, as it's his place to
do, but he's that flustered with all this. You'll have noticed,
I dare say, as his head's not very strong. Now, I'm different. I'm one of the noticing sort. I may have been only a
month with the Admiral, but a woman that's experienced
—and I've been in many places in my time—don't take
long putting two and two together. Oh, I could size up
Miss Elma all right. Ah! Emery *has* remembered his duty
for once, I'm glad to say."

The door opened and Emery poked in his melancholy
head.

"Here's two newspaper gentlemen waiting to see the
Inspector."

Rudge was about to consign the newspaper gentlemen to a warm spot, when it occurred to him that all God's creatures have their uses. He glanced at the card held out to him, and observed that it bore the magic words, *Evening Gazette*.

"I'll see them," he said, shortly.

The two newspaper gentlemen were ushered in—a breezy man with a cropped head and horn-rimmed spectacles, the upper portion of whose face appeared to have been darkened by some ineffectual form of sunburn application ("all handsome men are slightly sunburned"), and a morose man with a camera.

"Now," said Rudge, "how did you boys get on to this?"

Cropped-head grinned.

"Information received, eh, Inspector? 'If it's not in the *Gazette* then it hasn't happened yet.' We had it on the streets in the twelve-thirty. Do your best for us, won't you?"

"Well," said Rudge. He thought for a moment and then gave them as much information as he thought was bound to come out in any case.

"*That's* O.K.," said Cropped-head. "Now, as regards yourself, Inspector. Our readers will want to know all about you. Perhaps you would be good enough to come and be photographed in the boat-house? Adds interest to the picture, you know. Well, that's awfully good of you. It won't take a minute. Is that the Admiral's boat? Just point carelessly towards it. That's fine. Make a good picture, eh, Tom?"

Rudge, in spite of himself, felt rather flattered.

"We shall say, of course, that you have the case well in hand and that there's obviously no need to call in Scotland Yard. Just so. Now, how about this niece? Could we get a word with her at all?"

"No," said Rudge. "As a matter of fact," he added handsomely, "I don't mind telling you something about her."

The reporter was eagerly attentive.

"She went off to London this morning," said the Inspector impressively, "and got married—to a man called Arthur Holland, a trader, from China."

"Did she? Quick work. That'll make a good story. Why the haste?"

"I can't tell you that yet. But look here. If I let you have that story exclusively, will you do something for me?"

"Sure thing."

"I want to find out about Admiral Penistone's past career. Why he sent in his papers at forty-three, and why he rejoined the Navy afterwards and all about it."

"Oh! I can tell you something about that," the reporter laughed. "I got that out of a man I know in the Chinese Embassy. The old boy got into trouble in Hong Kong in 1911. Some private matter. Something to do with a woman. One of the things that aren't done by naval officers. He was requested to send in his papers. No public scandal—you know the sort of thing. My man didn't know all the details, but he promised to get them for me. I'll let you have anything I get hold of. I dare say we shan't print it all, because some of the parties may be alive, but I'll send you the dope on the whole thing. And, I say—if there's anything coming along that you feel you can let us have straight from the gee-gee's mouth, you will, won't you? That's a bargain."

Rudge agreed readily enough. This was a great deal more hopeful than unwinding red tape from the Admiralty. Trouble in Hong Kong in 1911? That explained matters. No doubt as Penistone was a smart officer they were glad enough to let him rejoin in 1914. But it would have made a difference to him, naturally. Soured the old boy's temper a bit, no doubt. Was it possible that the murder was the aftermath of that old affair? It seemed a long time to keep up resentment, but where Chinks were concerned you never knew. And, by the way, Holland had lately come from China. What was that Mrs. Emery had said about Holland? He had said he might walk over to Rundel Croft after eleven. Suppose he had done so?

Obviously Holland and Elma must be got hold of. They would have to be subpœnaed for the inquest in any case. He must tackle the coroner about that. A little job for Sergeant Appleton. He returned to the house and despatched his subordinate with a note. Hardly had he done so when the telephone rang.

Mr. Edwin Dakers was on the line. He was indeed grieved and horrified to hear of the Admiral's death. He thought he had better come down to Rundel Croft at once. As Miss Fitzgerald's trustee and representative, it would be necessary for him to see her without delay. Doubtless she was greatly upset by this melancholy occurrence.

"I haven't noticed it," replied Rudge, with a sort of grim satisfaction. "In fact, no sooner did Miss Fitzgerald hear of her uncle's death than she went up to town and got married to a Mr. Holland. I should be glad, sir——"

"*What!*" said Mr. Dakers, in a tone so aghast that it seemed to shake the instrument.

Rudge repeated his information.

"God bless my soul!" said Mr. Dakers, and paused for such a long time that Rudge began to think he had fallen dead with horror. Then he said:

"This is very unfortunate indeed, Inspector. I am more than shocked. I am horrified."

"It certainly looks a bit unfeeling," said Rudge.

"Unfeeling?" said Mr. Dakers. "It may be most gravely prejudicial to her monetary interests. Can you tell me where to find her?"

"They were staying at the Carlton, she said," replied Rudge. "Miss Fitzgerald—that is, Mrs. Holland——" (Mr. Dakers groaned faintly) "mentioned that they were going to a dance this evening. I should be glad, sir——"

"A dance at the Carlton?" interrupted the lawyer. "She must be out of her senses. T'chk, t'chk, t'chk. Most distressing. I am not quite clear upon the point of law involved, but if I remember rightly, the Master of the Rolls held in the case of—dear me! I think I shall have to take Counsel's opinion. In the meanwhile I thank you very much for apprising me of these events. I shall go and see my client immediately, and——"

"I hope you will, sir, and I should be very glad if you could persuade her to come back at once. Mr. and Mrs. Holland will be subpœnaed, of course, but in the meantime it would be desirable——"

"Of course, of course," replied Mr. Dakers, "most unfortunate and unbecoming. I shall make a point of advising her to return home without delay."

"Thank you, sir, and I should be very glad, sir, if I might have a word with you at some time myself. There are one or two little matters which I should like to have cleared up, in connection with a document we have here."

"Oh!" said Mr. Dakers. "Yes?"

"In connection," pursued Rudge, "with a copy of a will, sir, made by John Martin Fitzgerald in 1915."

"Ah!" said Mr. Dakers. His voice sounded cautious. "Yes. Yes, I see. In what way, precisely, are you interested in that will?"

Rudge coughed.

"Well, sir, in a general way, as you might say. There's a brother mentioned in it, for example, and one or two other points that might be of interest."

"Yes, I see. Well, Inspector, I think the best way will be for me to see you myself. I will endeavour to bring Miss Fitz—that is, Mrs. Holland, down with me, but in any case, I shall arrive at Lingham to-night. Where shall I find you?"

"I shall be at Rundel Croft, sir."

"Very well. I will telephone you when to expect me. When are you holding the inquest?"

"I should think the day after to-morrow, sir."

"Yes. I shall be there, of course, to represent Mrs. Holland. I think I should have been notified of this matter earlier. How is it that you did not ring me up till one o'clock?"

The Inspector would have liked to say that it was not his business to notify the solicitors of suspected or suspicious persons, but he replied meekly that he had been busy and had only just had time to digest the contents of the will.

"It is unfortunate," he added, "that Mrs. Holland did not herself acquaint you with the state of affairs."

"It is; very," replied the lawyer, dryly. "Very well, Inspector, we will leave it like that."

He rang off.

"And that's that," thought Rudge, discontentedly. "Nothing for it I suppose but to wait for the old blighter. Still, if he brings the Hollands back, that's something to the good. It's a pity there seems to be so little one can get on with. Hollands gone to town, Denny gone to town. Well, what about those cuttings?" He had not yet looked through the file of newspaper cuttings. They might perhaps suggest something in connection with Penistone's mysterious past. Or there might be other papers of interest.

The cuttings, as he had rather expected, seemed mostly to have to do with China, though a section of them seemed to be concerned with naval affairs. They dated from two years before the War and were neatly numbered and docketed to correspond with an alphabetical index in the Admiral's handwriting. Rudge noted a small bunch of cuttings collected under the heading, "Denny, W." These he turned over eagerly. They told him that Sir Wilfrid Denny had been for many years in the Hong Kong customs, retiring in 1921 with a title and pension. Apparently Denny had only come to Whynmouth in 1925, having previously lived in Hertfordshire. He was a widower of sixty-four, his wife having died fifteen years previously, in China. He had no surviving children, his only son had been killed in the War.

This was interesting. Sir Wilfrid, then, had also been connected with China. No doubt his friendship with the Admiral had dated from the latter's period of service on the Chinese station. Rudge returned the cuttings to their folder and was about to replace them in their file, when he noticed an endorsement on the folder "See H 5 and X 57."

What this cryptic reference might mean he could not think. He tried number five in the H file and found that it referred to a single cutting about an Able Seaman named Hendry who had been killed in a brawl in Hong Kong some years previously. This looked hopeful, but in turning to file X, he found no entries under that awkward letter. And indeed fifty-seven entries under X would, he thought, be unusual. "X" must refer to something different. To what?

He turned to the alphabetical list, and under the letter

F his eye was arrested by another entry. "Fitzgerald, W. E." The missing brother of Elma! Surely this would be of interest. Eagerly he turned up the file.

The folder marked "Fitzgerald, W. E." contained nothing but a slip of paper on which was scribbled in pencil, "See X."

"Damn X!" thought Rudge, "where the devil has 'X' gone to? Perhaps it was particularly private. The old boy may have hidden it in some safer place."

Filled with excitement he began a thorough and careful search of the cabinet and the desk. The cabinet yielded nothing, nor, on a superficial examination, did the desk. At length, however, after lifting a mass of receipts and old cheque-books out of the well of the desk, Rudge came to a sliding bottom. He pushed this back and disclosed a key-hole. A little search of the Admiral's key-ring revealed a key of suitable size. He fitted it in. It turned easily. The door slid back and disclosed a folder similar to those in the cabinet and marked "X."

Before he had lifted it out, Rudge knew that he was to be disappointed. The folder lay flat as a visiting-card, and was, in fact, perfectly empty.

He was still gazing at it in chagrin, when the door opened to admit Jennie with a tea-tray.

"So you're back, Jennie," said Rudge, pleasantly. "It's very kind of you to bring me tea. Is your mother better?"

"Well, she's none so good, Mr. Rudge, thank you. Doctor, he says it's her back. He's been down to her twice to-day and she's a bit easier now, but she's still very low."

Rudge expressed his sympathy and noted that the sick mother seemed to be genuine enough. When he had eaten his tea, he continued his search for the missing contents of the folder, but without success. Three telephone calls came to break the monotony: one from the coroner, ask-

ing Rudge to come and see him first thing next morning;
the next from Mr. Dakers to say that he was still trying to
get in touch with the Hollands and would be down on the
eight-fifty; the third, much later, from the Vicar.

"I am speaking from the Charing Cross Hotel," said
the crisp Oxford voice. "I find I shall be obliged to spend
the night in town. I will ring you up again in the morning."

Rudge thanked him, and rang off. Then after a minute
or two he took an obvious precaution. He rang up the
Charing Cross Hotel.

"Have you a Mr. Mount—Rev. Philip Mount—staying
in the hotel?"

A slight pause; then: "Yes, sir."

"Is Mr. Mount in the hotel?"

"I will enquire; will you hold the line, sir?"

A subdued babel; then the metallic clack of advancing
footsteps and the rattle of the receiver.

"Hullo, yes: who is it, please?"

"That's him all right," thought Rudge. Aloud he said,
"I just remembered something I wanted to ask you, sir,"
and repeated his question about the length of the painter.

The Vicar confirmed Peter's statement and Rudge
thanked him and rang off.

"All O.K. so far. I didn't like him going off like that,
but he seems straight enough. Hope he is, because of these
kids. But that rope's a teaser and no mistake."

The eight-fifty arrived at Whynmouth in due course,
and presently a taxi drew up at Rundel Croft. Rudge
heard it turn up the drive and stop. His hopes rose, then
sank again as he heard the door-bell.

"Mrs. Holland would have walked in," he muttered,
disappointed. "But no!" He cheered up again. "The door's
locked, of course, because of possible intruders."

Emery's steps shuffled through the hall. The study door opened and a tall, thin, grey-headed man was shown in—alone.

"Mr. Dakers?" said Rudge, rising and executing something between a salute and a bow.

"Yes," said the lawyer, "and you, I take it, are Inspector Rudge. Quite so. Well now, Inspector, I am sorry to say I have failed to see either Mr. or Mrs. Holland. They are certainly staying at the Carlton, and were expected back to dinner. I have left a note for Mrs. Holland expressed in such terms that I think she can scarcely fail to pay attention to it. I need not say again how shocked and grieved I am at the whole occurrence."

"I quite see your point of view, sir," said Rudge, "and I may add that the absence of Mr. and Mrs. Holland is making my own task none the easier. By the way, sir, I am in a somewhat peculiar position in this house, with Admiral Penistone dead and nobody else in charge, so to speak, but I dare say I shan't be out of order in asking you if you have dined, before we go on to business."

"Thank you, Inspector, thank you—but I require nothing. I am obliged to you. I should like to hear at once all the details of this sad affair."

Rudge rapidly outlined the circumstances of the Admiral's death and the departure of his niece, while Mr. Dakers contributed a running commentary of "Tuts" and "Dear, dears."

"There seems to be no doubt then, that Admiral Penistone was murdered."

"None at all, I am afraid, sir."

"He could not, I suppose, have—er—made away with himself and thrown the weapon into the river."

This solution had not presented itself to Rudge, but he replied that judging by the position of the body and the

general circumstances, he thought it almost outside the
bounds of probability.

Mr. Dakers nodded mournfully.

"I take it," he said, with the air of a man taking a
ferocious bull by the horns, "that there is—er—no suspicion attaching to my ward or her husband?"

"Well," said Rudge, cautiously, "I couldn't say that
suspicion attaches to any particular person so far. And
other things being equal, the crime is certainly not the
kind that we would suspect a young lady of. We know
very little as yet about Mr. Holland. Possibly you can
help us there, sir?"

Mr. Dakers shook his head.

"I know very little about him, beyond his name, and the
fact that he was, in a manner, engaged to my ward."

"Did the engagement have Admiral Penistone's consent,
sir?"

The lawyer looked very shrewdly at him.

"I see what is in your mind, Inspector. Well, I suppose
that is only to be expected, and it is quite useless for me to
attempt to disguise the facts. So far as I know, Admiral
Penistone, while reluctant as yet to give his consent to the
marriage, had not definitely forbidden it. That is as much
as I can tell you."

"I see, sir. Now about this will of John Martin Fitzgerald; I presume that Mr. Fitzgerald is dead, since you
and the late Admiral were acting as trustees for Mrs. Holland. Is this the copy of the actual will that was proved at
the time of death?"

"It is. My friend John Fitzgerald was a solicitor; he died
in 1916, and this was his latest will. I cannot say that it was
a will I should have cared to draw up for him myself, nor
was it, I think, a will he would willingly have drawn for
one of his clients, but you know, Inspector, solicitors are

notorious for making bad disposals of their own property."

"What was the will proved at?"

"At about £50,000. That," said Mr. Dakers,"did not represent the rewards of the law; the greater part of the money was inherited. But I had better begin from the beginning. John Fitzgerald married in 1888 Mary Penistone, the sister of the late Admiral. She died in 1911, and left two surviving children: Walter Everett, born in 1889, and Elma Mary, born nine years later, in 1898. When Walter was twenty, he got into some kind of trouble at home. I think it had to do with a young woman who was attached to the family in a dependent position—in fact, the governess. His father was extremely angry and there was a terrible quarrel. Young Walter ran away from home and disappeared, and for some time his name was not allowed to be mentioned. You know the kind of thing. Elma, of course, was too young to be told what the trouble was about, but Mrs. Fitzgerald always considered that her husband was too hard upon the boy.

"She died, as I say, in 1911, and I really think the worry about Walter helped to break up her health—in fact, as we used to say, it broke her heart. I know John Fitzgerald thought so, and it had a very softening effect upon him. He made efforts to find Walter, though without success, and he executed a will, dividing his property between Walter and Elma.

"Nothing was heard of Walter till the early part of 1915, when he sent his father a letter written from 'Somewhere in France.' He expressed himself as sorry for his previous bad behaviour and six years of neglect, hoped he was forgiven, and said that he was now endeavouring to turn over a new leaf and do his duty to his country. No word about where he had been in the interval. At the same time he enclosed 'in case of accident' a will drawn in favour of his sister Elma. His father and sister wrote back at once telling him to come home as soon as he got leave, and that all would be forgiven and forgotten. He never did come home, though he wrote from time to time, and after the disastrous battle of Loos his name appeared in the lists of 'missing, believed killed.' His father was at that time a very sick man. He was suffering from Bright's disease, and had not very much longer to live. He absolutely refused to believe that Walter was dead. He had turned up before, he said, and would turn up again. Having in the meantime come into a large property, he re-drafted his will of 1911, leaving the disposition of his estate the same as before, but with certain additional clauses.

"I must now say a word about his brother-in-law, Admiral Peniston. He—you may know something about his history?"

"I have heard that there was some sort of interruption to his career in 1911."

"Oh, you know about that? Yes, a disgraceful business. I need not go into details, but the affair was one which made it extremely unsuitable that he should be appointed as guardian of the young girl. Understand me, I express no opinion as to whether Captain Peniston (as he was then) was actually to blame in the matter. But the mere fact that his name had been connected with such an unsavoury business should have been sufficient. However, John Fitzgerald, who never would believe ill of anybody——"

"An unusual trait in a lawyer," Rudge could not help remarking.

"My good man, a lawyer in his private capacity and in his professional capacity may be two very different people," retorted Mr. Dakers, with some asperity. "John Fitzgerald could not think ill of his wife's brother. He maintained that Penistone had been unfairly treated, and by way of showing the world what he thought about it, he made him Elma's trustee, and inserted that preposterous clause about her marriage."

"You yourself," suggested Rudge, "accepted co-trusteeship with Admiral Penistone."

"And if I had not," said Mr. Dakers, "he might have appointed some other black sheep who needed whitewashing. No. I made the best of a bad job, out of consideration for my poor friend's daughter. And I must say, in justice to Admiral Penistone, that I have had no cause to complain of his management of his ward's affairs. Although his manner was abrupt and at times disagreeable, I believe him to have been a perfectly honest man as regards money, nor was there anything unbecoming about the household he set up for his niece. Had there been, I should, of course, have interfered."

"By whose wish was it that Miss Fitzgerald went to live with her uncle?"

"By her father's. I thought it unsuitable, but I could produce no valid grounds of opposition. Elma's share of the money was invested, by my advice, in sound securities, and the payments made to her quarterly by the trustees."

"A very nice little income," remarked Rudge.

"About £1,500 a year."

"It surprises me a little," said Rudge, "that the Admiral did not keep up a more elaborate establishment for his niece. This house is pleasant enough, but it is very remote, and they did not see much company, or so I understand."

"That is true," admitted Mr. Dakers, "but it was not altogether Admiral Penistone's fault. He himself naturally shrank from going much into society, and from 1914 to 1918 he was, of course, on active service, but he put no restrictions upon his niece. She was given a good education and had the advantage of two London seasons under the chaperonage of a very suitable lady, but I fancy that society life was distasteful to her."

"Odd that she should not have got married earlier," said Rudge. "A young lady with £25,000 or so should have had plenty of offers."

The lawyer shrugged his shoulders.

"I fancy that Elma was—a little difficult," he said. "She is perhaps not—attractive, in what I may call the marrying sense. There were some—needy persons, of course, but they were not encouraged. Admiral Penistone would not have dreamed of consenting to a marriage except with a man of independent means. And then, unfortunately, there was the scandal about Walter."

"What was that?"

"Why, that happened in 1920. Obviously the first thing that seemed advisable was to obtain from the Courts leave to presume Walter's death. We could not do anything till 1919, after the release of the British prisoners of war in Germany. His name was in none of the lists, and we expected to encounter no difficulty. Curiously enough, however, a man turned up who had been in Walter's unit in 1915, and this man stated that he had seen Walter alive in Buda-Pesth after the cessation of hostilities. He said he had not spoken to him, but that he had no doubt whatever of his identity. Walter was, I believe, a strikingly handsome man—he certainly was handsome as a boy. He was very like his mother, who was a most beautiful woman, much better-looking than her brother the Admiral, though there was a strong family resemblance.

"Well, of course, that meant further delay and more enquiries. We could get no news of Walter at all, but in view of the evidence of the soldier, the Court refused to presume death—naturally. Meanwhile, the affair had a very unfortunate sequel. As soon as it became known that Walter had probably not been killed during the War, we got the news that there was a warrant out for his arrest in Shanghai for forgery, if you please."

"In Shanghai?"

"Yes. The warrant dated from 1914. Apparently Walter, when he left the country in 1909, had entered the employment of the Anglo-Asiatic Tobacco Company. He was in Hong Kong at first and in 1913 was transferred to Shanghai. He got into some sort of financial difficulties, I suppose. Anyway, he forged a signature of a client of the Company to a large cheque and ran away. The War broke out just about that time, and I suppose that in the general confusion the matter was held up or overlooked, till the news that Walter was supposed to have been killed in 1915 put an end to it. However, when it appeared likely that Walter had survived after all, up it all came again. The Admiral was very greatly distressed. This further scandal, cropping up just when his own old trouble seemed to have been forgotten, soured his temper completely."

"I take it Admiral Penistone had rejoined the Navy during the War."

"Yes. He was a fine officer, and they were glad to get him. He did good service and finally retired for the second time at the end of the War with the rank of Rear-Admiral. But if other people had forgotten his previous troubles, he hadn't. They preyed on his mind, and this business about Walter finished him altogether. One man who had been semi-engaged to Elma withdrew rather pointedly when he heard about the brother, and Admiral Penistone said that he would not have his niece subjected to insult. He packed up bag and baggage and took her away with him to live in Cornwall. And there they stayed until a month ago. All this happened in 1920. Nothing has been heard of Walter since. So you see that the situation is rather a peculiar one."

"Yes," said Rudge thoughtfully. "Walter seems to be awkwardly placed. If he comes forward and shows himself, he probably goes to penal servitude. If he doesn't come forward, he can't get his money."

"That is the situation precisely. On the other hand, if he is dead, his share of the money goes to Elma under his will of 1914. Provided, of course, that is, that the witness was correct in stating that he was actually still alive after his father's death. If not, it still goes to her as residuary legatee under her father's will."

"In that case Walter's death would be to his sister's financial advantage. I see. But now, Mr. Dakers, how do things stand with reference to Mrs. Holland's own share of her father's money? I presume that, the Admiral being now dead, the clause about the consent to the marriage becomes void."

"That is exactly the difficulty," replied Mr. Dakers uneasily. "The point of view taken by the Court in such cases is that the testator cannot have required the beneficiary to perform impossibilities. Thus it has been held, over and over again, that in the case of the condition becoming impossible of fulfilment, through Act of God, the gift remains."

"Act of God?" queried Rudge.

"Yes. In the case of consent being required to a marriage, for instance, if the person whose consent is required dies before the marriage, then the condition is impossible of fulfilment, and the gift stands."

"Quite so," said Rudge, "but what does Act of God mean precisely?"

"Well," said the lawyer, a little reluctantly Rudge thought, "that means—well, practically speaking, it means, under conditions which the beneficiary could not have prevented."

"Let us speak quite plainly," said Rudge. "If Elma Holland should be found to have been concerned in Admiral Penistone's murder——"

"Of course, in *that* case," said Mr. Dakers, "there would be no question of her inheriting. The law expressly forbids a criminal to profit by the fruits of the crime. But surely that question does not arise."

"I should hope not," said Rudge. "Then so far as I can see, Mrs. Holland is now entitled to her inheritance?"

"Ye-es," said the lawyer. "I hope the Court will look upon it from that point of view. The difficulty lies in the extreme haste with which the marriage followed upon the death. I will be frank with you, Mr. Rudge. I think it would be possible to contest the case, and I think that, if that occurred, we should have to take one of two lines about it. We could, of course, say that she intended to ask the necessary consent before the marriage and that, but for the death, she would have had time to ask for it. Now, of course, she did ask for it—several times."

"With any reasonable expectation of ever getting it?" asked Rudge. "Mr. Dakers," he added, as the lawyer appeared to hesitate, "I will go so far as to tell you that I have witnesses here who are prepared to say that the Admiral appeared not to approve of the marriage."

"Precisely," said Mr. Dakers; "I must admit that there was—an appearance at any rate of objection. And that being the case, I do not quite know what the Court would think of a marriage so hastily concluded. It might be inferred that the Admiral was violently opposed to the marriage, and that, therefore, the marriage was undertaken with a definite intention of frustrating the object of the testator. The indecent haste attending the ceremony affords, you see, in itself a presumption that the death of the Admiral removed the only obstacle to the marriage."

"And that being so," said Rudge, "an allegation might be made that the Admiral's death was not altogether— shall we say, by Act of God."

"If such a monstrous allegation were made," replied Mr. Dakers, "it would have to be refuted; in which case, the mere fact that the hastiness of the marriage might jeopardise the absolute right to the estate would constitute a very good answer to the charge."

"Yes," said Rudge, seizing on the weak point of the argument, "provided the beneficiary was aware how the law stood." He considered for a moment, and then said:

"And your second line of defence would be?"

"To show that the ceremony was not arranged until after death had made it impossible to obtain consent. If it were so—though I do not see how a licence could have been taken out in the time—it would be a complete answer to the contesting party. It has frequently so been held. For instance, in *Collett v. Collett,* the mother, whose consent was required, died in 1856. In 1865 the daughter married. The Master of the Rolls held that the gift over (that is, to the person who was to get the money in case the condition was not fulfilled, you understand) will not take effect, if the performance of the condition has become impossible through the Act of God and no default of the person who had to perform it." (Mr. Dakers, reading these words from a note-book, glanced over his pince-nez at Rudge, who said nothing. He resumed.) " 'Here it is reasonably certain that the mother, if she had lived, would have given her consent to this marriage, one eligible in all respects.' There, you see, Inspector, is our difficulty. The Court seems to have based its decision to some extent on what the mother might reasonably have been expected to do."

"I see," said Rudge. "And in this case the Admiral's consent could not very well be presumed with any certainty."

"There again," said the lawyer, "who is to say? If the eligibility of the marriage, as such, is a factor to be taken into consideration, there seems to be no reason why Admiral Penistone should not have consented. Holland, so far as I know anything about him, seems to be a respectable man of suitable age and standing and with sufficient money of his own to take him out of the class of mere fortune-hunters. It is a very pretty case, Mr. Rudge, and if I were not personally concerned it would give me great pleasure to see it thrashed out."

Rudge was about to reply, when the sound of an approaching car was heard. A slight commotion followed at the front door. Voices and footsteps sounded and a minute after, the study door was thrown open.

"Inspector," said Arthur Holland as he followed his wife into the room, "we owe you an apology for running off like this, but we were in a hurry and were afraid you might delay us. Is this Mr. Dakers? How do you do, sir? My wife and I received your note, and thought we had better come and set your mind at rest."

"Thank you," said Mr. Dakers, rather dryly. "Well, Elma, you have married in very great haste. I trust you will not have to repent it at leisure."

Elma laughed. There was a faint flush of colour in her usually pale cheeks and she looked, Rudge thought, rather a prey to some consuming excitement than radiant with the happiness of a newly married woman.

"You have made a mistake, Mr. Dakers," she said. "I haven't jeopardised anything or compromised anything. Look at that."

She handed him a sheet of paper. Mr. Dakers settled his glasses more firmly on his nose, read it with a "Tut-tut" or two of astonishment, and handed it over to Rudge.

"That solves our problems, I think, Inspector."

Rudge looked at the paper. It was typewritten, with the exception of the signature, and ran—

> *"I willingly give my consent to the marriage of my niece, Elma Mary Fitzgerald, with Arthur Holland.*
> "(*Signed*) H. L. PENISTONE."

It was dated the 9th August.

Inspector Rudge looked at Holland.

"When did this come into your possession, sir?"

"My wife gave it to me this morning," he said. "She had it last night from the Admiral."

"At what time was that, ma'am?" enquired the Inspector.

"Just after midnight," replied the girl, in a curious flat tone which reminded Rudge of his interview with her earlier in the day.

"After midnight? Did you see your uncle alive after midnight?"

"Why, of course," interrupted Holland. "I saw him myself. Yes, I know, Inspector! I didn't want to tell you about that because I was afraid you might stop us from going to town. But I'll come clean now. I saw the Admiral alive here in his study at a quarter past twelve last night."

CHAPTER VIII

By Ronald A. Knox

THIRTY-NINE ARTICLES OF DOUBT

IN THE nature of the case, a policeman's life is bound up
with surprises. A considerable part of the community is
only too ready to set playful booby-traps for him, stretching wires across garden-paths or waiting in dark alleys
with half a brick concealed in the foot of a stocking.
Rudge had not risen to his inspectorship without some ex-
periences of the kind, and he had come near to achieving
that unwondering attitude which is (the old poet assures
us) part of the stuff of happiness. But this sudden admission almost caught him off his guard. Grice's statement that
the body had been a corpse since some time before midnight had seemed so evident a point of departure; all the
other features of the case had grouped themselves round it
so obligingly—the possibility of a journey into Whynmouth and foul play down-stream, the visit of the strange
car, the darkness, the loneliness, the set of the tides. (By the
way, why had he been so certain about the tides? Oh, yes,
Neddy Ware; odd that Neddy should have been so positive about it.) Too late he realised that no single piece of
evidence, except the misleading infallibility of the expert,
had excluded the possibility of a murder well after midnight. And this, it seemed now, was what must have happened. Of course, Holland might be lying, but it was diffi-

cult to see his motive; why abandon a first-class alibi at
the Lord Marshall for the honour of being the last man
who saw deceased alive? It would be a fool's game, and
Holland did not look like a fool.

In a moment, habit reasserted itself; he had drawn out
the inevitable note-book, and was turning over the pages
to a blank, remembering not to moisten his finger as he
did so. "I think I ought to tell you, sir," he explained, "that
you are not bound to make any statement. You know well
enough that you will have to be called at the inquest; and
if you prefer to reserve——"

"My defence?" interrupted Holland, with heavy rail-
lery. "It is too kind of you. But, you see, here I am, all
ready binged up with a cock-and-bull story carefully prepared to mislead you; it would be a pity not to get it off
my chest while I'm word-perfect. You would like to get
me in jug first, wouldn't you, and take down my statement with no witnesses, so that you could cook it afterwards? I prefer the present occasion, if you don't mind."

Rudge just checked himself in time from reminding the
unseasonable jester that he wouldn't do himself any good
by this kind of thing. After all, Holland evidently be-
longed to the opulent classes, who get the benefit of the
doubt. "Certainly, sir," he amended, with some frigidity
of manner. "But I think perhaps if Mrs. Holland——"

"You mean you want to be certain that we both pitch
the same yarn? Well, it's bad luck, for a man on his honeymoon. But perhaps, Elma, if you wouldn't mind——"
A rapid look passed between them; on his side, it registered adoring confidence; on hers, was it a frown over his
reckless demeanour? Or was there not, after all, a faint
suspicion of disgust? Mr. Dakers saved the situation, by
indicating that nothing would suit him better than a turn
in the garden with—in short, with Mrs. Holland; there

was much that needed discussion, he felt. And Rudge was left alone with his chief witness.

"Now, sir," he opened briskly, "when we last met you told a tale which was, you will admit, in contradiction with what you said just now?"

"These giant intellects! Yes, I told you I was in bed at Whynmouth. Actually I was here. A discrepancy."

"Excuse me, sir, but what I'm getting at is this—was it *all* untrue, what you told me? For instance, I have it down here that you were not seen by anybody after eleven o'clock. Do you still stick to that? It doesn't seem quite so likely, does it? Perhaps you would try to remember anybody you passed on your way out here—you will have walked, I suppose? Or did you come by the omnibus?"

"The last 'bus, my dear Rudge, as you and I know very well, leaves at half-past ten. No, I walked; and I passed some of the gentlemen who had recently left the Lord Marshall, but they did not look as if they were likely to preserve a clear memory of their impressions. There were some lovers about, but I am afraid I cannot swear to their features, and I doubt if they could to mine. I had no speech with anybody."

"Didn't meet one of our men, for example?"

There was a fraction of a pause, almost as if a ready invention were suddenly at fault.

"No, I think not," was the answer given. "Once I looked up a side-street, and thought I saw a policeman's lantern being flashed, but it might have been somebody lighting a bicycle lamp. I can't remember which street it was, now."

"And you would be coming straight along the main road?"

"All the way."

"Now, then, sir, let's get at this, if you don't mind. Were you meaning to pay this rather late visit all the time?

Or were you delayed on the road? Or did the idea just come to you suddenly, when it was already closing-time or close on it?"

"My dear Inspector, you are a little elementary. I have no doubt the Boots told you that he saw my shoes out in the passage. And therefore the story I have decided to tell you is that I was already in process of going to bed when an accident made me alter my purpose. Looking out from my window, I saw a man turning away from the front door whom I seemed to recognise by the set of his shoulders. Then I told myself I was a fool; something about the hat convinced me that he was a clergyman. Then reflection told me that clergymen are not thrown out of pubs at closing-time. And I felt convinced, I don't know how, that it was poor old Penistone. I wanted to see him, as you know; I threw on the rest of my clothes hastily and went out into the street. There was no sign of him then, of course, but I hurried down the road I supposed he would be taking; and in the end—well, in the end I came all the way here."

"On the off-chance of finding him still awake, late at night like that?"

"Inspector, I do not know whether you are a married man, or whether your bosom has always been impervious to the softer emotions. But if you will ask anyone who has been violently in love, he will tell you that a lover thinks nothing of walking a mile or two merely to stand outside a window and sentimentalise among the rhododendrons. That is all I would have done, if I had not found the lights going strong in the poor old Admiral's study."

"You saw them as you came along?"

"Do you know, you would get much more information if you didn't try to catch a fellow out all the time. Of course, I didn't see them from the road. I had come round into the lawn, and saw them from there. I went up and knocked, and the Admiral let me in through the french window. He told me I had come just in time, 'quite dramatic,' he said—he was in the act of making out for his niece the document we had been waiting for these weeks past, his consent to our marriage. And, sure enough, it was on the table when we came into the drawing-room."

"That would be—about a quarter past twelve, you say?"

"I didn't notice the time exactly. But I had started from the Lord Marshall soon after eleven, which is closing-time. I walked slowly after I had got out of Whynmouth, so I can't have been here till twelve or so; that's how I worked it out."

"Yes, I see. Now, was it your impression that Admiral Peniston was just meaning to turn in when you came? Was he in his dressing-gown, for example? Was he smoking, or drinking a whisky and soda or anything? You see what I mean, sir—I want to find out if he went outside after you had left, and if so, why."

"Well, I can't help you much there. He had a pipe in his mouth part of the time, to be sure. The only thing which made me feel he had not thought of bed-time yet was the litter on that desk; papers lying there, you know, taken out of their pigeon-holes. The Admiral wasn't the kind of man to go to bed without putting his papers to bed first."

"Ah, that's very interesting. And you haven't any idea, I suppose, what papers?"

"Not the least, I'm afraid. I dare say in your job you sometimes have to look over a man's shoulder to see what he is reading, but we have a stricter code in the jute trade."

Rudge felt the offensiveness of the reflection, but he achieved a passable smile. "You didn't stay long, then? Just thanked him, maybe, and said you'd be getting back to Whynmouth?"

"Hardly more than that. He let me out at the french window again, and I went back to the Lord Marshall in that frame of mind in which a man finds himself, my dear Inspector, when he realises that the greatest dream of his life has come true. That is to say, walking on air, and not noticing much that went on round me."

"Not even how you unlocked the front door of the hotel?"

"Why, I am afraid I had taken my precautions about that. I knew that Boots is fond of going to bed as early as he can, and does not like to have his sleep disturbed. So I was careful to leave the back-yard door on the latch—you will find that it has no bolts on it—and Mrs. Davis, I am afraid, was none the wiser. I thought best not; she talks."

"You're right there, sir. All the same, I wish you had been a little less quiet in your comings and goings; they'll put you through it properly at the inquest. But, of course, you'd leave your boots outside the door, so we'll have evidence that you were in before the front door was opened?"

"My dear Inspector, you think of everything. You want me to say that I was wearing, at a quarter-past eleven on the way to Rundel Croft, the same pair of boots which were outside my door at half-past. Believe me, your technique is improving. But the sad truth is that when I got up and followed my phantom Admiral, I put on another pair —suède shoes, which one does not have cleaned, if one is wise, at the Lord Marshall."

"Ah, that explains it. I suppose you did not by any chance bring a copy of the *Evening Gazette* with you to Rundel Croft?"

"I never read it. Its politics nauseate me."

Rudge held his note-book at arm's length, as if studying an artistic effect.

"Well, that gives a clear account of your movements,

Mr. Holland. Now, there are one or two questions I would like to ask; but, as they don't bear directly on what happened last night, I shan't be surprised if you won't tell me. The first is just this: Why was it that Admiral Peniston at first didn't want to see you marry his niece, and then changed his mind?"

"I think you must be very busy looking for mysteries if you make a mystery out of that. If you come to think of it, I have only known the family a matter of three or four weeks. I first met my wife, since you are kind enough to be so interested in our private affairs, at Sir Wilfrid Denny's, just after she came here; and it was love at first sight with both of us. The Admiral—well, he was a man of circumspection, and he wanted to see more of me, I suppose. When his niece wrote telling me to come down to Whynmouth again, because she had good news for me, I only just dared to hope it was this. (That was when I got the licence.) But it seems my respectability was more self-evident to him than it is to you."

"Oh, come now, no offence taken, I hope. And then there's this second question, which sounds impolite, but I must ask it. Why were you in such a hurry to get married, Mr. Holland?"

Holland paused this time quite unmistakably; but his face did not suggest guilt or duplicity; he looked more like an honest man who knows more than he is at liberty to tell, and is not quite sure how much he can tell without a breach of trust. That, at least, is how Rudge read his expression for the moment or two while the embarrassment lasted. Then: "Inspector," said Holland, with a more serious note in his voice, "you mustn't ask me to be responsible for a woman's fancies. I know you think it was very shocking to go and get married like that; very quietly owing to mourning in the bride's family, funeral bake-

meats scarcely cold, and so on. But, well, I think the truth
is Elma is far more nervous than her self-command lets
you see. I think she was altogether rattled by what happened here that night, and she felt she was in danger here;
who could tell she would not be the next victim of this
mysterious vendetta, or whatever it was? She wanted to
get away from the place, and she wanted to have a man
close to her, now that her uncle was gone, who would have
a natural right to be her protector. There's that about me,
you see; I may not be worthy of Elma, but I've got the
right *format* for a chucker-out. And I suppose that's how
she looked at it."

"Yes, I see that. Now, may I ask you this?—did Admiral
Penistone himself, when you last saw him, give you any
idea of what had made him change his mind? Did he explain at all?"

"If you'd known him, you'd know that he wasn't a man
for explaining things. He was short and sharp in conversation—hated to waste a word. And that night, why, he
hardly said more than 'Good evening,' and 'Come this way,
I've something to show you,' and 'There, will that make
you any happier?' Otherwise he just puffed at his pipe; that
was his idea of conversation."

"Ah, he was a great smoker, was he? Always the same
pipe, I'll be bound; your true smoker never uses more
than one."

"He wasn't, then. Why, you can see for yourself how
they're scattered over the mantelpiece. If one wouldn't
draw, he'd take to another."

"I wonder—do you think it possible that he had anything on his mind, and that was why he said so little? Of
course, I'm anxious to find out whether the unfortunate
gentleman knew at all what was coming to him. Did he
look worried or tired, for example, when you saw him?"

"Not that I noticed. No, not that I noticed. Of course, when I saw him in the study the only lamp burning was that reading lamp just beside you, which has a thick, green shade over it, as you see; you don't see much of a man's face when he is standing up and the light is all being thrown on his desk. But if you ask me whether his tone of voice suggested excitement or worry, I'd say, No."

"Well, Mr. Holland, I think I've asked you all that I wanted. Oh, except this—he wasn't wearing an overcoat, was he, by any chance?"

"In his study? On a hot summer night? You might as well ask whether he was wearing chain armour."

"I know it sounds unlikely, sir. But there it is—he was in a great-coat when he was found. And of course . . . by the way, Mr. Holland, when you thought you saw the Admiral outside your window, would he be wearing a great-coat then?"

"Now, what a fool one is about noticing things! I see him as in a great-coat now; but then, I know about the body . . . I feel as if he hadn't had a great-coat on; but then, I may be arguing with myself; I may be saying to myself that I must have noticed it if it had been worn, on a hot night like that. If only my memory worked by eye! No, Inspector, you may put me in jug, but I should be misleading you if I tried to give you a plain answer to a plain question."

"Well, thank you for what you *have* told me, sir. Now, about Mrs. Holland . . ."

"If you ask me, I expect Mrs. Holland will want her dinner. It doesn't seem to occur to you that you're rather spoiling our honeymoon. Look here, we've booked rooms at the Lord Marshall. Elma said she couldn't sleep in this house just yet. I don't dare to think what Mrs. Davis's dinner must be like when it gets cold. Can't you leave it till to-morrow and put my wife on the rack then?"

"Well, sir, it's like this. I've got to see the coroner to-morrow morning, and I've got to give him as full an account of the case as I can; and you and Mrs. Holland, look at it whatever way you will, are going to be important witnesses. But if you think Mrs. Holland would sooner see me first thing to-morrow, why, there's a policeman on duty in the Square, and if I may pass the word to him, I'll feel certain I know where to find you. Perhaps if I was to climb up behind, you wouldn't mind giving me a lift as far as Whynmouth?"

"For fear we might be tempted to take a wrong turning? Well, Inspector, I suppose we've deserved that. All right, come on; we'll play fair this time."

Rudge sat in darkness at the back of the car, instinctively spying on the two figures whose outlines were blurred against the illuminated patch of road. The impressions he had already formed of the couple were on the whole confirmed; there was little talk between them, and when there was any the initiative seemed to come from Holland; you saw, in the attentive droop of his shoulder sideways, the model of the deferential lover, whereas Elma looked straight in front of her and hardly moved when she answered. But then, she was tired, no doubt; she had much to think of; perhaps she even felt sorrow for the old man whose fortunes she had shared for so many years, now lying under that dust-sheet in the mortuary.

Rudge made an excuse to follow them into the hotel; he was privately concerned to make sure about the locking of that door into the back-yard. The Lord Marshall is an old-fashioned hotel, and there is no private entrance for visitors; they have to pass along a narrow passage, with a slight recess in the middle of it which gives you a back

view of the gentlemen who are refreshing themselves at
the public bar. One of these made a half-turn as they entered, and Rudge had two simultaneous impressions—that
he recognised the man, and that the man did not want to
be recognised. At least, he shrank back as they approached,
and his face was hidden in the darkness of the space under
the stairway. Returning from a mercifully brief interview
with Mrs. Davis, Rudge found him again and verified his
guess. It was Cropped-head, the *Gazette* reporter. By a
promise of seeing him next day, Rudge managed to stave
off his eager questionings about the progress of the case.
Then he had a word with the policeman in the Square, and
went back to the seclusion of his own rooms.

Inspector Rudge, we must regretfully admit, was a quite
ordinary man. He did not solace himself with the violin,
or the cocaine-bottle; he did not tie knots in string, or
collect scarabs, or distinguish himself in any way by side-
lines. The rooms to which he returned were quite ordinary
rooms, from which he had not even troubled to remove the
landlady's decorations; the whisky he took out of the cupboard was so well known that the mention of its name
would be an unnecessary advertisement; the same may be
said of the tobacco with which he filled his pipe. If the full
truth must be confessed, Inspector Rudge was so far
human that he took off his boots and replaced them with a
pair of dressing-slippers. Then he got down to the night's
work; and that consisted in selecting from the mass of
material he had accumulated during the day the points
that seemed most likely to repay investigation. These points
he jotted down, in the form of questions; he added no
written comment, except an occasional memorandum; but
as each question was reduced to verbal shape he looked up
at the ceiling and let his mind play around the possibilities
which it suggested. The questions are here reproduced,

with a summary of the cogitations to which each one led. When he counted them up, his orthodox mind was delighted to find them exactly thirty-nine in number.

1. *Why did Penistone come to Lingham, and why did Sir Wilfrid mind?* Altogether, there was too much of the China Station about this business. On the face of it, there was nothing particularly improbable in the fact that two men well acquainted with China should be living at such close range. But Mrs. Davis, representing the local gossip, had seen some significance in it; and, quite unexpectedly, she had volunteered the information that Sir Wilfrid did not seem over-pleased at the neighbourhood. Was it conceivable that there had been a connection between them in the past? A guilty connection? If so, on which side did the guilt lie? On Sir Wilfrid's surely. Rudge's mind, do what he would, was apt to travel in official grooves; and the notion of blackmail forced itself on him. The more so, because Sir Wilfrid appeared to be in straitened circumstances. *Mem.—Apply to the bank in the hope of getting the Admiral's passbook; hardly possible to have the handling of Sir Wilfrid's.*

2. *Why did Jennie think that Penistone and Elma seemed more like husband and wife than uncle and niece?* Probably mere gossip. Jennie had, after all, seen the couple but a short time; the fact that they managed the household— presumably—in financial partnership would give them, to the girl's mind, the air of equals. Once again Rudge's fancy toyed with the idea of an impersonation; yet it seemed quite impossible that any such impersonation should long persist; Dakers would see through it if nobody else did.

3. *Why was Elma so familiar with the French maid? And why did the French maid leave so suddenly?* The two questions could be treated as one; if there was any signi-

ficance in the former it would probably provide an explanation for the other. The allegation that Célie had found the place dull was surely a mere excuse; a Frenchwoman who had stood years of Cornish exile would necessarily take more than a week to grow tired of Lingham; Whynmouth, after all, boasted a picture-palace. It might, of course, be some romance or tragedy below stairs which happened to have come to a head at the moment. But it seemed more natural to assume that the move was the cause of the flight—yes, you might almost call it a flight, since there was money owing. Of course, if Célie were not a mere servant, it might be that money was no object to her. But why leave just after a move? Surely it would have been more plausible to give notice when the move took effect. And that meant—that ought to mean that Célie, on coming to Lingham, had found something there which was unexpectedly disconcerting to her; or that circumstances arose at Lingham which would not have arisen in Cornwall. Too short a time for romance. Had Célie been in Lingham before? *Mem.—Trace, if possible, Célie's present whereabouts and past references.*

4. *Why, again on Jennie's testimony, was so little love lost between Elma and Holland, on her side at any rate?* Once more, it might be mere gossip. Who was it who was credited with a "miserably low standard of intoxication"? Perhaps Jennie had an unusually high standard of walking-out. Jennie peered at you; and a couple of shy lovers might have been at pains to disengage their hands at the warning of her heavy-footed entrance. But if there was anything to it, it suggested that the marriage, on one side at least, was a *mariage de convenance*. On which side? Hers, according to the evidence; and, to be sure, she had had an earlier disappointment; her youth was slipping from her. It might be, too, that she was anxious to deal with her capi-

tal, instead of having the interest doled out to her by
trustees. But where was the need here? She lived simply;
she dressed dowdily. Holland, of course, might be an ad-
venturer; but, if so, he was a clever feigner of love.

5. *What did Elma do with her money?* This question
arose naturally out of the last. How simple life would be
for the police, if we all audited our accounts, like the public charities! Rundel Croft was not a house of pretensions;
its grounds were negligible. Even if Elma paid more than a
half-share—and the Admiral must have had *some* money
—it was hard to believe that £1,200 a year could be needed
for upkeep. Yet the capital was hers; there was no obvious
need of saving. Once again the word blackmail suggested
itself; but this time it seemed to be the wrong way about.
If Sir Wilfrid were the blackmailer, why did his victims
settle so close? And why did he manifest annoyance? *Mem.
—Once more, consult the Admiral's pass-book.*

6. *What part did Walter play in the background of these
lives?* If he was dead, then his influence only persisted in so
far as he was keeping Elma out of half of her inheritance;
and this, in view of her already comfortable circumstances,
seemed a factor that could be neglected. But if he were
alive—what would be his influence then? Was he popular
with his family, or had the story of his disgrace obliterated
all affection? It was odd, when you came to think of it,
that a household so connected with a soldier who disappeared in the War should have no photograph of him ex-
posed in study or drawing-room. And yet—there was the
scandal of the cheque; awkward, perhaps, to have visitors
saying "Who's that?" If he were alive, what was he doing;
what would he be doing? It seemed unlikely that a man of
his antecedents would let a fortune pass him by without a
struggle. Yet, granted he were alive and were attempting
to reinstate himself, what could he stand to gain by com-

mitting a crime of this sort, or inducing others to commit it? "Point is, disappearance of valuable uncle," Rudge found himself quoting. The corpse of one trustee does not make a legacy.

7. *Why did Ware think the Admiral had altered since he last saw him?* People do change their looks, of course, and a man labouring under a long grievance may be excused for losing something of his old cheerfulness and vitality. But the photographs at Rundel Croft, evidently dating back to the period of Ware's reminiscences, bore a quite unmistakable resemblance to the man found drowned. Again the wild suggestion of an impersonation flooded across the Inspector's mind; again common sense told him that a long-sustained impersonation is a practical impossibility. Was it conceivable that Ware did recognise the corpse he fished out; then, for some reason, pretended not to; then, by way of explaining his lapse of memory, invented this story of altered looks? But again, why should Ware pretend ignorance? Why not have said, "I've seen the man before somewhere, but I can't remember the circumstances"? *Mem:—Ask Dakers about this.*

8. *Does Mrs. Davis's allusion to a runaway wife at the Vicarage lead anywhere?* It seemed a long shot; but so far, apart from Elma, there was no woman in the case except the woman in the car, untraced, and this phantom from Lingham's past, who might surely be expected to give the place a wide berth. It has been suggested that Rudge's mind ran obstinately in grooves of police experience; and *cherchez la femme* is almost the first item in the policeman's decalogue. But how to make enquiries about Mrs. Mount's history since her elopement? The Vicar could supply the name of his guilty rival, but it would be brutality to ask him; and even so the traces of a ten-years-old disappearance would almost certainly have been obliterated

by now. No, Rudge decided, he was becoming fantastic. Mrs. Mount had never lived at Lingham; presumably her husband had never heard the names of Denny or Penistone at the time of her desertion. There was not even a loose thread to be picked up here.

Rudge drew a line across this page. So far, his questions were all questions which might have been asked, though there would have been no reason for the police to ask them, yesterday afternoon, when the river ran peacefully between the Vicarage and Rundel Croft, the two boys sporting in it with no shadow of a tragedy to overawe their high spirits; when the Admiral's brisk walk and sharp voice proclaimed him very much alive, and no pale corpse rested in the Whynmouth mortuary. Now he must get on to the crime itself; its circumstances and the traces it had left. He hitched his chair up a little closer to the table, took a meditative pull out of his glass, emptied out and refilled his pipe, then returned methodically to his self-imposed catechism.

9. *Why did Elma dress up that night to meet the Vicar?* Here again you were dealing with impressions, the impressions of a rather fanciful servant-girl. But one must not despise the testimony of the expert; and a lady's maid, in the little world of her own limited interests, is an observant critic. Any deviation from the normal, however slight, is worth watching as a possible hint that crime did not come altogether like a bolt from the blue; that somebody was up to something beforehand. But in this case who was up to what? If Elma thought she was going to meet Holland that night, odd that it should have been her uncle, not she, who was in a hurry to get back to Rundel Croft. And if a meeting was projected, it was evidently a secret one; no need, then, to draw attention to it by tricking herself out for the occasion. On the other hand, Mr.

Mount seemed hardly the man to appreciate a lady's costume; hardly the man whom the most enterprising of adventuresses would have set out to vamp. Old English sports, No. 82, Vamping the Vicar. Was it conceivable that Elma was up to some game which involved leaving Rundel Croft later that night; that she meant to change her clothes for the purpose, and was at pains to put on elaborate evening dress so as to make the later change a more effective disguise? *Mem.—Ask Jennie if any other wardrobe items showed signs of disturbance or hasty folding this morning.*

10. *Why did she hide the dress afterwards?* At least, that was going a little too fast. But she had certainly made a point of packing the dress, and of packing it herself. The conclusion, though not irresistible, was certainly probable, that there was something about that dress which she did not want even a confidential eye to discover. But that meant, unless she was going to tell a quite different story under to-morrow's cross-examination, that Elma had something to conceal, and was giving a false account of her movements. If, after leaving the boat-house, she went straight to bed, it was impossible that any tell-tale evidence —a split or a stain—should have made its appearance since her good night to the Admiral. The trouble was that since Elma had moved to the Lord Marshall, Jennie was no longer in a position to report. *Mem.—If there is a chambermaid at the inn who doesn't talk, ask her to find out whether that dress ever came back from London.*

11. *Was it Penistone who went down to Whynmouth that night?* The evidence came from two sources; both were uncertain, one quite possibly mendacious. Rudge had satisfied himself that the lighting outside the Lord Marshall was particularly inadequate. The direct statement made to the Boots, who could hardly be lying, showed that

the man who called at the door was either the Admiral or an impostor who was impersonating him. If Holland's account were true, it confirmed the notion that some deliberate attempt had been made at disguise; Holland did not overhear the visitor's conversation, and yet thought there was a look of the Admiral about him. But then, was Holland telling the truth? Assume that it was the Admiral; why did he suddenly want to take that late (and bad) train up to London? In the alternative, why did he want to create the impression that he had intended doing so? Either supposition implied that there was some mysterious dealing on the Admiral's own part, which no other evidence, except perhaps his impatience to get away from the Vicarage, suggested. Assume that it was not the Admiral; then what was the point of this elaborate frame-up? To implicate Holland in the crime? But there was no foretelling that Holland would not remain fast asleep at the Lord Marshall; nothing but his own evidence served to connect him with the mysterious caller. To deceive the public about the spot at which the murder was committed? Yes, there was something in that; it might help out an alibi. But would not the bogus Admiral have been at pains to leave other evidence of his visit, besides that of a sleepy and stupid hotel servant?

12. *If it was the Admiral, did he travel by road or by river?* According to the Vicar's evidence, which must be genuine since it could be checked, the Admiral had a game leg, and did not walk if he could help it. It seemed unlikely that he could have taken out the car without waking some of the household. The boat remained as a possibility; and if the Admiral went secretly down the river in a boat, where was he going to put it when he took the London train? Abandoned, it would invite theft; moored among other boats it would bear testimony to his movements. It was

hardly to be supposed that he meant to leave Whynmouth for ever. The suggestion seemed to be that all this talk about the train was a blind. Once again, for what purpose? The only thing which seemed certain was that the Admiral's boat had been taken from its moorings that night, and had been restored to the boat-house by somebody who was not the Admiral.

13. *Why did the visitor, whoever it was, ask for Holland and then refuse to see him?* If it was a bogus Admiral, the answer was not in doubt; the man had asked for Holland so as to get an excuse for mentioning the Admiral's name; possibly also to implicate Holland in the trouble which was to follow. He did not actually meet Holland, for fear of detection. If it was the real Admiral, a motive was harder to assign. His behaviour seemed that of a man who wants to make sure that a hotel guest has really arrived, or that he is really in the hotel, and yet does not trouble to conceal those inquisitorial methods from the person against whom they are directed. If Holland's story were true, the Admiral might have contemplated a real visit, so as to reassure him about the consent. But why, after taking so much trouble, should he go away without leaving any significant message?

14. *Did Holland really see anybody in the street?* Answer: Yes, and it means that Holland's story is true up to a point; he really was in the Lord Marshall, or near it, as late as closing time. But there was that hesitation about the great-coat; was that genuine? Or was the ignorance affected, to avoid possible traps? Answer: No, and it means that Holland still possesses knowledge which he is concealing. Either he knew that the Admiral intended to make that visit, or he was privy to the plans of the fellow who impersonated the Admiral. In either case, his mention of

the visitor would be an attempt to prove that he was really
in the hotel at closing time; this smelt of an alibi.

15. *Did Holland really go to Rundel Croft that night?*
Against the story was its extreme vagueness; the absence of
clear motive, the care he took to explain why no witnesses
of his journey were likely to be forthcoming, his selection
of a fresh pair of shoes, the alleged secrecy of his exits and
entrances. On the other hand, if Holland was lying, it was
hard to suppose that he was lying to screen himself; bed
was his best alibi. The evidence of the Boots and Mrs.
Davis would be a difficult defence for the police to get
over, without some positive clue to implicate Holland—
and no such clue existed. Instead of sticking to his first
story, that he had slept soundly in his bed, he had gone
out of his way to confess himself a liar, had told a story,
fantastic in many points, about a visit to Rundel Croft
which no witness could attest, and in doing so had deliberately claimed the position of the last man who had seen
Penistone alive. He seemed to be running his head deliberately into a noose; why should he do that, unless to divert
suspicion from the real criminal? And that meant . . .
yes, it would hang together. He had told the truth this
morning; since then, fresh knowledge had come to him
which induced him to put a halter round his own neck.
But then, *was* Holland lying? Would he not, by now, have
contrived to make up a more plausible story, accounting
for his presence at Rundel Croft?

16. *If he went, did he go by appointment?* Such an appointment might have been made either with the Admiral
himself or, more probably, with Elma. If the former were
true, nothing could bring the charge home except some
record of a message; if it was brought by note, somebody
had brought the note; if it was sent by telephone, the call
could probably be traced. Also, to be sure, a message sent

by telephone to an hotel meant that the receiver would be lifted off by an hotel servant, and the circumstance, at that hour of the night, would probably be remembered. When you came to think of it, the message (if there was one) must have come from Elma, or Holland must have supposed that it came from Elma. Otherwise, he would have had no reason to conceal it; and he could have made his own story much more plausible by admitting it. *Mem.— See Mrs. Davis about the message: enquire if necessary at the telephone exchange.*

17. *Who was the woman who went through Lingham at a quarter to eleven?* At least, that was really the wrong way to put it; you could hardly hope to know who she was, at this stage. But it was worth considering whether her arrival could have had any influence on the situation. Her car, which might or might not have contained another occupant, would reach Whynmouth in time to deposit the mysterious visitor at the Lord Marshall. Alternatively, it would have been possible for the occupants of such a car to be at Rundel Croft in time for the murder, even if you dated the murder early. They might have gone round by Fernton Bridge, the enquiry for the Vicarage being merely a blind; or they might have stopped close to the Vicarage, and ferried themselves across by making free with Mr. Mount's boat. This last plan would have the effect of bringing the Vicarage boat on to the scene of action; a point deserving to be considered, from the detective's point of view. But Rudge found himself instinctively recoiling from such an explanation. For it would mean that the criminal or criminals came and went by car, their base presumably London. It was not possible for the Whynmouth police to search for suspicious characters in London; Scotland Yard might have to be invoked, and that always meant that the credit went to Scotland Yard.

At this point the Inspector drew a fresh line across his page. He had reached the end of the enquiries which were antecedent, or seemed at first sight antecedent, to the murder itself. It was time now to come on to a fresh set of problems: those created by the circumstances in which the corpse was discovered. The pipe needed to be re-lit; and, for that matter, another tot seemed indicated; the indication was allowed to have full weight. Now for the *facts*. Human testimony was a slippery and uncertain thing to deal with; what you were told was a photograph fogged, as it were, by the shadow of the man who told it you. But Nature did not lie; tides ran, dew formed, blood flowed, doors opened and shut, on uniform and ascertainable principles. The clues pointed you on to the actions which had produced them, and then hinted entrancingly at the motives which lay behind the actions. Well, then . . .

18. *Here is a man murdered; who had a motive, and what motive, for murdering him?* Ordinarily, one would expect a local quarrel; though the knife, as Mrs. Davis acutely noticed, is not the English criminal's weapon. But a month's residence hardly gave time for any supposition of the kind here. A Cornish enemy would have found it difficult to track his man down, would have delayed longer to ascertain the lie of the land. The quarrel, then, which found its satisfaction in that grisly wound, must be a quarrel dating from past history in the Admiral's life. Further, you could assume with some certainty that the murderer either knew the habits, or possessed the confidence, of his victim. A man is found murdered in the Vicar's boat on the very night when he has been dining at the Vicarage; in his pocket is a copy of that very newspaper to which he is in fact a subscriber; the murder is somehow connected with a visit, alleged or real, to a neighbouring hotel where an acquaintance of the victim is in fact staying. All

this betrays a knowledge of relevant circumstances; the mysterious Chinaman of the story-books can be ruled out of the list of suspects; he would not have committed the murder just so. That narrowed down the search to people who knew something about the Admiral. Who did? His neighbours: Neddy Ware (not much), the Vicar, the Vicar's sons, Sir Wilfrid Denny, still an unknown quantity. His servants: but they had given, so far, no ground for suspicion. His family and those concerned with its fortunes: Elma, the problematical Walter, Holland, Mr. Dakers. Of these, which had a motive—a strong one? Elma had a weak one, the desire to get her money absolutely. Holland had a stronger one, to overcome an obstacle to his marriage; but was it strong enough? Not unless and until it could be proved that the typewritten consent was a forgery. Mr. Dakers hardly came into the picture at all; Walter, if he was alive, was a tough customer no doubt; but how exactly did he stand to gain by his uncle's disappearance? This absence of motive was a puzzling feature; was it possible that some guest of Sir Wilfrid Denny's was implicated? *Mem.—Trace Denny as soon as possible.*

19. *Why was a knife chosen as the weapon?* Stabbing usually meant murder in hot blood, or as the result of panic; a thought-out crime would ordinarily depend on safer weapons. Its use suggested that the murder took place at some spot where the report of fire-arms would have been heard, and would have brought rescue; near the house, for instance. Grice had been away all day, and had as yet made no investigation of the wound since the loss of the Norwegian knife had been discovered. If that knife seemed likely to be the weapon, it would look as if the criminal's first plans had not involved murder, or, at least, murder done in that way.

20. *Why was the body found in a boat?* No use to suggest that the murder had been done in the boat, and the
body, from fear or disgust, left where it lay. In the first
place, it is very hard to murder a man in a boat; you must
be in it yourself, and that means looking at one another all
the time—no chance for a sudden attack. And in this case
the blood must have flowed, yet there were no marks on
the white paint. The body, then, had been deliberately put
into the boat; why? For convenience of colportage? That
was possible; but granted that your corpse has got to
make a journey by boat, it does not follow that it is best
left there. Suppose it had been thrown overboard, with a
couple of stones tied to it? The Admiral's disappearance
would have caused alarm at first; but a report from the
Lord Marshall that he had been seen in Whynmouth that
night, just *en route* for the late train would have dissi-
pated the rumour of murder until the river gave up its
dead; and by that time the murderer might be anywhere
—China, for example. The murderer's instinct is always to
hide his victim, at least for the moment; this murderer had
deliberately put the corpse on show, with the certainty of
its discovery next morning. What did that mean? It suggested, at least, that the whole circumstances in which the
corpse was found were a deliberate frame-up; the criminal felt certain that suspicion would not fall on him, so
long as he left evidence which would fasten the suspicion
on other people. Granted that frame of mind, you could
just account for the boat. A boat travels with the stream
or with the tide at a more or less uniform pace; a floating
body, by itself, might get held up by any overhanging
branch, any patch of shallows. It might be that the criminal wanted to suggest, by the position in which the body
was found, that the murder had taken place at a different
hour or at a different spot from the actual hour, the actual

spot. Best to ask Neddy Ware to say exactly what combinations of times and places would have brought the boat to the spot at which he found it, e.g., Whynmouth, Fernton Bridge, the Vicarage, as alternative sites; 10.30, 11.30, 12.30 as alternative times. *Mem.—Look up Neddy Ware again.*

21. *Why was the body found in that particular boat?* An easy answer suggested itself, "To throw suspicion on the Vicar"; for which reason, too, the hat was doubtless thrown in. To suppose that the Vicar, if he were really privy to the murder, would allow his connection with it to be thus blatantly advertised was ridiculous. But then, was it not almost equally ridiculous to suppose that the criminal had chosen the Vicar as his scapegoat? The frame-up, in that case, was inconceivably clumsy work. The simple bluff of pretending that the Vicar was the criminal seemed too simple; the double bluff of pretending to have pretended that the Vicar was the criminal seemed too complicated. Yet, for what other purpose could the Vicarage boat have been dragged into the story at all? It might indicate that the murderer had started from the other side of the river, and had found that a borrowed boat saved the trouble of going round by the bridge. On the other hand, it might indicate that the murderer had wanted the police to think just that, having in fact started his operations from the Rundel Croft bank. There was not much to be made of this clue, and yet it haunted the imagination.

22. *Why was the Vicar's hat left behind?* Assuming for the moment that Mount was the criminal, the question admitted of no ready answer. On the whole, people are hat-wearers or bare-headers; the former class will notice the absence of the familiar feeling as a kind of discomfort. You would expect the murderer, passing his hand over his forehead, to cry out instinctively, "Good heavens, where is my hat?" An unconscious exchange of hats between the

murderer and his victim seemed just possible; Holland had
fancied a clerical appearance about the hat which the
Admiral, if it was the Admiral, had worn that night.
Again, assuming that the murderer came from the direction of the Vicarage, it was possible that he had found the
hat lying derelict in the summer-house, and had borrowed
it for his own purpose—to hide his face, for example.
*Mem.—Examine the hat on the off-chance of finding lay
hairs adhering to it.*

23. *Why was the key to the french window found in the
bottom of the Admiral's boat?* This key business was less
puzzling. Presumably, when Elma left her uncle to lock
up the boat, she took the key up with her, and left it in
the french window, on the outside, so that he could let
himself in later. Did he so let himself in? It looked as if he
must have, to find his great-coat. Then, if he ever went out
again alive, he would lock the window from the outside
and slip the key into his pocket. It might fall out of his
pocket, easily enough, when his dead body was put into
the boat. Alternatively, if the Admiral was in fact killed
in his garden before he had time to re-enter the house, the
criminal would no doubt use the key to let himself in,
when he was in search of the hidden papers. Once he had
got those papers, and the Admiral was dead, it did not
matter what he did with the key; indeed, it was necessary
to get rid of it somehow.

24. *Why was the Admiral's boat moored, contrary to
custom, by the bows?* Here was a point of genuine significance. It meant that this boat, too, had figured somehow
in the movements of that August night. Either the Admiral had been abroad on her, and had been caught in the
middle of his travels; or else the criminal, having despatched him in his own garden, had made use of two
boats in disposing of the body, or possibly in securing his

own escape. And for some reason, a baffling one, surely, he had thought it more important to leave the Admiral's boat moored than the Vicar's. Inexplicably, he must have thought that things looked more natural this way. Another pertinent consideration arose: Elma must surely have known her uncle's little fad about the mooring of boats; and therefore if she or anybody acting under her immediate direction had been guilty of the murder, it was hard to believe that the boat would not have been found in the morning moored as usual.

25. *Why is a whole length of the painter missing?* And such a small length; not as much as you would naturally cut off if you needed the rope for some unusual purpose; to tie a man's hands, for example. No, the Vicar's boat had first been cut loose from its moorings, and then it had been tied up again, either to some other post or to some other boat, and once more it had been necessary to cut it with a knife instead of untying it. This was puzzling, because ordinarily what man has done man can undo, if it is the same man. You had to allow for accident; e.g., two ropes might have been tied together, and then swelled through being left in the water; or some sudden need for haste might have arisen, so that there was no leisure for untying knots. But following out the indications of the painter for what they were worth, you were led to the conclusion that the painter had been twice cut; that a different person had been responsible for the second cut, and that this new person was shorter than the other. The Vicar, for example, who was tallish, might have cut the rope in the first instance; but if it was he who re-tied the boat, he would naturally do so at a height which would make it possible for him to untie it again without difficulty. This new figure in the story might be called x-n, the original painter cutter being labelled x. Now, it was possible that x-n was

simply the Admiral. But the question arose whether you
had not to allow for two people besides the Admiral, both
concerned in the doings of that night, x and x-n. Holland
might be x, but such was his height that he might have
been expected to untie the boat even from its first moorings.

26. *Why was the body found in a coat?* It was a pity,
when you came to think of it, that that question had not
been put down immediately after No. 20. It would have
been a rhyme. Rudge, in his youth, had tried to fill up the
last lines of limericks, but he had never claimed to be a
poet, and it was a new experience for him to find himself
in the position of the young Ovid, writing verse unconsciously. Yes, to be sure, that great-coat. If the Admiral
really went into Whynmouth, and really meant to catch
the late train, it was conceivable that he would have taken
a coat with him to protect him against the chill of the early
morning. But Rudge was altogether inclined to discredit
that projected railway journey. If the Admiral really went
to Whynmouth, or to any other point along the river, in
a boat and with the intention of returning in a boat, he
would only have encumbered himself with a fairly sub-
stantial overcoat for one reason—he must have anticipated
having to hang about somewhere waiting for somebody,
talking to somebody, in the open air, and was afraid that
he would get a chill after taking exercise without this precaution. On the other hand, the great-coat was a loose one;
what they call in the shops "something in the style of a
Raglan." It would have been quite possible, then, for the
murderer, unless he were squeamish about handling corpses,
to pull the overcoat on to a dead body in a perfectly convincing way. Now, what would that mean? Probably, that
the murderer was elaborating a "frame-up" as before; having disseminated the idea that the Admiral meant to go up

to London by the late train, he went on to give that idea
corroboration by vesting his victim suitably for such a
journey.

27. *And now, why the newspaper in the pocket?* If the
Admiral had really intended a train journey, and had gone
into the house to get his coat with that in view, was it not
humanly certain that his eye would have fallen on the
newspaper close by, and that he would have crammed the
familiar copy in his great-coat there and then? The train-
service from Whynmouth to London is not distinguished
for speed, and most residents arm themselves with some
kind of literature before they set out on it. But this the
Admiral had not done; the second copy found in the hall
the morning after the murder was the genuine article, for
it was marked "Admiral Pennystone," with one of Mr.
Tolwhistle's characteristic mis-spellings. Where did the un-
marked copy come from? The shops and the bookstalls at
Whynmouth were all shut by nine; and there were no
longer any street vendors—Whynmouth is a sleepy place,
and the last optimist who had tried peddling alleged "late
editions" had gone out of business some months earlier.
The Admiral had not gone into the Lord Marshall; could
not, then, have picked up a copy there and walked off with
it. If he was really in possession of it while still alive, it
followed that he must have called somewhere else that
night. Sir Wilfrid Denny's house suggested itself as a possibility. If, on the other hand, the paper had been thrust
into the pocket after his death by the man who murdered
him, that could only have been done with the intention of
falsifying the evidence. Falsifying it how? In point of time,
by suggesting that the murder took place, say, after nine
instead of having taken place before nine? But that would
bring the real time to an impossibly early hour. In point
of place, then; the murder really happened in some place

at a distance from Whynmouth; and the murderer, by
thrusting the *Gazette* into the dead man's pocket, had tried
to create the impression that the murder took place at
Whynmouth, or at least while the victim was on his way
back from there. Read so, this piece of evidence chimed
in with the conclusion which had already suggested itself
—that the murderer wanted it to be thought, falsely, that
the Admiral was in Whynmouth that evening. If you accepted this argument, a further consideration arose. The
murderer was somebody who did not know Whynmouth,
or whose knowledge of it was not up-to-date. A resident
—the elusive Sir Wilfrid, for example—would not have
made the mistake of imagining that the *Gazette* was still
on sale at eleven o'clock in the evening.

28. *Of what nature were the documents marked* "X"?
That they were secret, that they were valuable, went without saying. What was much more remarkable, if you came
to think of it, was that any reference to "X" should have
been given among the files at all. The Admiral himself,
though he was one of the few admirals who had not pub-
licly attested his indebtedness to any system of memory-
training, was clearly not absent-minded beyond the aver-
age of humanity; why then should he need a reference to
remind him where these all-important documents were
kept? Yet, if the references were not for the Admiral's
own benefit, who else could profit by them? In the event
of his desk being broken open, would it not have been
safer to leave the very existence of "X," as well as its
whereabouts, a secret? It looked almost as if the Admiral
had expected the fate which ultimately came upon him—
after all, there was that loaded revolver in the desk—expected that a police officer sooner or later would rummage
in his desk, and would need a pointer to inform him that
secret papers were concealed somewhere. It would appear

that Sir Wilfrid was somewhat involved, also the nephew, Walter. It seemed probable that the background was Chinese. Was it blackmail? If so, Sir Wilfrid must surely be the victim of it, not Walter; you cannot threaten with exposure a man who has disappeared from human ken.

29. *Were they destroyed, or stolen? And by whom?* It was just possible that Penistone at some time had got rid of documents which would be damaging to himself or to someone he cared for. It was more natural to assume that the murderer was also a thief. But—here was an important point—the person who stole those papers must, almost necessarily, have been an inmate of the house; the desk had shown no traces of being rifled, there were no marks of violence about the secret drawer. If, then, the villain of last night had removed those papers, he had known exactly where to look for them, and had wasted no time over it.

Whew! There was a fresh section of the evidence concluded; that finished the clues which dated from last night. Rudge's left foot had gone to sleep, and he tramped his room for a bit, trying to map out what remained of his task. Yes, he must analyse the behaviour of the various people, against whom suspicion might conceivably lie, since the actual discovery of the corpse. The most noticeable feature, undoubtedly, was what you might call the drain of the rural population—the general dash for London. Very well, then:

30. *Why did Elma Fitzgerald hurry up to London?* The conclusion seemed inevitable that her flight was consequent upon the news of the murder. She was not fond of early rising, and her early rising that morning had been Rudge's own fault. The Whynmouth line assumes, like most railways, that you do not want to travel up to the metropolis much after ten o'clock; after that hour, the speed of the trains sagged noticeably, and day tickets were

no longer available. Consequently, if you were going up
to London you prepared for an early start. Elma had made
an early start, but she had not prepared for it. She had
not fled to meet Holland; for she knew, unless his overnight message had remained undelivered, that he was in
Whynmouth. She had not been to see Mr. Dakers—though,
of course, Holland's pursuit might have interrupted that
plan. *Better wait to hear what she will say to-morrow.*

31. *Why did Holland ditto?* This was plainer sailing.
Innocent or guilty, and whether he believed her to be innocent or guilty, he would naturally want to see Elma
and to discuss the situation. But, assuming that Holland
was himself innocent, it looked as if he must have believed
Elma guilty. Otherwise, he might at least have waited to
tell a true story to the police.

32. *Why did Sir Wilfrid ditto?* It was to be observed
that Sir Wilfrid, if his movements had been correctly re-
ported, was in the van of the movement. He had gone up
to London "by the first train," and that ran, when was it?
Soon after seven . . . anyhow, long before Elma was out
of bed. Not before the body was discovered, but surely
before the rumour of its discovery was likely to have
reached him. Either, then, the "call" which summoned
him had been accompanied by news of the tragedy—and
that meant Neddy Ware or the Vicar or Rundel Croft
as its source; or else he went up to London ignorant that
the murder had been committed . . . or at least ignorant
that it had been discovered. Well, well, it might be an accident after all; at least he must hear what the man had
to say. But what a curious influence Penistone must have
had, that his death seemed to scatter his acquaintances in
alarm, instead of rallying them in sympathy!

33. *Why did the Vicar ditto?* Once again, mere coincidence was possible; Mount might, quite possibly, have gone

up to chat to an archdeacon about dilapidations. But it
seemed more natural to connect his behaviour, too, with
the general upset. Now, what precise development in the
story had led to the Vicar's *Hegira?* The corpse had been
discovered, and he remained calm—comparatively calm.
The disappearance of Elma and Holland left him still un-
moved. What new factor could have arisen in the situation?
It looked very much as if the Vicar had made some discovery on his own, a discovery which he had not seen fit
to communicate.

34. *Was the Vicar telling all he knew?* Curious how
people differed under cross-examination. Elma Fitzgerald
had a natural pose of hostility; she so obviously resented
being asked any questions about anything, that it was
difficult to know whether she was embarrassed at being
asked these questions about this. Holland's contemptuous
joviality was no doubt a permanent mood with him; it
made him a difficult subject for interrogation, because you
never knew quite what allowances to make for his fun.
But Mr. Mount, now, he was evidently a man anxious, as
a matter of conscience, to tell the truth. But there was a
hesitation in his manner which seemed to suggest that he
was not quite sure which part of the truth to tell; not quite
sure how he ought to answer one question, for fear the
next should trench on ground where he was determined
not to tread. He was scrupulous about telling the truth;
and the scrupulous in this world are apt to be more of a
nuisance than the unscrupulous.

35. *Why did the Vicar water his garden?* It might, of
course, be nothing more than a horticultural *gaffe*. But,
if you were prepared to make a long shot, and suppose that
the Vicar came into it somehow, you naturally asked,
was he trying to hide traces? Indulge the fancy, and where
did that lead? Not his own traces, surely; for he would

be conscious of having left them, and would have had the elementary common sense to obliterate them earlier in the day, to obliterate them at some time when the police were unlikely to be about. The same consideration applied, though with slightly less force, if you thought of them as the traces of somebody of whose presence he had been conscious at the time when they were made. And yet he must surely have had some idea whose they were and how they came there, or his meticulous sense of justice would have induced him to point them out to the police. A long shot, but it needed thinking over.

36. *Why was the Admiral's pipe left in the Vicar's study?* Probably because the Admiral forgot it and left it there. He had been in a hurry, it seemed, when he left; and the most punctilious of admirals will have these lapses occasionally. And he was, as Holland had pointed out, a man of many pipes. But Rudge's brain was by now worked up into the state in which it could see significance in everything; and even this pipe—there was the bare possibility that the Admiral had left it there on purpose, in order to have an excuse for going back to the Vicarage (but apparently never went) ; or that the Vicar himself had found it in some place where it seemed all too likely to tell a story, and had for safety removed it elsewhere. Rudge, perhaps with a theologian's unconscious animus, was already thinking of Mr. Mount as the sort of man who would not tell a direct lie, but would be quite willing to let you deceive yourself ("lead you up the garden" was his own less technical phrase).

37. *Why were Holland and Elma in such a hurry to get married?* That the licence had already been procured before the murder took place, seemed evident. But this in itself need not suggest foreknowledge of the murder; Holland's own account—that Elma had encouraged him

by her letter to expect the Admiral's consent, and that
he had taken out the licence on the strength of that hope—
seemed sound enough as it stood. You could understand
why there should be haste in their proceedings while the
Admiral was still alive, and had given his reluctant consent. Who knew when he might change his mind? But,
once he was dead, that motive ceased to operate; you would
have thought it common decency to wait a little, and according to Dakers it would have been common prudence
too. There must be some reason, but what reason? Rudge
admitted that at this point the case defied him.

38. *Why did Holland conceal, at first, his alleged midnight interview?* His own excuse, that he had concealed
the whole story of his midnight journey simply to avoid
embarrassing questions when he was in a hurry, seemed
strangely inadequate. On the assumption that his first story
was true, and his second false, why should he cast doubt
on his own veracity by this curious *volte-face?* On the
contrary assumption, why did he not stick to his lie when
once he had told it? Having the typewritten consent in
his pocket, he could just as easily pretend it had been given
to Elma early on the previous evening, before the dinner-
party; what motive was there for insisting so strongly that
it had only been drafted at midnight? It looked as if some
piece of evidence must have cropped up during the day
which would make Holland's statement that he had slept
soundly at the Lord Marshall inconsistent with the genuine-
ness of the typewritten consent. What could that evidence
be? Rudge tortured his imagination vainly over the
problem.

39. *Why was the typewritten consent typewritten?*
There was no typewriter in the Admiral's room; the
documents in the files which were not holograph had
plainly been copied out by a professional. Moreover, the

amateur, to whom it is a matter of labour to fit his sheet straight into the machine, does not have recourse to his typewriter unless he has a document of some length, say four or five lines, to deal with. Improbable, then . . . unless the document was a forgery (a signature being much easier to forge, by mere imitation, than a whole line of writing). Or possibly the "consent" might have been extracted by some threats or violence, in which case it was likely enough that the criminal should have expedited matters by supplying a ready-made formula. *Mem.—Ask Mrs. Holland where and by whom she thinks the typewriting was done.*

And so, having got his ideas down on paper, Rudge went off to bed, comforting himself with the old, superstitious hope we all have sometimes, that he would wake up with an inspiration. But the night did not bring counsel. He did, indeed, dream that he saw the actual crime being committed. But as, in his dream, the author of the murder was Mrs. Davis, the victim Mr. Dakers, the weapon a rolled-up newspaper, and the scene of the whole incident the Charing Cross Hotel, he wisely concluded that oneiromancy has its fallible moments.

CHAPTER IX

By Freeman Wills Crofts

THE VISITOR IN THE NIGHT

INSPECTOR RUDGE woke next morning with a vaguely troubled mind. He had a subconscious impression that this was no ordinary day and that important duties were awaiting him. Then he remembered. His big chance had come! He sprang out of bed.

During breakfast he laid his plans for the day. First there was a conference with his chiefs. Superintendent Hawkesworth had been on leave when the murder took place, and though Rudge had wired for him directly he had heard of it, he was not expected back till early that morning. The Chief Constable, Major Twyfitt, had also been away, but he had returned last evening, and he also would want to hear the news. Then there was the interview with the coroner about the inquest, after which Rudge supposed he would be at liberty to take up one or more of the lines of investigation he had thought out on the previous evening.

He was a good deal worried that he had not yet been able to arrange for an adequate identification of the remains. Rudge did not himself doubt that the dead man was the Admiral, but this had not been proved, and it was his job to prove it. This question of identity would be the first to be raised by the Super, and it would probably be the only one in which at this stage the coroner would be interested.

Rudge walked round to the Lord Marshall on the chance that Dakers might be about. Dakers should be his man for the identification. By a chance which Rudge took as a good omen for the day, it happened that as he entered the porch he met Dakers coming out.

"Good morning, sir," Rudge said genially. "This is a bit of luck for me. I was just wondering if I could see you."

Dakers was polite, but not genial. He showed no enthusiasm for the meeting. "What is it?" he asked shortly.

"The identification of the remains, sir. May I ask how long you knew the Admiral?"

"How long?" the solicitor repeated slowly. "Let's see. Twenty-one—two—about twenty-two years; possibly twenty-three."

"Good enough, sir. And during that period you've seen him, I presume, at intervals?"

"Yes, at irregular intervals, I have."

"Then, sir, I should be obliged if when convenient you would run out with me to Lingham, where the body is lying, and see if you can formally identify it."

"I should like to have my breakfast first."

"I said, sir, when convenient. Would ten o'clock suit?"

Dakers agreed and Rudge went on: "There's another thing I'd like to ask you about while I have the opportunity, and that is the late Admiral's consent to his niece's wedding. Do you happen to have it in your possession?"

"You mean the typewritten statement?"

"Yes, sir."

Dakers considered. "How do you come to be interested in that?" he asked.

"In the same way, sir, that I expect you're interested

in it," Rudge returned promptly. "We both, I take it, want to be sure that it was really given by the Admiral."

"You mean," said Dakers frigidly, "that Mrs. Holland is either a liar or a forger or both?"

"No, sir," Rudge answered imperturbably. "Mrs. Holland didn't say she got it from the Admiral. Mr. Holland said that. My question is really in Mrs. Holland's own interest. I take it that that document will have to be proved before she can inherit, and I was going to suggest that the sooner its authenticity is established, the better."

Dakers became if possible even more frigid.

"Thank you, Inspector, but I shall endeavour to look after my client's interests without the help of the police."

Rudge shrugged. "As you will, sir. But you must realise that the police will have to examine that document, and I was merely suggesting that if you could see your way to work with us in the matter it would save time and trouble. But of course it's as you like. Till ten o'clock then, sir."

Superintendent Hawkesworth was waiting for Rudge at the station, and within a few minutes Chief Constable Twyfitt arrived. Rudge at once gave a detailed account of what had happened and what he had done, with the steps he next proposed to take. The two men heard him without interruption, Hawkesworth scribbling copious notes.

"That seems all right, Rudge, as far as you have gone," the Superintendent said, glancing at his superior.

"Yes," Major Twyfitt agreed. "I think Rudge has done quite well. And his proposals for carrying on seem sound."

"Yes, but there's too much in them for one man," Hawkesworth decided. "We'll have to divide them up. Just let's settle what everyone's to do and then you, Rudge, can get along with that identification. Now let's see." For some moments he scribbled rapidly. "This'll do, I think," he went on. "I'll take on the China affair. I'll

get in touch with the Admiralty and the Foreign Office
and that newspaper man and any other place or person I
can think of. Then I'll follow up Denny: I dare say there's
some connection between the two. Sergeant Appleton
we'll put on to Holland: Holland's doings in this country,
that is: Holland in China will come under me. If necessary, Appleton can go up to the Yard and get some help
there. At the same time he can find out if those two were
really married in town. Constable Hempstead seems to
have done well?"

"He certainly has, sir. He's no fool, is Hempstead."

"Very well, we'll give him his chance. We'll let him
search the river, both banks, over the length along which
the boat could have floated. He's to look out for traces
of any kind, particularly for footprints on the bank,
signs of a struggle, places where the body might have been
lifted into the boat, and that missing bit of the painter.
That'll keep him busy. You yourself, Rudge, take Rundel
Croft and the people in it, excluding the dead man, who I
think will come into my department. That covers things
in the meantime?"

"Yes, sir, I think that's all right."

"Well, you get along now. Then you're going to see the
coroner? Formal identification and an adjournment of
course?"

"Of course, sir."

Fifteen minutes later Rudge and Dakers reached the
public house at Lingham where the body of the deceased
was lying. Dakers had recovered his good temper and had
chatted pleasantly enough during the drive.

"Well, sir?" Rudge asked, when the solicitor had stared
for some moments at the dead features.

Dakers seemed to awake as from a reverie. "Oh yes,"
he said without hesitation, "it's Admiral Penistone right

enough. No doubt whatever." He appeared somewhat touched. "Poor old fellow," he went on, "I'm sorry to see him like that. We didn't see eye to eye in everything, but still—judging people as you find them, I could say nothing but good about him." He turned away with a sigh. "I suppose you want me to give evidence of identity at the inquest?"

"It would save Mrs. Holland," Rudge pointed out.

"Very well. When does it take place?"

"To-morrow at ten, sir."

"I shall be there."

"Thank you, sir. I suppose, sir." Rudge smiled as if to discount the saying of a stupid thing: "I suppose Mrs. Holland really was the late Admiral's niece? You see, no one here knows the family. As you are aware, they moved here about a month ago."

"Of course she was," Dakers answered testily. "I'm afraid you won't get far on those lines, Inspector."

"We have to question everything, sir, as you know. Well, sir, I'm obliged to you for doing the identification. Where would you like to be put down?"

They drove back to the Lord Marshall and Dakers got out. Rudge was turning away, but the solicitor stopped him with a gesture.

"About that consent, Inspector. I've been thinking over it and after all I don't see any reason why you shouldn't see it. I haven't got it myself at the moment, but when I get it I'll let you know."

Rudge thanked him again and the two men parted. Rudge was pleased with his day so far. He was certainly making progress. Already some of his theories had been eliminated and bed-rock fact was beginning to emerge from the mass of speculation in which the case was smothered.

Rudge's business with the coroner was soon settled. It was obviously impossible to complete the inquest, and Mr. Skipworth agreed that all that was now necessary was to carry on the proceedings far enough to enable a burial order to be given. This procedure had already been tentatively agreed on by telephone, and the meeting was really to run over the required evidence and make sure that no unforeseen factor had arisen.

For the rest of that day Rudge busied himself in trying to glean information about the Rundel Croft household. He did not learn much, it must be admitted, but he initiated a series of enquiries about each member, the replies to which, when received, should prove valuable. Among the Admiral's papers he found the Cornish address from which the deceased man had moved, and he telephoned to the Superintendent of the district for all available details of the family. He interviewed Elma Holland, though unfortunately without much success. He found out where the servants—the butler and his wife, and Elma's present maid—had been engaged, and wrote to their former employers for further particulars of them. Lastly, he made a general search of the house, which, however, proved quite fruitless.

At a few minutes before ten next morning Rudge entered the hall where the inquest was to be held. To tell the truth, coroners' enquiries were formalities which completely bored him. A waste of time, he considered them, indeed worse than a waste, for he believed the time could always be used more profitably in carrying on the normal investigation.

As he had foreseen, the proceedings afforded little of interest. The eleven jurors did not elect to view the body, and as soon as they were sworn, evidence was taken.

Neddy Ware first told in detail of his discovery of the

body. Then Mr. Dakers swore that he had seen the body and that he identified it as that of Rear-Admiral Hugh Lawrence Penistone. He gave a short outline of the Admiral's life, explained how he came to know him, and then stood down. Next Dr. Grice stated the cause of death, a wound in the heart from a knife or dagger with a long thin blade. A post-mortem had shown that the Admiral was in reasonably good health for a man of his years.

This brought the proceedings to a close, the coroner stating that in order to enable the police to make further enquiries he would adjourn the inquest till that day three weeks.

Once again Rudge was struck by the keenness of his reporter friend from the *Evening Gazette*. The man simply pestered him for news. A growing shortness in Rudge's manner had no effect whatever, and it was not till he threatened to give anything available to a rival journal, that the man became reasonable.

Another person who developed a surprising curiosity was Mr. Mount. Mount was the first man Rudge had seen on reaching the coroner's court. This was not surprising in a way, because Rudge had himself told the Vicar that his presence at the inquest would be required. But owing to the decision only to take evidence of identification that morning, Mount had neither been sent a summons to attend, nor been officially informed of the place and hour. But there the man was, and not only so, but he was evidently in an extremely curious as well as apprehensive condition.

On leaving the room Rudge found himself button-holed by the Vicar. Under the thinly veiled guise of a clergyman's natural interest in his parishioners, Mount made a really blatant attempt to learn the extent of the police knowledge of the case. But Mount was a child in the In-

spector's experienced hands. Rudge replied readily and with
a convincing air of candour, while warning the Vicar not
to repeat his confidences. But Rudge knew that when the
Vicar came to think over what he had been told, he would
be hard put to it to find out what those confidences were.

Rudge wondered if he had given enough attention to
Mount. Sitting down in his room, he ran through his notes,
transcribing anything he had learned about him.

In the first place, Mount was evidently already on intimate terms with the Rundel Croft people. Then it was
in his, Mount's, boat that the dead man had been found,
and more significant still, Mount's hat had been in the
boat. Then there had been Mount's sudden journey to London; there had been his watering of the garden, and now
there was this deep anxiety about the case. The more
Rudge thought over it, the more he felt impelled to the
conclusion that Mount must somehow be implicated.

Rudge considered the above points in turn, but the only
one from which he thought fresh light might be obtained
was the man's visit to London. He recalled the details.

It was between twelve and one o'clock that Mount
had sent his note saying that he was anxious to go up that
afternoon to town on an urgent matter connected with
his clerical duties. Now that must have been a very sudden
decision. He, Rudge, had been speaking to Mount earlier
in the morning, and the man had said nothing about this
visit then. Rudge did not know much about ecclesiastical
matters, but he doubted that business was done at that
rate. Most professional visits to London would mean for
clergymen meetings arranged a considerable time earlier,
or interviews with dignitaries, also arranged some time
beforehand. He was inclined to doubt that the clerical
duties in question had much to do with the church.

Rudge wondered what he should do. Mount bore a

high reputation for probity, and if the matter were put directly to him, he might give the required explanation. Then Rudge saw that he would probably do nothing of the kind. He, Rudge, had nothing to put which would demand an answer.

Mount had hurried up to town. But so had Elma, so had Holland, so had Denny. Was it possible to believe that there was no connection between all these visits? Suddenly it seemed to Rudge that his best plan would be to try to trace Mount's movements in town. It shouldn't take long and it might lead to something vital.

Rudge went in and put his views before Superintendent Hawkesworth. Hawkesworth was impressed, and agreed to release Rudge for a couple of days.

"You'd better advise them at the Yard what you propose to do," said Hawkesworth. "I'll ring them up that you'll call."

The first question was: How had Mount made the journey? Mount had a car, but most persons of moderate income went by train, rail being so much cheaper for the long distance. Mount had been at the Vicarage at one o'clock, and he had rung up Rudge from the Charing Cross Hotel at nine. There were two, and only two, trains he could have used, the 2.5 from Whynmouth, which reached Waterloo at 5.45, and the 4.25 from Whynmouth, arriving at 8.35.

Rudge began by calling at the office of the local newspaper and getting a photograph of Mount. Then he went to the station and began his enquiries. He learned at once that Mount had been seen on the day in question. He had been noticed particularly by both the booking-clerk and the ticket-collector, and for the same reason. He had, it appeared, bought a London ticket, but he had not travelled by a London train. He had gone by the 1.30 which con-

nected at Passfield Junction with the 11.0 a.m. express
from Waterloo to the west. He had explained that he
wished to break his journey and would go on to London
by a later train.

As Rudge jogged along in the next train to Passfield
Junction, he reminded himself of the lie of the land. The
main line of the Western Division of the Southern Railway ran from Waterloo to Devon, past Whynmouth. It
did not, however, go through Whynmouth; it ran at this
point some ten miles inland. Whynmouth was the terminus
of a branch which left the main line at this Passfield Junction, a small roadside station some fifteen miles away in
the London direction. The nearest town to Whynmouth
on the main line was Drychester. It lay on the Exeter side
of Whynmouth, twelve miles away by road. There was no
direct rail connection between the two places, the route
being by Passfield Junction.

At each of the small stations between Whynmouth and
Passfield Junction Rudge jumped out of the train and enquired if the Vicar had been seen alighting on the day
in question. But it was not till he reached the junction
that he got any information.

Mr. Mount was slightly known to the stationmaster, and
he believed he had seen him on that day entering a third-
class carriage of the down express. Rudge went at once to
the booking-office, and there he learned that only three
third-class tickets had been issued by that train—a single
to Exeter and two returns to Drychester. From this it
seemed pretty clear that Mount had booked to Drychester.

In due course Rudge reached Drychester. But here he had
not the same luck. Drychester station was a busy place,
very different to the small roadside junction. No one knew
Mount and no one had noticed a clergyman resembling
him.

It looked, however, as if Mount had reached Drychester at 2.40. If so, he would have been too late to have caught the earlier of the two trains to town, and must therefore have gone by the second, leaving Drychester at 4.50. That is, he would have had two hours and ten minutes in Drychester. What could he have done in that time?

Rudge could form no idea. He thought first of going down to the cathedral and making enquiries of the vergers, but he wasn't anxious that it should be known that he was making this investigation. At last as a sort of forlorn hope he decided to interrogate the taxi-men at the station, on the off-chance that Mount might have driven to his destination.

Armed with his photograph, Rudge went round the men. He did not expect to get much, and he was therefore agreeably surprised when he suddenly found he had struck oil. But he did not realise, not for a long time after, how deep and how rich was the well he had tapped.

When he showed the photograph to one of the men, a little weazened rat of a fellow, it produced a reaction.

"Aye," said the man, "I've seen the gent all right, I 'ave. But not 'ere. I've seen 'im in Lingham."

"Oh," said Rudge, "in Lingham, have you? That's no good to me. I'm looking for traces of him here."

"I didn't see 'im 'ere, guv'nor. Never seen 'im but the once; in Lingham."

Rudge's fate, Mount's fate, and the fate of several other persons trembled in the balance. Rudge was about to pass on to the next driver, but fortunately for himself, he didn't. Fortunately for himself, he asked the fateful question: "When was that?"

"Last Tuesday night," the taxi-man replied, "at a 'ouse near Lingham, about a 'arf a mile beyond the village, an' down on the river."

"Beside the church?"

"That's right, guv'nor."

"And what time was that?"

The man paused in thought. "About midnight or a bit after."

Rudge's heart gave a sudden leap. Midnight or later on the night of the crime was a very critical hour in the case. At midnight the terrible drama which led to Admiral Penistone's death must already have been under way. What the Vicar was doing at midnight was something that he would be extraordinarily glad to know.

"Better tell me all about it," Rudge suggested, carefully keeping the eagerness out of his voice.

But the man's story, instead of clearing up the situation, seemed only to make it still more incomprehensible. It seemed that on that night, the night of the crime, he had been on duty when the last train arrived from town, the 7.0 p.m. from Waterloo. It arrived at 10.20, and he got a fare from it. It was a lady, a small, middle-aged woman with a bright, quick manner. As far as the taxi-man could see in the somewhat poor light of the lamps, she was elegantly dressed and very good-looking. Quite an attractive lady, he evidently thought. She had asked him to drive her to a house in Lingham which she would point out, wait for her for a few minutes, and bring her back to the Anglers' Arms at Drychester.

Except that it was rather late to pay a call, this seemed reasonable to Rudge. He knew the trains from town. The last train having a connection to Whynmouth left Waterloo at 5.30. The 7.0 from town did not stop at Passfield Junction, and the only way in which a passenger by that train could reach Whynmouth was by driving the twelve miles from Drychester.

"I follow you," Rudge said. "Go ahead."

The man had driven his passenger to Lingham and she had directed him to the house he had mentioned, near the church. She had asked him to wait on the road, so as, she said, not to rouse the children with the sound of the engine. She had said she would not be long. Then she had disappeared in the direction of the house. That must have been a few minutes before eleven.

The taxi-man settled down to wait, and wait he certainly did. The few minutes passed three or four times over, and still there was no sign of her. He began to get impatient, and getting out of the taxi, he walked up the short drive till he got in sight of the house, which had been hidden behind a small plantation. The house was dark and silent and no one seemed to be about. The taxi-man grew anxious about his fare, and he went forward and knocked at the first door he came to. Rudge recognised it as the side-door. For a time no one answered, and the taxi-man knocked louder and louder. At last a window opened upstairs and this parson put his head out. What was it: a sick call? The taxi-man gave him clearly to understand it was not a sick call, and the parson said he'd come down. He came down and asked what was wrong. The taxi-man asked would his passenger soon be out, as he had an early job in the morning and he didn't want to spend the night waiting at the gate. The parson evidently didn't know anything about the lady, but he asked for a description of her. Then suddenly he seemed to recognise her. He appeared upset for a moment, then he said it was all right, that he thought the lady was a friend of the housekeeper's, and if the taxi-man would wait a moment longer he would find out when she was leaving. He disappeared for three or four minutes, then he returned to say that the lady had been taken with a fainting fit, and in the excitement the taxi had been forgotten. The lady was not well enough to go back to Drychester that night, but would stay with his housekeeper, and he would pay the taxi. He had done so. The taxi-man had returned to Drychester, and that was all he knew about it.

Here was a fresh complication! Rudge swore. Instead of things straightening themselves out, the tangle was getting worse.

"Tell me," said Rudge, "you drove through Lingham, didn't you?"

"Correct, guv'nor."

"Did you stop there?"

"Not above a minute or two. I stopped and the lady directed me which way to go."

Here was at least something. This must have been the car Constable Hempstead had seen. So far as it went, Hempstead's report was corroboration of the story.

Rudge postponed consideration of the affair, and walked to the Anglers' Arms, which was near the station. And there he got some news which, he thought, entirely justified his suspicions.

It seemed that about seven o'clock on the evening in question, a telegram had been received from Waterloo, to the effect that the sender, Mrs. Marsh, was going to Drychester by the next train and required a room to be reserved for the night. Also, she wished the hotel to be left open, as owing to having to pay a call on arrival, she could not reach it till midnight or later. The room had been duly prepared and the porter had waited up till nearly two, but the lady had not turned up, nor had anything been since heard of her.

This certainly did back up the tale that the lady had intended to return from Lingham Vicarage to Drychester. So far the thing looked *bona fide* enough. It would, however, be easy to get the details at the Vicarage. In the meantime Rudge must not lose sight of his present quest: what was Mount doing at Drychester?

He produced his photograph and asked if the hotel manager had ever seen the original. And then came the information which brought all his suspicions of Mount back with a rush and made him congratulate himself on having followed up this line of the case.

Mount, it appeared, had called at the hotel on the day following that on which the telegram had been received, and Rudge saw that he must have gone there immediately on arrival in Drychester. He had stated that he was conducting a delicate enquiry on behalf of a member of his church. It concerned an unhappy marriage; he hoped the manager would not ask for details. His parishioner's wife had intended to meet her husband on the previous night with reference to a possible reconciliation, returning afterwards to the Anglers' Arms and there spending the night. But she had not turned up and his friend was very distressed about her. He, the friend, wishing to keep his family skeleton hidden, had not himself come to the hotel to make enquiries, but had deputed him, the Vicar, to do so in his stead. Could the manager give him any information about the lady? The Vicar could not say under what name she might have registered.

Though the manager did not personally know Mount, he had seen him at functions at the cathedral, and was satisfied of his *bona fides*. He therefore gave him all the information at his disposal. Mr. Mount had thanked him and had at once left.

Rudge imagined that this interview had probably constituted Mount's whole business in Drychester, but to make assurance as sure as possible, he went to the cathedral and in the guise of a former parishioner, asked the head verger if he had ever heard of his old rector, the Rev. Philip

Mount, who he believed was now in charge of a parish
somewhere near. From this beginning it was easy to steer
the conversation in the way it should go, and Rudge was
soon convinced that the Vicar had not been at the cathedral on the day in question.

Rudge caught the last train to town that night. Next
morning he was early at Scotland Yard, where he explained that he wanted to make some enquiries at the
Charing Cross Hotel and possibly elsewhere. He was asked
if he required help, and on his saying that he did not, he
was told to go ahead and ring up if he was stuck.

Assured of a free hand, Rudge went on to the hotel.
There with the aid of his photograph he had no difficulty
in establishing the fact that Mount had arrived at a few
minutes before nine on the evening he rang up, evidently
from the train arriving at Waterloo at 8.35. So far as was
known he had not gone out that night. Next morning he
had paid his bill after breakfast and left.

So far it had been plain sailing for Rudge. Enquiries
at the reception office and from waiters and chambermaids
had quickly brought him his information. But now he was
up against something stiffer. In vain he questioned porters
and messenger boys. The head porter remembered seeing
the Vicar, but he couldn't remember how he had left. He
or one of his staff might have got a taxi for him, but they
got so many taxis they couldn't be sure.

Rudge was extremely persistent, but success did not
crown his efforts. Mount had gone, but no one knew how.

Rudge went out into the square in front of the station.
In all probability Mount had walked to where he had
wanted to go, or, if not, had taken a 'bus or gone down to
the Underground. If so, Rudge did not see how he could
possibly get on his track, and he would be forced to return
to Whynmouth and fall back on the chance of getting a

statement. Such a statement Mount might, of course, refuse to make, and Rudge didn't see how he could force it from him. No, if he, Rudge, could find out what Mount had done in town, it would be infinitely better.

He wondered whether Mount might not after all have taken a taxi. The porters might have forgotten the circumstance, or Mount might have come out into the square and hailed one himself. Rudge decided to make enquiries of those drivers who used ranks near the hotel.

He began at once, and a long job he found it. To man after man he showed his photograph and asked if he had taken the Vicar up. And man after man shook his head and said he had never seen the gentleman.

But Rudge persevered. These enquiries were his only hope, and he would be quite sure they led nowhere before abandoning them. And then at last his perseverance reaped its just reward. A driver came in from a job and took his place at the tail of the line. Rudge went up to him with his photograph.

The driver was by way of being discreet. He had seen Mount, but he didn't know what business of Rudge's that was. A little judicious backsheesh, however, overcame his scruples, and he told what he knew. Mount, it appeared, had hailed him from the station square and told him to drive to Judd Street, to a private hotel. He didn't just remember the number, but he could find the place again.

"Then find it," said Rudge, getting in.

Presently they drew up at Friedlander's Private Hotel and in a couple of minutes Rudge was interviewing the manageress. Yes, the clergyman of the photograph had called on the morning in question. He had asked to see Mrs. Arkwright, a lady who had been staying with them for some three weeks. But Mrs. Arkwright had gone away unexpectedly the evening before and had not yet returned, so the clergyman was disappointed. He had left his name and address: Rev. Philip Mount, Lingham Vicarage, Whynmouth, Dorset, and asked that Mrs. Arkwright be requested to ring him up when she returned. He had then gone away.

Rudge turned the conversation on to Mrs. Arkwright. The manageress was reticent, but still he managed to pick up a good deal. Mrs. Arkwright was middle-aged, small, active and vivacious. She was decidedly good-looking and always dressed well. Though evidently not rich, she seemed comfortably off. The manageress was not certain that she might not be French. They had a French girl staying at the hotel, and Mrs. Arkwright spoke French to her as fluently as she spoke English to the others.

Rudge felt he was getting on. That this Mrs. Arkwright had unexpectedly travelled from London to Drychester on the evening before the crime now seemed clear. Having during the journey mysteriously become Mrs. Marsh, she had driven to the Vicarage and there vanished.

Rudge would have liked to search the lady's room and belongings, but he had no warrant and he did not think he could manage it otherwise. However, by judicious pumping he obtained a little more information from the manageress.

Mrs. Arkwright was pleasant-mannered and a favourite among the residents. She had not, however, many friends of her own, by which the manageress meant visitors. Indeed the manageress might say she had only one visitor, a man who called at irregular intervals. He was tall and distinguished-looking, and his forehead was bronzed, as if he had lived in some hot country. The manageress indeed had seldom seen so good-looking a man. His name was Mr. Jellett.

Rudge was in a reflective frame of mind as he left the

hotel and automatically turned his steps to the nearest tube station. There was something very puzzling about this whole business. That this Mrs. Arkwright or Marsh had gone to the Vicarage on the night of the murder, there could be no doubt. But it wasn't at all certain that she had seen Mount. From what he had said to the taxi-man it was difficult to believe that Mount knew she was there. At the same time Rudge found it equally difficult to believe the story about her visiting the housekeeper and getting a fainting fit. In either case where had the woman disappeared to? It almost seemed as if Mount himself did not know and that his journeys to Drychester and London were simply an effort to find out.

To Rudge it looked very much as if there had been some secret negotiations in progress between the Vicar and this woman. Whether he had seen her on the night of the crime or not, something had happened to make him want to see her the next day. And there was an element of secrecy about the whole thing which looked anything but well.

Then Rudge remembered something he had been told by the garrulous landlady of the Lord Marshall Hotel at Whynmouth. This man, Mount, had had trouble in his life. His wife had run away from him with some man. Now could it be . . . ?

Rudge whistled softly between his teeth. If Mrs. Arkwright-Marsh were really Mrs. Mount, it might at least partially account for these mysterious proceedings. Some question, possibly that of a divorce, might have been raised, which would have necessitated an immediate interview. This would account for the visit to the Vicarage and Mount's subsequent journey to town, though it might not explain Mount's denying knowledge of her call. Oh, yes, it might, though. Rudge saw that he had been wrong. In the excitement of discussing a divorce the taxi might well have been forgotten, and when Mount found it waiting he might have invented the story about the housekeeper to allay possible scandal.

On the whole Rudge thought this theory promising enough to justify further enquiry into it. He did not see, it must be admitted, how it was connected with the death of Admiral Penistone, but that connection was suggested by the boat, the hat, and particularly by the Vicar's eagerness at the inquest.

How, Rudge wondered, could he find out about Mount's erring wife? He thought for a while, then, returning to the Yard, borrowed a Crockford. From this he found that Mount had been in his present position for ten years, before which he had been a curate in one of the Hull churches. Rudge immediately put through a call to the Superintendent at Hull, asking him to try to obtain a description and if possible a photograph of Mrs. Mount.

In a couple of hours there was a reply to say that a photograph and description had been obtained and were being sent up to the Yard.

On Monday morning they arrived. The photograph had been got from one of the local newspaper offices, and showed the lady in a hospital committee group. The description gave Rudge a thrill of satisfaction. It looked as if he were on the right track.

In half an hour he was back in the hotel in Judd Street. He was sorry to trouble the manageress again, but would she be good enough to tell him if Mrs. Arkwright was among this group?

The manageress hesitated a little, but when he explained that the photograph was ten years old she became quite certain. Yes, that fourth lady from the left was undoubtedly Mrs. Arkwright.

Full of self-satisfaction, Rudge took the first train from

Waterloo. Determined to be thorough, he went to Dry-chester and saw his friend, the taxi-man. Here he had not such definite confirmation, though the man agreed that his passenger might well have been the original of the photo.

It was with the gratifying consciousness of something attempted, something done, that Rudge returned to the police station at Whynmouth that afternoon to report his progress to Superintendent Hawkesworth. Hawkesworth, however, took the disappointingly narrow view of achievement so frequently displayed by Authority.

"Huh," he said when Rudge had finished, "it looks to me like a wash-out. This blessed parson is considering making things up with his wife or divorcing her or whatever you like to make it. But that won't help us any with the question of who killed old Penistone. What do you propose to do now?"

"I thought, sir, of going to Mount and asking for an explanation."

Hawkesworth frowned. "An explanation of just what?" he asked.

"An explanation of where Mrs. Mount went to that night. The boat was gone; it was connected with the murder; who took it? Did Mrs. Mount? I think, sir, we could press that question under the circumstances."

The Superintendent considered, then nodded shortly. "Very well; try it. You may as well, now you've gone so far."

Rudge was bitterly indignant as he drove out to Lingham Vicarage. This was always what happened when you took trouble and did anything specially well! What sort of mind had Hawkesworth? Surely to goodness it was clear that this information about Mrs. Mount was vital? Her unexpected visit to the Vicarage on the night of the crime; her unexpected disappearance after arrival there; Mount's

ignorance or assumed ignorance of the whole affair. The
boat; the hat; Mount's sudden attempt to find his wife;
Mount's subterfuges to keep his real business from leaking
out—ecclesiastical matters, he had said to Rudge; a parishioner's unhappy marriage, he had told the Drychester
hotel-keeper; family news, he had explained to the lady in
Judd Street. . . .

In fact the whole thing was darned fishy, and he would
be bound to get some valuable information from Mount.
Somewhat cheered, Rudge set out for the Vicarage.

CHAPTER X

By Edgar Jepson

THE BATHROOM BASIN

POLICE CONSTABLE RICHARD HEMPSTEAD had been cherishing his aunt, Mrs. Emery. At first when she returned to her native neighbourhood and settled down at Rundel Croft, he had showed himself nephewly, but in moderation, certainly not to the point of cherishing her, and even now the cherishing, it is to be feared, was not a natural effusion of pure nepotic feeling. It was the result of feeling, indeed, of two feelings: a strong feeling, a hunch, in fact, that the secret of the murder of the Admiral was to be found in Rundel Croft, and a scarcely less strong feeling that the society of Jennie Merton was good for him.

So it came about that during the last week he had been often in the house. When he was on his round, all kinds of reasons for just looking in on his aunt occurred to him; the house being empty, except for her and Jennie and Emery, burglars might have broken in, or the chickens might have been stolen; or he had to ask her some question, connected with the mystery, of no great importance; or he had to give her some information, of no great importance, about the progress of the police towards the solution of it. He was gifted with a quite decent creative imagination, which, doubtless, was often of use to him in the witness-box. When he was off duty he would, in nephewly fashion, drop in to tea or supper.

It is to be doubted that Mrs. Emery, who had rather more than her fair share of womanly intelligence, as the wives of the Emerys of this world generally have, ascribed his assiduity to the finer feelings of a nephew. She perceived that Jennie was, as a rule, at hand—she would have a good view of the drive from the windows of the upper part of the house, where most of her work lay—to open the door to him when he called. Also she had once heard her say, as she was bringing him from the back door to the kitchen: "Oh, go hon, Mr. Hempstead!"

Well, as Mrs. Emery saw it, Jennie was a good girl, as girls go nowadays, and showed quite a lot of sense in the way she was picking up cooking, and cooking was what a man really wanted when he was married; and in any case Dick was one of those pig-headed young men, who will go their own way, and he might do worse. Anyhow, who was she to interfere with love's young dream?

So it came about that Hempstead had had the run of Rundel Croft, for Elma Holland and her husband had not been in his way. If sometimes he was not alone, but accompanied by Jennie, when he was having the run of it, it did no one any harm. Also, he was a useful man to have about, for in a big house like Rundel Croft little things were always getting out of order and going wrong, and he was useful with his hands. Mrs. Emery soon fell into the way of getting him to set the little things right that the Admiral had been used to set right, putting a spring in a lock that had ceased to work, restoring a patch of paint that had been rubbed off, to maintain in fact the spick and spanness the Admiral had demanded. He was a useful visitor.

He had inspired into Jennie his strong opinion that the solution of the mystery of the murder was to be found in the house, and though she would have helped him in his search, or at any rate superintended it at intervals, in any case, that identity of opinion made her help him with enthusiasm.

Together they searched the house with uncommon thoroughness, every nook and cranny of it, especially the Admiral's study and bedroom and Elma Holland's sitting-room and bedroom, hunting above all for the missing white frock in which Elma had dined at the Vicarage.

"Mind you, Jennie, I don't say as you're wrong in thinking that she packed it up that morning and took it to London with her," he said. "But there's a possibility that she rolled it up small and stuffed it away in some hole or corner, and if so be as we could find it, I'll eat my helmet if we don't find it marked in some way or another that would be a useful clue. It might even be blood-stained."

"It might truly," said Jennie in thoughtful agreement.

They found several holes and corners in which the frock might have been hidden; but they did not find the frock.

Then on Monday afternoon as they were finishing their tea (and it was just about the time that Inspector Rudge was reporting at Whynmouth police station) Mrs. Emery said: "There's one thing, Dick, as you might have a look at before you go, and that's the basin in the bathroom. Miss Elma complained, when she came back, that the water ran out of it very slowly and now it's quite choked up and it won't run out of it at all. It's a job for a plumber, I know; but you might be able to do something with it."

"Well, that's easy, Aunt," said Hempstead with manly confidence. "It's just a matter of clearing out the trap."

He finished his tea—he was always rather longer about it than his uncle and the two women—and having gathered the tools he wanted from the house tool-box, he and Jennie went up to the bathroom, and he got to work. It was an easy job, for, after he had taken up the linoleum, he found the board in the floor above the trap loose, to enable the inevitable plumber to get at the trap easily. He unscrewed the nuts and lifted the cover off the trap. The trap was choked with hair, and he began to pull it out. He was struck by its coarseness and paused to examine it.

Then he said: "This is rum. If I hadn't seen the beard on the Admiral's chin, I should have said as he'd shaved it off."

"It is like the Admiral's beard," said Jennie. "Only it's not so grey."

Hempstead picked the rest of the beard out of the trap carefully and put it in the little enamel basin he had brought up with him to hold the debris that was choking the trap, with a very thoughtful air.

Then he said: "Aunt said that Mrs. Holland complained of how slowly the water ran out of the basin when she came back from London after getting married. I don't suppose anybody had used that basin between then and the morning after the Admiral was murdered."

"I don't suppose they did," said Jennie.

"So, if anyone was shaving off his beard——" said Hempstead thoughtfully and stopped short.

He had said enough. It was no good talking about things. Besides, he wanted to think it out.

"I shouldn't say anything about this, not even to my aunt or uncle," he said. "It may be important."

"Of course not," said Jennie. "And certainly not to your aunt. It would be all over the place before night."

"And you might find me a piece of thick brown paper. I can't dry this hair in front of the kitchen fire 'cos my aunt would see it."

"Of course you can't," said Jennie, and she went in search of brown paper.

Presently she came back with it. Hempstead squeezed the water out of the shaved-off hairs and wrapped them in

the brown paper and put the little packet in his pocket.
They went down to the kitchen.

"I suppose nobody used that basin between Mrs. Holland's going away to get married and coming back, Aunt?"
he said.

"Nobody that I know of," said Mrs. Emery.

"Well, I've cleaned out that trap for you, and the
water's running quite free again," he said and took his
leave of them.

He went away thoughtful, thinking it out, in search of
Inspector Rudge.

He found him just outside the Vicarage gates, displayed
his find and told him where he had come across it.

"It is," said the Inspector, "a rum go—in the trap of the
bathroom basin at Rundel Croft? Well, well."

His eyes brightened as he began to perceive the implications of the discovery.

"Yes, sir. And Mrs. Holland complained that the water
was running slow out of the basin when she came back
after gettin' married, and nobody seems to have used that
basin between that and her going away. It looks as if there
couldn't have been any hairs in that trap when the Admiral
went off to dinner at the Vicarage the night he was murdered. There certainly hasn't been anyone with a beard in
the house since Mrs. Holland went away the morning after
the murder."

"What you mean is that whoever shaved off that beard
shaved it off on the night of the murder?" said the Inspector, frowning thoughtfully.

"That's right, sir."

"Mr. Holland didn't wear a beard by any chance?" said
the Inspector.

"No, sir: I saw him about three or four times when he was
courting Mrs. Holland and he was just the same as now."

"Ah," said the Inspector, and he went on frowning.

Then he said: "But whoever it was called that night at the Lord Marshall and asked for Mr. Holland, did have a beard, and it seemed to me pretty clear that it wasn't the Admiral at all, and this seems to settle it. Whoever wore the beard, he went back to Rundel Croft and shaved it off."

"That's right, sir," said Hempstead.

"Well, he couldn't have done that, unless he knew some-one at Rundel Croft very well, and it could only have been the Admiral himself or Mrs. Holland. If the Admiral was alive, it might have been him; but if the Admiral was dead, it could only have been Mrs. Holland," said the Inspector.

"But it could hardly have been the Admiral, sir, because whoever it was shaved off his beard, he shaved it off because he didn't want anyone to know that he'd been pretending to be the Admiral," said Hempstead.

"Exactly, and it doesn't seem likely that the Admiral should want anyone to pretend to be him. But it was some-one who knew one of them, right enough."

"But the very last place that anyone who'd committed the murder would want to be seen in, is about here," protested Hempstead.

"M'm," said the Inspector. "If you'd seen the silly things murderers do that I've seen. Besides, there are some people who call themselves criminologists, who say that a mur-derer always goes back to the scene of his crime."

"Does he now?"

"No, he doesn't," said the Inspector.

He was silent, considering the possibilities opened up by Hempstead's discovery.

Then, glowing with quiet cheerfulness, he added: "Well, what we want is a man with a beard who has shaved it off. Now, where have I seen a man lately who'd shaved off his beard? I fancy I have."

CHAPTER XI

By Clemence Dane

AT THE VICARAGE

RUDGE rang, and, getting no answer, rang again. He could hear the bell jangling in the deeps of the house, but he could not hear any sound of footsteps. The peace of summer which lay upon the garden had had its effect, apparently, upon the house itself. All its blinds were down and he could hear the loud ticking of the grandfather clock in the hall. Putting his eye to the key-hole, he observed: (*a*) That there was no key in the lock, and (*b*) that the hall was empty. No guilty Vicar was standing within upon the mat, quaking in his shoes, afraid to ignore the summons yet afraid to open. All was a tea-time quiet, yet there was no pleasant chink of china, no tinkle of spoons. "Doubtless," thought Inspector Rudge, "the maids are taking tea out of doors. Girls often carry out their sewing to a paddock. I'll go round."

He went round. The neat, flagged courtyard at the back was, however, equally deserted. The kitchen door was locked, and there was nobody in the sheds at the further side of the yard. On the kitchen door, however, a card was pinned, a white card such as is used at funerals, and on it was inscribed: BACK AT SEVEN-THIRTY.

So that was that! Unwillingly, for in spite of his professional zeal Inspector Rudge would have enjoyed a cup of

tea, he tramped out of the little yard. The noisy echoes of
his feet breaking the silence, he skirted the garden. He
should have gone straight out into the street, and knew it.
Unless he were doing his official duty he was a trespasser
without rights. But he had two hours to put in before he
could return. Virtuously, he resolved to wander about the
village, dropping questions casually, as Cockneys drop
aitches, and perhaps visit that village sphinx, old Wade, in
the hope of gleaning some stray straw of information. Still,
it was exceedingly hot. Why hurry? Besides, wasn't that a
greengage tree strapped up like a flogged prisoner to the
wall at the corner of the garden?

Now, if Inspector Rudge had a weakness, it was for that
deceptive fruit, the greengage. The Londoner knows gages
only in boxes or barrow-tainted, knows that you have to
eat three brackish spheres plucked too early, for the sake of
the one sugary perfection plucked too late. But a small boy,
Tommy Rudge, had stayed at his grandmother's somewhere up in Norfolk, thirty years earlier, and had eaten
Norfolk gages from just such a wall. Memory, the experienced harpist, plucked at the Inspector's heart-strings.
There was the tree: there were the greengages, each with
the golden crack of perfection widening on its jade cheek.
The Inspector o'erleaped the years and the three feet of
lettuce-bed at the same moment. He plucked, ate, dripped
juice from chin and fingers, and dropped the stone at his
feet.

As he did so a glint of light caught his eyes and made
him peer downwards. The glint explained itself quickly
enough, but it was not the bit of broken bottle winking in
the sun which held his attention after that first preliminary
glance: yet his attention was held—held by a couple of
greengage stones, not of his spitting-out, but not yet dry.
By them lay a handkerchief, juice-stained, rolled into a

ball, and on the bare ground at the foot of the tree were
footprints, small, neat footprints. "Size three," thought
Rudge, mechanically appraising, "and French heels at
that!"

Stooping without moving in his tracks, he drew the
handkerchief to him, shook it out. It unrolled easily, for it
was still wet: somebody clearly enough had wiped finger-
tips messed with juice upon it. Then, unsteadily rising, still
careful not to disturb the neighbouring tracks, he examined his find.

It was stained, it was crumpled; but the linen was fine,
the embroidery delicate. "Two-fifteen a dozen," estimated
the accurate Inspector Rudge, who had a gift for acquir-
ing information of the oddest kind, and whose mother, a
lady's maid in her day, had always seen to it that his information was correct. "Two-fifteen at a guess, unless it's
sales," repeated Inspector Rudge thoughtfully, when, fin-
gering the corners, he discovered in one of them, small,
detached, not part of the pattern, the initial C.

Very thoughtfully Inspector Rudge smoothed and folded
the handkerchief, produced from his note-book a clean
envelope, tucked it in, and restored the whole to an inner
pocket. Yet more thoughtfully he glanced about him, hesitated over the stones, shook his head, considered the footprints, shook his head again, then, with a precaution entirely unlike his impetuous arrival, high-stepped off the
bed on to the path, and began pacing majestically to and
fro once more.

The late afternoon sun poured down upon his bowed
shoulders till his blue serge suit shone sordidly, as blue serge
will on a fine day. An inquisitive robin, mistaking him by
his gait for the gardener, kept pace with him in the bushes.
So slow was his progress that Michaelmas daisies, swaying
over the path and pushed aside as he passed, had time to

beat his broad back resentfully. For the Inspector was deep
in thought and something more than thought. He was
floundering, as once or twice before in his strange life he
had floundered, out of the shallow of common sense into
the unplumbed deeps of instinct. A mood was on him:
that part of his mind which, as he put it, "felt through his
elbows" was in charge. Something was wrong, somewhere,
somehow, and Inspector Rudge knew it. There was no one
in the house as far as he could tell. He had spied into the
hall and found it empty: the placard on the back door was
explanation enough. Someone might be hiding in the house,
of course. But why should they be? There was no sense in
it. And Inspector Rudge had nothing at all to go upon, not
even his own shrewd reasoning powers, not even his fac-
ulty of putting two and two together and making twenty-
two of them. No, he had nothing but the handkerchief
with the stained proof that someone had recently been in
the garden, and his own feeling in his elbows that something was wrong.

There was no one in the house as far as he could tell, but
he had the oddest feeling that there was someone in the
garden. So strong a feeling was it that twice he stopped and
turned round sharp to stare down the overgrown glories of
the long, straight path. Empty of course. Only an honest
blaze of sunshine greeted him. Red, white, blue and yellow heat blazed up again from the mounds of pyrethrum,
the early purple daisies, the phloxes. The guardian holly-
hocks stood motionless in the heavy, sun-saturated air.
What's wrong with honest sunshine and rejoicing flowers?
What's wrong with the Vicarage garden, just after tea-
time on an August afternoon? He turned and resumed his
slow pacing. Something was wrong.

If "C" were Mrs. Mount, then within the last quarter of
an hour Mrs. Mount had been in her former husband's gar-

den, eating her former husband's greengages, perfectly comfortably and at home. And now she was—where? In the house? Why should she be? But she might. He had never seen her handwriting, and it was just possible that she had written BACK AT SEVEN-THIRTY on the funeral card. And where did she get such a card unless she had been in the house? It was the sort of card you would find in a parson's study, but hardly in a fashionable handbag. Had she written the message, written it, knowing that the servants were out, in her late husband's study? For whom was the message? For the incomprehensible Vicar? For the handsome unknown who occasionally came to see her at the hotel? Why half-past seven? Suppose she hadn't written the message. Suppose a maidservant had written it? Or the Vicar?

He had an impulse to go to the door and remove that telltale card, then restrained it. The card was a message for someone. Suppose that someone had not yet arrived and read it? Better not disturb the situation.

Unregretfully the Inspector cast aside all thoughts of a hot potter through the drowsy village, of unprofitable conversations with tinker, tailor and candlestick-maker, and another interview with old Neddy Ware. And more regretfully he cast aside also the pleasant, planned finale to that hot potter. No arrival at the local inn for Inspector Rudge, no deep draught of delicious beer, cooled in the well. Instead, instinctively and professionally the Inspector abandoned the open path for the little strip of lawn that ended in a shrubbery, and insinuated himself between the laurels. These began where the kitchen garden ended, and swept round the front garden, thus protecting by a twelve-foot belt of foliage the lawn and the house from the view of passers-by in the road.

The Inspector knew his duty. He glanced at his watch:

it was nearing six. If anybody arrived at the Vicarage between that hour and the seven-thirty of the notice at the
back door, Inspector Rudge intended to know of it. The
laurels were dirty, as laurels are even in the depths of the
country, and the ground below them was dusty. His coign
of vantage was airless and intolerably hot. Nevertheless,
there Inspector Rudge intended to remain until the writer
of the card returned or its destined reader arrived.

He made himself as comfortable as he could, though he
did not dare smoke; but he kept chewing-gum for such
emergencies and played noughts-and-crosses with himself,
patiently; for the loam upon which he lay was dry and
loose as sand. As the shadows lengthened the air grew
cooler and he suffered less from heat but more from
midges. But it was not until the village church had struck
seven that his devotion was rewarded. Voices, cheerful and
unlowered, struck upon his ear. The hidden gate of the
drive creaked and banged again. Footsteps sounded the
other side of the impenetrable wall of laurels and holly that
divided the lawn from the entrance. Two figures swung
round it deep in conversation, reached the porch, dived
into its shadows, and the taller figure tugged at the bell.

Inspector Rudge gripped the tough laurel stems in his
amazement. The last people in the world he expected at
this hour in this place were the Hollands, husband and
wife. What were they saying? What were they doing? He
could hear the bell jangling, but he could not hear their
words: and the porch was so deep in shadow that he could
not watch their faces. Should he emerge and cross-question?

While he hesitated they turned in the doorway and Holland's voice rang clear.

"We may as well wait."

His wife came out on the gravel.

"What's the time now?"

Her husband looked at his watch.

"Just past seven."

Elma hesitated.

"I'm not coming all this way for nothing."

"Have you considered," Holland said uneasily, "that it may be a trap?"

"A trap? How could it be?"

"Well——" He hesitated. "How much does Célie *know*?"

"Oh, don't fuss so, Arthur. It's hot and I won't be harried. Sit down a little." And, crossing the lawn, she sank into the worn hammock that swung between two boughs of the giant cedar, while her husband flung himself on the grass beside her.

For some ten minutes the two sat there, saying little. Inspector Rudge cursed his luck. Nine out of ten women would have talked a rope about their necks in ten such idle minutes. It was his luck to be suspecting a woman outside his experience, a woman who could sit still and say nothing. Even when she tired of her immobility still she held her tongue, gave neither watcher a reason for her sudden movement. But when she swung her feet to the ground and began to stroll towards the house, her husband instantly rose and joined her. Had she signalled to him? Did she know herself watched? wondered Rudge. But he was sure that he himself had not stirred; nevertheless he remained perfectly still. Elma Holland, Inspector Rudge considered, was quite capable of setting a counter-trap. Meantime the pair had reached the house once more, and Holland's voice came ringing over the grass.

"I say, the door's ajar."

"She must have come in without our seeing," the woman's voice answered him. "Come on! Let's go in! She must be somewhere," and they disappeared.

Inspector Rudge drew a deep sigh of relief. At last he could move, could yawn, could stretch himself, could lift the weight of his body off one unfortunate foot, which, doubled under him, was almost asleep. It was a very bad attack of pins and needles indeed. He was just beginning gently to massage it when he was nearly startled out of his senses by the sound, faint but unmistakable, of a scream. He stiffened where he sat. Then, pulling himself to his feet, was preparing to grope his way into the open, when nearer, much louder, much more vigorous, came a second scream, a whole series of screams; and there burst out of the dark open entry the figure of Elma Holland.

Once out of the doorway she appeared to have no further power to walk, though she laboured forward a short step or two as if she were thrusting her way through an invisible hedge. Her face was white as the washed walls of the house, and as her husband, who came racing the next moment across the threshold, reached her, she fell back into his arms like a stuffed sack.

The Inspector was not much less swift, but as he broke through the bushes and ran across the lawn to them, his thought ran ahead of him—"What has she seen to break *her* nerve like that?" Then, as he reached the huddled pair, he noted the condition of Holland's hands and, first crying: "Here! Out of my way!"—added "and stay where you are!" pushed past them, leaped up the steps, dashed across the hall and flung open the dining-room door. Empty! So was the drawing-room. But the door of the Vicar's study was open. In went Rudge and cast a hurried glance about him.

Very still was the study, barred with sun and shadow, very cool, very dark. It was a pleasant coolness and a pleasant darkness after the glare of the lawn. "Quiet as a tomb," thought the Inspector to himself. "So what's she screaming about?" Then, as he moved to the writing-table, which was set at an angle to the window, rampart-wise, he saw what Elma Holland had screamed about.

Slid down upon the floor between the desk and the wall lay the body of a woman. Her eyes were open and glazed like the eyes of a carefully painted waxwork; on her cheeks the make-up stood out in hectic patches on the skin. Her two hands were clasped upon her breast, not peacefully, but in a last gesture of energy. They were clasped about a knife-handle, whose blade was sunk in the stained folds of her flowered summer dress.

CHAPTER XII

By Anthony Berkeley

CLEARING UP THE MESS

RUDGE plumped down on his knees beside her, heedless of the blood which lay everywhere on the carpet. The woman was still warm, and the blood had scarcely ceased to flow from her breast. But quite certainly she was dead.

A voice from the doorway brought the Inspector to his feet again.

"We were in the hall when she did it. We actually heard her fall." Holland spoke gravely, but without any traces of panic.

Rudge frowned. "I thought I told you to stop outside, sir."

"Oh, damn your rotten little orders, man. Here's a woman stabbed herself; it's no time to stand on ceremony. Is there anything we can do? *Is* she dead? Are you certain?"

Rudge got slowly to his feet. "She's dead right enough. Must have died just about the time you were in the house."

"She died in my arms, then," said Holland sombrely.

Rudge glanced at the blood on the other's hand, and Holland nodded.

"I held her up for a second," he said. "I thought she was dead, so didn't disturb her hands or take the weapon out."

"That was wise of you, sir."

"You know who she is, of course? My wife's French maid—Célie."

"Ah!" said Rudge. "I shall have a few questions to ask you and Mrs. Holland."

"Later," Holland said, in his masterful way. "My wife's very much upset at the moment. Naturally. I can't have her worried till she's had time to recover."

Rudge lifted his eyebrows slightly, but all he said was: "I must ask you not to leave these premises for the present, either of you. Where is Mrs. Holland now?"

"I put her in a hammock, on the lawn. I must get back to her. We'll wait for you there, Inspector. Anything we can tell you, of course, we will."

There was the sound of footsteps on the gravel outside, which marched without hesitation into the hall. "Anyone about?" called a voice. The next moment the figure of the ubiquitous reporter from the *Evening Gazette* appeared in the doorway. With a muttered word Holland slid past him and out of the house.

A shaft of sunlight from the window flashed cheerfully on the reporter's horn-rimmed spectacles. "Hullo, Inspector. Didn't expect to see you. Is the Vicar about?" He caught sight of what lay at Rudge's feet. "My God—what's this?"

"I understand it's Mam'selle Célie," Rudge replied austerely, "Mrs. Holland's late maid. And I must ask you to leave me alone here, *if* you please. I'll see you get your story later. There are——" Further sounds of footsteps outside caused him to break off short. Both men listened intently. Again the footsteps progressed without hesitation into the house, and along to the study. The Vicar came into the room.

"Why, Inspector," he said in surprise. "I didn't know you were to be present too. Has—*oh!*" For a moment he

appeared too frozen with horror to move. Then he threw
himself on his knees beside the body with a little cry.
"Celia!"

"Don't touch her, please, sir." Rudge bent down as if to
guard the body from the Vicar's ministrations.

The latter turned a ravaged face up to him. "She's
dead?"

"I'm afraid so, sir."

"She hasn't—killed herself?"

"It looks uncommonly like it, sir."

Mr. Mount dropped his face into his hands and remained
motionless for nearly a minute. When he spoke again it
was with more self-possession.

"Inspector, you know who this poor soul is?"

"She's already been identified, sir, as Mrs. Holland's late
French maid."

"Yes." The Vicar paused for a moment, as if to stiffen
himself in a resolve. "Inspector, there are many things connected with this tragedy that I cannot tell you. My lips are
sealed by the confessional. But if it will serve the interests
of justice this much I can say: this poor woman is my wife.
And alas, I fear that it is I who drove her to this terrible
deed."

2

"You, sir?" said the Inspector sharply. "How is that?"
Then catching sight of the newspaper man, he added:
"Here, I told you to clear out." He was about to seize the
fellow by the shoulder and hustle him out of the room, by
way of some physical vent for the various emotions that
were boiling inside him, when he saw from the other's
white face and shaking hands that it was not just callous
professional curiosity which had kept him there; the man
looked indeed almost incapable of walking. Rudge laid a

gentle instead of a ferocious hand on his arm, and led him towards the door. "In the War, weren't you?"

The reporter mustered up a shaky smile. "Yes, but we didn't kill—women. I think I'm going to be sick."

The Vicar pushed past the Inspector and took charge, leading the man into a small lavatory that opened off the hall just inside the front door. "Stay there till you feel better," he nodded, and returned with the Inspector to the study.

"Turns some people up, blood does," commented the latter. "Now, sir—you were going to tell me?"

They stood side by side, looking down on the dead woman. "Poor soul, poor soul," muttered the Vicar. "The mother of my boys, Inspector. Perhaps I was too harsh with her. Too narrow, perhaps. Yet what else could I have done? My creed expressly forbids divorce. 'Those whom God hath joined together let no man put asunder. . . .' It's too explicit."

"She wanted you to divorce her?" Rudge gently dropped the question into the Vicar's musings, which seemed to be addressed more to himself than to the Inspector.

"Yes. I never knew the name of the man who induced her to run away with him; she always refused to tell me; perhaps it was better so. But he seems to have been kind to her, according to his lights." It was plain that the Vicar was trying hard to be just. "At any rate, he was faithful to her; and she to him. They wanted to marry. They always have wanted to marry. But I could not reconcile it with my conscience to divorce her. Then last Tuesday— the night of the murder, in fact . . ."

"Yes?" Rudge almost held his breath. At last something was going to come out about that night's hidden happenings.

"She called upon me here, quite late, and urged me once

more to reconsider my decision. She was very upset—agitated—quite distraught, in fact . . ."

"Ah!" breathed Rudge.

"I had the greatest difficulty in soothing her. Especially in view of what I had to say."

"You repeated your refusal, then?"

"What else could I do?" asked the Vicar piteously. "I considered that I had no choice. The injunction is too explicit. It distressed me very much to have to say so, but conscience," added the Vicar, with a wan smile, "makes brave men of us all."

"And what time was this, sir, when the lady called?" It distressed the Inspector too to have to continue his cross-examination in these circumstances, but his duty was no less plain.

"I saw her soon after midnight."

"But we have information that she arrived here at about eleven?" Rudge said gently.

A slight flush appeared on the Vicar's cheekbones. "I repeat, I saw her soon after midnight. About a quarter past twelve, so far as I can say. I brought her into the study here, and we talked for nearly an hour."

"But what was she doing between eleven and a quarter past twelve?"

The Vicar's lips stiffened. "That I cannot tell you, Inspector."

"Meaning that you won't tell me, sir, or you don't know?"

"I have nothing further to say."

The two men eyed each other steadily.

Rudge gave up the point. "And this afternoon? Had she made an appointment with you?"

"She had, for seven o'clock, and with Mr. and Mrs. Holland too. Unfortunately, most unfortunately, I was late.

Otherwise," said the Vicar, with a little break in his voice, "who knows but what I might not have prevented—this?"

"And you had been——?"

"At the Ferrers Abbas flower-show. The maids are there still, and my boys. The house was quite empty."

"Why did Mrs. Mount make this appointment?"

"She did not say, in so many words."

"But you gathered, sir?"

"I think," said the Vicar, a little uneasily, "that she had come to some decision regarding certain information she considered she had concerning Admiral Penistone's death."

"And that information is known to you?"

A look of obstinacy which Rudge in his exasperation characterised privately as mulish, spread over the Vicar's face. "I told you just now, Inspector, that on some points my lips are sealed. That is one of them."

Again the two looked at each other.

But this time an interruption came from without. Once more footsteps sounded on the gravel drive, to be followed this time by the jangling in the back regions of an old-fashioned bell.

The Vicar went out into the hall, and Rudge followed him.

Standing in the open front door was a small, elderly man, whose not very spick-and-span suit was set off by a smart grey trilby hat set at a jaunty angle. "Ah, Mount," he said. "Sorry I'm so infernally late. Is the conference over?"

"Conference?" repeated the Vicar stupidly.

"Yes. Seven o'clock I was told to be here. I couldn't quite make out what it was about on the telephone, but the —the lady sounded pretty urgent."

"She—rang you up?"

"Yes." The new-comer looked more than a little embarrassed. "Sounded like a cock-and-bull story to me. Well, she said she was your *wife*."

"She was," said the Vicar sombrely. He turned to Rudge. "Inspector, I don't think you know Sir Wilfrid Denny, do you?"

"By sight well enough, sir. I'm glad to see you've come back, Sir Wilfrid. I've been hoping to have a word with you."

"About this terrible business at Rundel Croft? Yes, of course. I got back this afternoon. It never occurred to me that you'd want to see me, or I'd have come back sooner. I had to go to Paris."

"Denny . . ."

The Vicar was obviously going to break the news of the latest tragedy, and, not wishing to intrude on the scene, Rudge turned away. Out of curiosity he opened the door of the lavatory where the sick reporter had been parked, and glanced inside. It was empty. Evidently he had recovered.

Before returning to the study to mount guard over the body and telephone to the Super and Dr. Grice, Rudge indulged his curiosity once more. He took a couple of steps outside the front door and glanced across the lawn. The result gratified him. In the hammock sat Mr. and Mrs. Holland, side by side; Mr. Holland's arm was about his wife, and Mrs. Holland's head was on her husband's shoulder. Even as Rudge glanced at them she raised it and spontaneously kissed him.

"So she *is* human after all," said Rudge to himself as he hurriedly turned away. "And now she's found out that she loved him all the time. Well, they say it takes a shock to make some of 'em realise it."

3

Rudge had handed over to Superintendent Hawkesworth.

Major Twyfitt, the Chief Constable, had motored back home, but luckily he had not taken back Hawkesworth to the county town with him. Together the two, as soon as Dr. Grice had arrived, had searched the house, but nothing had been discovered to throw any further light on the death. The Superintendent was now making arrangements for the removal of the body, and Rudge found himself at liberty for a few words with Mr. and Mrs. Holland.

Mrs. Holland was still in the hammock. That she had received a severe shock was obvious, but already she was showing such signs of recovery that Rudge, who wished to put his questions while impressions were still strong, thought himself justified in over-riding Holland's objections to an immediate interview. He dropped, with a carefully unofficial air, on the grass beside the pair.

"It's unfortunate, sir, I agree. But you'll understand that I must do my duty. Now would you be good enough to tell me first of all what you know about this appointment? When did Mrs. Mount make it, and what reason did she give?"

Rudge had addressed his question to Elma, but it was Holland who answered it. "She rang us up at the Lord Marshall just after lunch to-day, and asked us to meet her here. She gave no reason."

"But you would have inferred one?"

"No."

"Was it you who spoke to her on the telephone?"

"No," said Holland—a little reluctantly, Rudge thought. "It was my wife."

"I see." Rudge turned pointedly to Mrs. Holland. "What reason did you infer then, madam?"

"None." Elma's tone was as curt as ever.

"You did not ask for any?"

"No."

"But it must have seemed strange to you that your late maid should want to meet you at the Vicarage?"

"I imagined she was upset about something and wanted advice, and did not care to come to the inn, where she might be recognised."

"But why shouldn't she be recognised?"

Elma shrugged her shoulders. "That I can't tell you."

"Did you know that she was Mrs. Mount?"

"Certainly not."

"It surprises you?"

"Very much."

"Perhaps," said Rudge tentatively, "you can see some way in which that fact may throw light on your uncle's death?"

"I'm afraid I can't," Elma retorted. "But of course it gives a reason for her having left me—my service so abruptly."

Rudge nodded. "Yes, that's true enough. By the way, you say you imagined she was upset about something. Did she sound upset on the telephone?"

"Agitated, perhaps," Elma said slowly. "Yes, she did."

And yet not too agitated, Rudge thought, to eat greengages before the conference she had called.

"It never occurred to you," he went on, "that the advice you thought she wanted might be on some matter connected with your uncle's murder, Mrs. Holland?"

"Certainly not," Elma replied sharply. "Why should it?"

Rudge might have given more than one reason for his

question. Instead, he asked, slowly and significantly: "How much did Célie—*know?*"

His shot got home. Elma paled, then flushed, and sent a glance towards her husband which was a patent appeal for help. Holland supplied it at once.

His words took Rudge by surprise. He did not bluster or attempt to end the interview, merely remarking: "It's curious you should say that, Inspector; I asked my wife that identical question not an hour ago. I too had considered the possibility that she might be about to give us some information on the Admiral's death. But my wife was positive she could have known nothing."

"How could she?" asked Elma, in relieved tones.

Rudge glanced from one to the other. He knew very well that Mrs. Holland had said nothing of the sort, at any rate just then. He was not sure that he had been wise. In an attempt to frighten information out of them, he had intimated to the pair that he had overheard their conversation while they were waiting; and Holland, of course, had seen him come out of the bushes. They could not know for certain that he had not been able to hear them too while Elma was in the hammock. And yet Holland had not been in the least frightened. He had taken the thing quietly out of Rudge's hands, reassured his wife, and returned an answer which was admirable in its noncommittal quality. Rudge had to console himself with the fact that without doubt Elma had, just for an instant, lost her grip. These two *must* know something—but Rudge recognised that there was not the faintest hope of getting it out of them by direct questioning.

Anxious not to put them too much on their guard, he tried another line. "Now, will you tell me, sir, exactly what happened when you got into the house? You noticed the front door open, I think, and followed Mrs. Holland inside?"

Holland smiled slightly. "As you saw, Inspector, from your laurel bush, yes. By the way," he added, more sternly, "had you some idea that anything like that was going to happen? Because if so . . ."

"I had no idea, sir; no more than yourself. Now, will you kindly give me those facts?"

"Well, I followed my wife into the hall. We thought that Célie—Mrs. Mount—must have come, as the door was ajar. We looked into the drawing-room first, then the dining-room. I think it was while we were in the dining-room (which adjoins the study, you know) that we heard a scream——"

"A *terrible* scream," put in Mrs. Holland with a shudder.

"Yes, it was terrible. I've never heard anything so—well, *awful*—producing awe. It was just like an animal. I dashed out of the dining-room and into the study, but before I got there I heard a thud, which must have been made by her fall. And there she was, on the carpet, and the blood streaming out. As I told you, she died in my arms."

"Oh-h-h-h-h-h," shuddered Elma.

"I see. Thank you, sir. And you, Mrs. Holland? That coincides with your own impressions?"

"Yes. I think so. Perhaps I should have said myself that we heard her fall before my husband moved, but I couldn't be sure."

"But you think not, sir?"

Holland considered. "I couldn't say. Perhaps. I suppose we stood still for a few seconds. Sort of frozen, you know. Yes, perhaps we heard the thud before I moved. I'm not sure we didn't, now I come to think. But in any case there couldn't be more than a second and a half in it either way."

"And then you followed your husband into the study, madam?"

"Yes," Elma faltered. "And saw—and saw . . ." She covered her face with her hands and her body shook.

Holland leapt up. "Inspector," he said, in a low voice, "get out."

Rudge got.

In any case he had not expected to learn anything more.

4

"Of course it's suicide," growled the Superintendent. "The doctor says her grip on the dagger must have been applied during life; there's only her prints on it; the Hollands were within a few yards of the room when she did it, and actually heard her fall; Rudge had command of the front door, and the back door remained bolted on the inside, and when he searched the house there was no one in it. How could it be anything but suicide?" The Superintendent spoke scornfully.

Rudge said nothing, but his ruddy cheeks grew a shade ruddier still.

"You don't agree, Rudge?" said the Chief Constable.

"No, sir, I'm afraid I don't. The way I look at it is this. Would a woman going to commit suicide fill up the time beforehand by eating greengages? It isn't natural."

"Then are you saying Holland killed her?" asked the Superintendent sharply. "Because there's no one else who could."

"No, sir, I'm not saying that either."

It was the following morning, and a conference was being held at Whynmouth police station. Already there was tension in the air, and further tension threatened. The pos-

sibilities of Mrs. Mount's death being due to suicide or
murder had been discussed already for at least half an hour,
and no decision had yet been reached. The Superintendent
was all for suicide, and the Chief Constable had to agree
that the logic was on his side; Inspector Rudge obstinately
clung to murder, and when challenged to produce his
proofs could only mutter puerilities about things being
"natural" or the reverse, and "feeling things in his bones";
no wonder the Superintendent snorted. Major Twyfitt had
persevered nobly in a Chief Constable's first duty, that of
holding the balance between two disputing subordinates,
but did not know how soon it might not escape from his
grasp.

He determined now to shift the ground of discussion.
"Well, of course, Rudge, if you feel that way you'll do all
you can to collect evidence to support your ideas. Otherwise I think we can leave it for the time being to the coroner. Now, about the murder of Admiral Penistone. You
told us last night of the dead woman's identity with Célie
Blanc, the lady's maid, which does definitely connect the
Vicarage with the tragedy, as you've felt all along," said
the Chief Constable soothingly. "And you told us about
Hempstead's discovery in the bathroom at Rundel Croft.
Now, have you any ideas where all this is going to lead
us?"

"I have, sir," replied the Inspector grimly. "I've a very
good idea indeed."

"Ah, that's good. What is it?"

"I'd rather not say, sir, if you don't mind, until I've
collected a little more *evidence*," Rudge answered, with a
side-glance at the Superintendent.

"Yes, yes, of course. So long as you're working on definite lines. Well, the Superintendent has got the details from
the Admiralty now about that episode at Hong Kong,

which you'd like to hear. Just let Rudge have the facts, Superintendent."

Superintendent Hawkesworth drew a folded paper from his breast-pocket, opened it, and in a totally expressionless voice read:

" 'Captain Penistone was involved in a disgraceful scene in Hong Kong in 1911. By his own admission he followed a girl, who was being ill-treated by a Chinaman, into a low-class den which was already unfavourably known to the authorities. After that he stated that he remembered nothing further. He was, however, seen, in an advanced state of intoxication, singing and dancing in the company of a number of seamen of both British and other nationalities, and Chinese coolies; and he was carried on board his ship the next morning, still under the influence of drink and opium, by a party of his own men who had recognised him the previous evening. In consideration of his record, Captain Penistone was permitted to send in his papers instead of being tried by court-martial. On the outbreak of hostilities with Germany, Captain Penistone volunteered his services in any capacity, and in view of the emergency he was reinstated temporarily with his rank of Captain. He served with distinction throughout the War, and so far as the Admiralty was concerned, the regrettable incident at Hong Kong was expunged from the records. The Admiral, however, expressed to several of the senior officers here his dissatisfaction with the affair, and his belief that a good deal more lay behind it than had ever appeared, and he used to state his intention of devoting his leisure on retirement to getting to the bottom of it; but as to whether there were any grounds or evidence for this belief, nothing is known here.' "

"I see," said Rudge. "Followed a girl in, did he? Well, that clears up one point, sir, doesn't it? File X!"

"You mean, File X contained the evidence he had collected to support his view that the incident was rigged?" nodded the Chief Constable. "Yes, that's the view we'd come to."

"And it gives you something else, Rudge," added Hawkesworth. "It gives you motive. Those papers had disappeared from the folder, hadn't they? Obviously they were taken after the murder, by the murderer. In other words, the Admiral was right. He'd got his evidence—and it was going to implicate somebody who didn't want to be implicated. So the Admiral was murdered to stop him blowing the gaff. Well, that gives us a pretty strong pointer. The murderer is a man who was in Hong Kong in 1911. Anything wrong with that?"

"Nothing," Rudge agreed. "That's right enough, sir. Must be. But there's one thing I can't understand, and that's Mr. Holland's story about seeing the Admiral, *in* his study, *with* a lot of papers on his desk, *after* midnight that night. According to what the doctor says, that's just the time the murderer ought to have been looking for File X."

"And perhaps so he was," said the Superintendent darkly.

"If you mean Holland, sir," said Rudge, returning to an old difficulty, "why did he want to come out with that story at all, when there was no evidence that he wasn't safe in bed and asleep at the Lord Marshall?"

"I don't mean Holland," snapped the Superintendent. "I mean the man Holland saw. The man whom he mistook for the Admiral. The man who was impersonating the Admiral—for the third time."

"The *third* time?"

"Yes. Once in the study, once at the Lord Marshall, and once—in Hong Kong!"

"*Oh!*" Rudge registered such genuine admiration that

the Superintendent forgave him his foolishness about Mrs. Mount. "That's a smart bit of work, sir, if I may say so."

"You can bank on it, that's the murderer," said the Superintendent complacently, and his tone added that that was not the end of the smart work.

"But wait a bit," cried the Inspector excitedly. "That means Mrs. Holland's in it. Holland gave it away that she was in the study too."

"And haven't you thought all the time that Mrs. Holland knew a good bit more than she let on?"

"I never thought she was actually mixed up in the murder," Rudge confessed.

With an air of triumph the Superintendent rose and unlocked a cupboard. From it he produced a package, and from the package a white chiffon frock. His large hands looked absurdly incongruous on the delicate stuff as he draped the dress over the back of a chair before the eyes of the Inspector. His reason for doing so was plain; there was no need for him to point to the rusty-coloured stain that smeared one hip. "The missing white dress. Got a warrant to search her room at the Lord Marshall, and found it at the bottom of a drawer," he said briefly.

"I *knew* she knew something!" exclaimed Rudge.

"Why *do* people keep damning evidence against themselves?" Major Twyfitt asked.

"Lucky for us they do, sir," said Hawkesworth. To Rudge he added: "Mind you, I don't think she was in it from the start. But she's an accessory after, all right. And that gives us another pointer. See it?"

"Oh, yes," nodded Rudge. "The brother, Walter. I've had him in mind from the beginning."

"You have, eh?" said the Superintendent, somewhat discomfited. "Why didn't you ever say so, then?"

"No evidence," replied Rudge smugly.

"Anyhow, it seems clear enough now," interposed the Chief Constable. "We can assume, I think, that if anyone has been impersonating the Admiral, either in Hong Kong or here, it must have been this Walter Fitzgerald. There must have been a strong resemblance. We've got evidence of that too, Rudge. Two witnesses who saw a man in Whynmouth on the day of the murder whom they mistook in the distance for the Admiral, and only realised when they were quite close that it was a younger man."

"Yes, sir? And that gives me another idea. May I put through a telephone call to London?"

"Of course."

Rudge consulted his note-book, and then gave the number of Friedlander's Hotel and asked for priority. The connection was made in less than two minutes. Rudge explained who he was, and said: "You remember telling me that Mrs. Arkwright only had one regular visitor, a tall man with a bronzed forehead? Did this man wear a beard? He did? Thank you." He rang off.

The other two looked at him enquiringly.

"That connects up something more." Rudge was unable to conceal his satisfaction. "The man who ran off with Mrs. Mount, the man whose name the Vicar never knew—that was Walter Fitzgerald too."

"Ah!" said two breaths simultaneously.

"It's beginning to work in."

The Superintendent cleared his throat. "Now, my theory of what happened that night is this. This man, this Walter Fitzgerald, came down—— Yes? What is it? Oh, come in." A loud knock at the door had broken him off in midsentence.

Police Constable Hempstead entered, looking thoroughly pleased with himself. In his hand he held a short length of manilla rope, knotted to another short length. "Hope I'm not disturbing you, sir," he said to Major Twyfitt, "but thought you'd like to know at once. I've searched both banks thoroughly this morning, from Rundel Croft to the sea, and found nothing except this."

"The missing bit of the painter!" exclaimed Rudge. "Where was it? Sorry, sir," he added perfunctorily to the Chief Constable, who nodded good-humouredly.

"Caught up in some bushes, 'bout half-way down, on the Vicarage side."

"Good man," said the Chief Constable as he took the rope, and even Hawkesworth grunted approval.

"Did you make any enquiries at the cottages?" asked Rudge.

"Every one, sir. Nobody heard or saw anything. But I've found out something else."

"You have, eh? What?"

"Well, you remember that set of photos you gave me, sir, of the finger-prints on the oars in the Admiral's boat? Well, I believe I've identified them." Hempstead produced a piece of paper, which the Superintendent took before anyone else could reach it.

He whipped another set of the photographs out of his pocket and pored over them for a minute. Then he looked up. "That's the man. Who is it, Hempstead?"

Hempstead beamed with self-importance. "Neddy Ware, sir."

5

When Rudge left the police station for a belated lunch he had a good deal to think about. The business was getting altogether too wide-spread for his liking. Half the inhabitants of Lingham seemed now to be implicated in the murder, or at the least accessories after it. The Vicar, Elma

Holland, and now Neddy Ware. There was another point against Neddy Ware too. The plaster casts which had been taken of the footprints on the bank showed a number which had been definitely identified as the Admiral's, several of his niece's, and just a few of a large, coarse sole, studded with nails, which could belong to nobody at Rundel Croft but a gardener; but they might belong to Neddy Ware. The impressions were good, and the Super was going to find out himself, after lunch, whether they were Neddy Ware's or not; but no one had any doubt now on the point.

He had been cunning, had Neddy Ware. The Inspector ruefully acknowledged to himself that he had been completely taken in by the old man. Neddy Ware had given him precisely correct information on all matters concerning the river and its tides which he could have checked from anyone else who was familiar with them; even on points which might have told against himself he had been accurate; but what about his speculations, which the Inspector had unconsciously put on practically the same basis as the rest? It was difficult now to disentangle speculation from fact, even in consultation with his note-book, but there seemed to Rudge two main ideas which Ware had deftly given him and which had lain in his mind ever since as a basis on which any theory of the crime must be founded: that if the Admiral had taken his boat out at all that night he must have taken it down-stream, and that it would have taken him an hour to row to Whynmouth. How did these two ideas look now?

For the first there really seemed no reason at all. Why must the Admiral have gone down-stream? So that the abandoned boat could have drifted to where it was found at the time it was found. But was it found at that time? And at that place? The whole of Ware's first story must now be viewed with the deepest suspicion.

What about the second point, then? From Rundel Croft to Whynmouth, by water, was about two and three-quarter miles. The Admiral must have started at between a quarter-past and half-past ten. At that time the tide was, even according to Ware's own information, at its strongest ebb. Could a lusty man not row a boat, with a swiftly flowing tide to help him, at faster than a slow walking pace? Nonsense; of course he could. Twice as fast. Very well, then. Neddy Ware had wanted to deceive the police as to the time the Admiral could have reached Whynmouth that night (assuming for the moment that on the other point he had been speaking the truth, and it was down-stream the Admiral had gone). Now why the deuce had he wanted to do that?

At this point the Inspector mechanically pushed his full plate of gooseberry pie away from him and allowed one of his landlady's best efforts to get stone cold.

There were only two possible reasons that Rudge could see; one, that somebody had an alibi for half-past eleven, but not for eleven o'clock; and the other, to make the police think that the man who called at the Lord Marshall just after eleven was an impostor—which was exactly what they did think. But in that case the man really was the Admiral. . . .

This was getting altogether too difficult. Rudge noted the point for future reference, and followed another line.

There was another advantage too in shifting forward the time of events by half an hour or so. Just after midnight the brother, Walter Fitzgerald, had been in the Admiral's study. This extra half-hour gave him plenty of time to get there, break the news to his sister, and begin his search for File X, by midnight. Without it, Rudge had found the time-table exceedingly cramped.

Well, there already were the answers to any number of

his thirty-nine articles of doubt. Rudge turned them up in his note-book and glanced through them, to see whether this intervention of Neddy Ware's cleared up any more puzzles.

It did, at once. 26: Why was the Admiral wearing a coat? Rudge remembered the difficulty. If it was the Admiral who had taken out his boat that night, and a fairly warm night at that, why wear a coat for hard rowing? But suppose it was not the Admiral who had been doing the rowing. Suppose it was Neddy Ware, who had not only brought the boat back but had taken it out too, with the Admiral as a passenger. There was a profitable line of enquiry. If only that were true, Neddy Ware must know not only where the Admiral had gone, but who had killed him. But how on earth to find out if it were true? Because quite certainly Neddy Ware would not give himself away on that point.

Well, there was only one possibility. The Vicar had been sitting in his summer-house. He might have seen. Rudge had had a suspicion already that the Vicar had seen something from that summer-house. Well, the Vicar had got to be made to speak, that was all.

Falling at last on his gooseberry pie, Rudge swept the plate clean in half a dozen gargantuan mouthfuls, followed them with a couple of bites of bread and cheese, and ran down to the street and his car.

Mr. Mount was in, and had just finished his own lunch. He received the Inspector in his study.

Rudge came to the point at once. "Sorry to bother you again, sir, but we've information that Admiral Penistone left Rundel Croft in his boat, at about ten-fifteen. You were sitting in your summer-house at that time, overlooking the river. Did you see him leave?"

The Vicar answered at once. "Since you ask me the direct question, Inspector: yes, I did."

"Thank you, sir. Is it any good my asking why you didn't let me have this information sooner? Although I never actually asked you, you must have known it would be very valuable."

"Certainly, I will tell you. It was because I feared that my knowledge might lead you to suspect an innocent man."

"I see, sir. Then you know who murdered Admiral Penistone?"

"No," the Vicar retorted, "I don't. But I'm pretty sure who didn't."

"Well, we'll leave that. Which way did the Admiral head, sir? Up-stream or down?"

"Down."

"And Neddy Ware was rowing him?"

The Vicar looked first startled, and then distressed. "Inspector, if you suspect old Ware of——"

"I don't, sir. Not of the murder."

"I have your word?"

"You have, Mr. Mount."

"Very well. Then I will admit to you that Ware *was* rowing the Admiral that night; and extremely surprised I was to see it. I had no idea they were even acquainted. But that is the reason why I said nothing of what I saw. We parsons have to rely a good deal on our estimate of people's natures, you know, and I would stake everything I have on the fact that old Ware is totally incapable of anything of that kind. I've known him ever since he came to Lingham, you see, so I feared that this information of mine would put you on an entirely wrong scent. I therefore determined to volunteer nothing myself, but to use what influence I may have with Ware to induce him to

come to you of his own accord and give you a full account
of his own knowledge of that night's happenings, whatever
it may be. I may say I have quite failed."

"He told you he wouldn't come to us?"

"More than that. He denies that he was in the boat at
all; he says that I was mistaken."

"We have quite definite evidence that he was, sir; his
finger-prints on the oars."

"Yes, I was quite sure I was right."

"Well, we must tackle Ware ourselves."

"I doubt whether you'll get much out of him."

"We shall see, sir. In the meantime, are you sure there
isn't anything else you'd like to tell us yourself, sir, about
that night—without necessarily incriminating anyone?"

"Nothing," said the Vicar firmly.

6

Rudge left the Vicarage in some elation. Not only had
his surmise been confirmed that Ware was rowing the boat,
but definite evidence was at last forthcoming that it had
headed down-stream. Curious that old Ware had been so
insistent on that point too. Except for the single suggestion about the length of time needed for the journey, it
seemed as if Ware had not been trying to deceive him at
all—almost as if he had been attempting to put him on
the right track. Was it possible that Neddy Ware's guilty
knowledge sat heavily upon him, that he thoroughly
wanted the Admiral's murderer to be caught, but that at
the same time, like a schoolboy, he would not directly give
him away? When one came to think of it, that really was
the only explanation of his behaviour. But if so it was a
pity in a way; for Rudge knew Neddy Ware well enough
to be quite certain that if the old man had made up his

mind not to give the murderer away, no possible means could be found of making him do so.

Anyhow, one could but try. Hastily obtaining permission from Major Twyfitt for the interview, and learning at the same time that the theory of the footprints had been proved correct, Rudge drove out to Ware's cottage.

The old man was sunning himself in the garden, and seemed thoroughly pleased to see his visitor.

"Well, Mr. Rudge, still puzzled about them tides?"

Rudge sat down on the same bench. "No, Ware; it's not the tides this time; it's something more serious. I want you to tell me what you were doing in the Admiral's company last Tuesday night—the night he was murdered?"

Old Ware looked the picture of innocent astonishment. "Me? I wasn't in his company. Whatever put that idea in your head, Mr. Rudge? I didn't even know him by sight. Didn't I tell you the next day I hadn't recognised him?"

"You did, and I'm afraid I can't believe you. Especially as you were in Hong Kong when there was that scandal about him, so you must have known all about that though you never let on a word. Now look here, Ware, I'm not threatening you, mind; I wouldn't do anything like that; but at the same time I'm ready to tell you that we've got evidence that you called for Admiral Penistone at Rundel Croft last Tuesday evening and rowed him down-stream at a quarter past ten. And what's more, I'll tell you what the evidence is: you were seen starting, there's your finger-prints on the oars, and there's your footprints on the bank. So you see there's no getting away from it. Now I needn't tell you this puts you in a nasty position. Mind you, *I* don't think you had anything to do with the murder, but there's others who might."

"I'm glad *you* don't think I had anything to do with the murder, Mr. Rudge," said Ware dryly.

"But there's others who might," repeated Rudge, "and will, too, unless you tell us all you know about that evening. Now come, Ware."

Neddy Ware drew a moment or two at his pipe before he spoke. "You're pretty sure it *was* murder, eh, Mr. Rudge?"

"Well, you don't imagine it's suicide, do you? And I'm afraid I can't see how that knife could have got into his chest by accident. Accident, suicide, or murder, it's got to be one of those three."

"Oh, no, it hasn't," retorted Ware. "Not by a long chalk it hasn't."

"What do you mean? Are you saying that the Admiral's death wasn't due to either accident, suicide, or murder?"

"Me? I'm not saying anything. That's your job, to find out what the Admiral died from. All I'm saying is that every death isn't due to one of those three. What about hanging a man, eh? What's that, Mr. Rudge—accident, suicide, or murder?"

"Well, never mind that," said Rudge impatiently. "What I want to know is, what did you do last Tuesday evening, and where did you take the Admiral? And I needn't repeat what I said about it being in your own interests to tell me."

Again Ware paused before replying, so long that the Inspector began to think that he was never going to reply at all; but at crucial moments such as these he had learnt that silent patience was the best policy.

At last the old man took the pipe out of his mouth. "This woman, now. What's all this about her? They're saying she's Mr. Mount's wife, and there's others saying she was the Frenchy maid that the Admiral's niece had."

"She's both," said Rudge, shortly, annoyed at this sidetrack but thinking it best not to bustle the old man. Rudge was something of a fisherman himself.

"Is she? That's queer now. And killed herself, they say."

Ware turned round suddenly and looked full at the Inspector. "Is that true, Mr. Rudge? Did she kill herself? What is it this time, eh? Accident, suicide, or murder?"

"The Super and Major Twyfitt are satisfied it's suicide," said Rudge, and did not add that he was not.

"Ah!" said Ware, and returned to his pipe again.

Once more the Inspector reminded himself that patience is a virtue.

And then Neddy Ware did a thing which surprised his listener. He voluntarily returned to the subject of his own doings. "So you want to know about me, Mr. Rudge? Well, seeing you know so much, perhaps I'd better tell you. I would have told you before, but it seemed better to say nothing about it, in case you might get foolish ideas into your head about me. That's why I said the next morning I didn't know him. Well, I *did* call for the Admiral, like you said. He'd offered me five shillings that afternoon, seeing me fishing near his place, to row him down to Whynmouth after late dinner, him not wanting to do any hard work with the oars just after eating a lot, you understand."

"And where did you take him?" Rudge asked eagerly.

"Why, where he wanted to go—Whynmouth. I put him ashore at the steps, and he asked me the quickest way to reach the Lord Marshall. And that's the last I see of him."

"You didn't wait for him?" Rudge said, disappointed.

"I did not. He said he'd be late, and come back likely by motor."

"You left the boat, and walked back?"

"I did not. I rowed it back, and put it in the boat-house for him all ship shape."

"Which end first?"

"I can't say that. Probably bow. That comes easier. Why, Mr. Rudge?"

"Oh, nothing. Do anything else?"

"I give her a bit of a swab out before I left her, that's all."

"What time did you get to Whynmouth?"

"Couldn't say for certain. 'Bout eleven, I suppose."

"And you rowed the boat back nearly three miles against the tide. How long did that take you?"

"Not much under two hours. Must have been—yes, nigh on one o'clock (*your* time) before I berthed her."

"And then you walked straight back to your cottage?"

"I did, Mr. Rudge. And that's all I know. So I'm glad *you* don't suspect me of murdering the Admiral, whatever others may think."

Rudge persevered for some little time longer, but could get no further information. As he returned to his car he was not altogether satisfied with what he had got. How far could Neddy Ware be trusted? If one accepted his story it seemed proved that the man who visited the Lord Marshall that night really was the Admiral: and that might well be the case. But the rest of the story did not seem to ring quite so true. Would it be likely, for instance, that the Admiral would saddle Ware with that two-hour pull back against the tide for the sake of the forty-minute run down with it? It was possible, of course, but somehow the Inspector had a strong feeling that it was here that Ware's story left the rails of truth. He was pretty sure that the old man had not told all he knew. Why, for instance, after getting to bed so late, was he up and fishing at such an early hour the next morning? It almost looked as if he knew what he was going to catch.

But for the present at any rate there was nothing to be done about it: and at least Rudge thought he might now

take it as established that it was to Whynmouth that the
Admiral had gone that night. But whom to see?

Whom but—his murderer?

Walter Fitzgerald had been in Whynmouth. With any
luck he had been staying there, and could thus be traced.
It was to Whynmouth that every signpost seemed now
to be pointing: and it was towards Whynmouth accord-
ingly that Inspector Rudge now headed his shabby little
two-seater.

7

Nevertheless his journey thither was occupied by reflections of a matter alien to his errand. The more he thought
about it the less satisfied he was that Mrs. Mount's death
was due to suicide, as the Super and Major Twyfitt were
so comfortably convinced. The matter of the freshly-
eaten greengages was only one of a dozen indications,
slight enough in themselves but in the aggregate formidable, that suicide had never been intended. It was quite
obvious that Mrs. Mount had been mixed up somehow in
the Admiral's murder. At any rate she must have known
a good deal about it—too much, Rudge fancied, for its
perpetrator. Her suicide was really too fortunate, for him,
to be true. And especially just before that conference
which she herself had summoned, and at which without the
smallest doubt she intended to shift at any rate some of
the burden of knowledge from her own shoulders. Would
it be likely that after summoning her husband, the Hollands and Sir Wilfrid Denny, Mrs. Mount should intend
to confront them with nothing less than her own corpse?
That would have been a grim joke indeed: but Mrs. Mount
had not been a grim lady.

No, it was altogether too lucky for Walter Fitzgerald
that she should have died when she did.

But how had he managed it? There the Inspector had to admit himself completely at a loss. As soon as his telephone messages had brought relief, he and the Superintendent had searched the house from attic to cellar, and had found nothing. Moreover, he was satisfied that nobody had escaped while he was still confined to the neighbourhood of the study. He had had both the front door and the kitchen regions continuously under his eye, to say nothing of the drive. If Walter Fitzgerald really had done the thing, he had done it exceedingly cleverly.

All the way to Whynmouth the Inspector beat his brains against this stone wall.

Nor did he have any better luck on his other errand. Though he spent the entire afternoon calling personally at every hotel, inn, public-house, and apartment-house in the place, no trace could he find of his bearded quarry. It seemed that the man had not been staying in Whynmouth at all.

Well, it did not really matter. The Admiral must have arranged to meet him there: but that did not necessarily mean that he would be staying there. It was quite possible to understand why the rendezvous had not been arranged for Rundel Croft; no doubt the Admiral would not have him in the place.

Rudge began to regret his lack of information about this nephew. It seemed impossible to get a line on the fellow from any angle. It was worse than useless to apply to the only person who could give any really valuable information, Mrs. Holland. Besides, in her present rôle of accessory after the fact Mrs. Holland herself was once more in the limelight of suspicion. The only possible hope was Sir Wilfrid Denny.

Rudge put his car up in Whynmouth and had himself ferried across the river to West End.

Sir Wilfrid was in his garden, syringing his roses for green fly with tobacco juice. A rose lover himself, Rudge was interested to notice now that the little rose-garden was the only part of the grounds which did not wear the same air of neglect.

Sir Wilfrid greeted him with a nod. "Afternoon, Inspector. I was rather expecting you to-day. Look—did you ever see anything more lovely?" He cupped a half-opened Emma Wright in two fingers and turned it towards the Inspector.

"Beautiful, sir," agreed the latter wholeheartedly.

"But she loses her colour almost as soon as she opens," mourned Sir Wilfrid. "That's the worst of these modern roses—at least, I class her with the moderns. They don't keep their colour. Give me the old-fashioned ones. That pink over there now. There's no modern variety to come anywhere near it, in the pinks."

"Madam Abel always has been a favourite of mine," Rudge nodded.

Sir Wilfrid beamed up at him. "You're a rose enthusiast too, Inspector? That's magnificent. I'll take you round. This is my latest importation. Mrs. G. A. van Rossem. Know her? I can't say I'm altogether satisfied. The usual mix-up of colours they seem to like so much nowadays. I must say I prefer my roses self-coloured. Mabel Morse, now. . . . Eh? Don't you agree?"

"Yes, I do, sir. Entirely. I think you're quite right. But to tell you the truth, I came to see you about something rather different."

"Ah, yes," Sir Wilfrid nodded, descending to earth. "Poor Admiral Penistone. I remember; you said you wanted to ask me something. Yes?"

"It's about his nephew. Walter Fitzgerald. Can you give me any information about him?"

"Walter Fitzgerald?" Sir Wilfrid looked puzzled. "No, I don't really think I can. Of course, Inspector, I never knew the Admiral really well. We'd been acquaintances for a very long time, but I can't say that we ever got much beyond that stage. I imagine," Sir Wilfrid added with a slight smile, "that few people did, with Admiral Penistone."

"You were in Hong Kong when he was stationed there, sir, weren't you?"

Sir Wilfrid nodded gravely. "Yes, I was. And when a certain incident took place. But no doubt you know all about that already?"

"Yes, we've heard about that. Did the Admiral ever refer to that incident to you, sir?"

"He did. Frequently," replied Sir Wilfrid dryly.

"Yes, I understand it was a bit of a bee in his bonnet. Do you agree with his idea, sir, that there was a good deal more behind it than ever came out?"

"I wish I could," said Sir Wilfrid, looking a little distressed. "But the facts were too plain. And I happen to know the authorities made a very searching investigation. It was always my belief that this idea of Admiral Penistone's was due to a kind of obstinate pride. It was his one lapse, you see, in a thoroughly honourable life; and he simply refused to face it."

"Then you don't fancy there was any possibility of the Admiral's having been impersonated on that occasion?"

"None. To anyone with even as little acquaintance as myself of service conditions, the notion's simply moonshine. Why, there were some of his own men there. How could they have been mistaken? No, I'm sorry to have to say so, Inspector, but Captain Penistone had no one else to thank but himself for the affair. That was the opinion of everyone on the spot. But in any case, this is all old history. It can't have anything to do with his death."

"No, of course not," said the Inspector tactfully. "Then you can't give me any information about the nephew, which is what I really came to see you about? You knew he was in Hong Kong at about that time too?"

"By Jove, I remember now. Yes, he did come to dine with us once. A tall, good-looking fellow. I remember. Pleasant chap, too. I heard he'd rather gone to the dogs, afterwards. Pity."

"Had he a beard, sir?"

"A beard?" repeated Sir Wilfrid, puzzled. "I don't think so. I don't really remember. Why?"

"Oh, just a small point. Then you never saw him again?"

"No, I think he only came once. But I wouldn't swear. We used to entertain such a lot in those days," said Sir Wilfrid, rather ruefully. "He might have come again, but I don't remember it."

"I see, sir. Thank you. Now there's one other point. Were you by any chance in the garden here last Tuesday evening?"

"The night of Admiral Peniston's death? Yes, almost certainly; though again I couldn't swear to it. But unless it's raining, I always have a stroll round the roses after dinner. So far as I remember it wasn't raining that night, so I expect I did. Why do you ask?"

"Because we have information that the Admiral landed from his boat at Whynmouth steps at about eleven o'clock that night, and as you know, they're almost opposite this garden. I was wondering if by any lucky chance you'd seen him and could confirm that?"

"No," said Sir Wilfrid decidedly. "Not so late as that, I'm afraid. And I'm pretty sure I had a couple of friends in that night. (Funny, isn't it, how hard it is to say for certain what one was doing only a week ago?) But what's all this about the Admiral being seen in Whynmouth that night? I'd gathered he was killed up-stream some-where."

"Why did you think that, sir?"

"Well, I don't know. Wasn't the boat floating down-stream at four in the morning? I took it for granted that must have meant it had been up-stream."

With a slightly superior air the Inspector explained the tidal vagaries of the River Whyn, and pointed his remarks by accompanying Sir Wilfrid over his own rather dis-hevelled lawn to the water's edge and illustrating his mean-ing on the spot. Sir Wilfrid, a somewhat mild little man, had the air of promising to know better next time.

Having delivered his lesson, the Inspector took his leave, with the unhappy reflection that he had really learned nothing at all from his visit. Sir Wilfrid's private opinion regarding the Superintendent's "smart piece of work" could hardly be called information.

Having walked, in full view of his host, out through the main entrance, Inspector Rudge doubled round to the back one. There he learned, after judicious and veiled questioning, that so far as was known Sir Wilfrid had not left the house at all last Tuesday evening, but had had two friends in to see him. "Leastways, the decanter had gone down by a tidy bit, it had, and there was three glasses to wash up the next morning, to say nothing of more cigarette-ends in the ash-trays than any one man could smoke, so it looks as if there was, don't it?" Rudge agreed that it did.

As has been said before, Inspector Rudge left nothing to chance.

8

Rudge called in at the police station in Whynmouth before going back to his lodgings, and found that Sergeant

Appleton had telephoned through his report from London. He had had no difficulty in obtaining information about Holland. Holland, it seemed, was thoroughly well known in his own line. Several important men had spoken of him to Appleton in the highest, not to say flowery, terms. He was known, apparently, not only all over the East but in London too as the very best type of trading Englishman—energetic, determined, dead honest and reliable, the sort of man whose word it was never necessary to obtain in writing; what he promised, he performed, and what he performed he performed just a shade better than anyone else. Appleton had been impressed, and said so frankly.

About the marriage too there was no room for doubt. It had been performed at a registry office in the West End, and Appleton had inspected the register and spoken with the registrar, who had described husband and wife exactly; he had taken particular notice of them, he said, because they were both so out of the ordinary type.

"Humph!" said Rudge to himself. "And yet according to the Super he's an accessory after. At least his wife is, which almost always means the same thing. Something funny somewhere."

He went back to his supper.

As usual he ruminated during the solitary meal. On the whole he was not dissatisfied with his day's work. It had not been true that he had learned nothing from Sir Wilfrid Denny. Going over the conversation again in his mind Rudge fancied that he had learned one thing of real value, which might lead to quite remarkable results—so remarkable, indeed, that when Rudge first began to realise their possibilities he feared that his imagination, goaded by the events of the last week, was running hopelessly away with him. And yet . . .

But it was useless to speculate. He must shelve that line of enquiry until there was evidence to support it. In the meantime he would turn his thoughts to the death of Mrs. Mount.

There was one point which told badly against murder, and Superintendent Hawkesworth had, of course, made the most of it. According to the doctor, if Mrs. Mount had been stabbed by some other person, her murderer could not have escaped being spattered, and liberally, too, with blood; her clothing had been of the flimsiest; it would have interposed only a feeble barrier against the stream of blood that must have spurted from a wound in such a position— as indeed the condition of the carpet plainly showed. And yet not a single person so stained had been seen by anyone. Therefore, argued the Superintendent, contemptuously logical, no such person existed.

Rudge, still obstinately fixed in his idea of murder, thought now that he saw a way round this difficulty; and it was a way, too, which might be made to carry several other of the peculiar circumstances of the death. Perfectly simple too: Mrs. Mount had been stabbed from behind, not from in front at all. And that argued that her murderer must be a man. But of this the Inspector was already convinced. If he was right and Mrs. Mount really had been murdered, the man who had killed her was the same as the murderer of Admiral Penistone. Rudge had no doubt at all about that. And he had killed her to close her mouth, which she was just about to open against him.

From the weapon, that usually hopeful source of enquiry, nothing could be learned. Mr. Mount had identified at once the knife that had been drawn from his wife's breast as his own, a steel paper-knife with a pointed end which lay habitually on the desk in his study. The only argument from that fact was that murder had not been intended from the first; circumstances had arisen in the course of the interview that must have taken place, which had made murder imperative. But it was not an argument on which one could really rely.

As to the Superintendent's chief objection to the theory of murder, namely, that murder was impossible since no murderer could have got away and yet no murderer had been found, Rudge was not disposed to bother too much about that. He already had a theory to account for that. Rudge did not believe that the murderer had got away at all.

His meal finished, he got up from the table and began to wander aimlessly about the room. He felt restless. Something must be done, and he did not know quite what. Finally he went down to his car and drove out to Rundel Croft. He would smoke a quiet pipe in the boat-house, looking out over the river, and see if that would help matters.

It did, but the pipe was hardly needed. Quite automatically the Inspector, as soon as he arrived in the boat-house, cast an official eye over the Admiral's skiff, and something took that same eye immediately. Caught in between two of the planks in the bow was something of a vivid red colour. Rudge bent over it. It was a head of valerian, drooping and sad, but not withered.

"Humph!" said Rudge.

This was extremely interesting. He knew where he had seen valerian last: that very afternoon, in Sir Wilfrid Denny's garden. There was a big clump of it growing close to the water, at one end of the landing-stage. And, so far as Rudge knew, there was no other on the river. But the really interesting thing was that this head had not been there when the boat was examined on the morning after the murder (Appleton would never have missed it in any case), as indeed its comparatively fresh condition showed. There were only two possible inferences: one, that the boat had been taken out to-day and had picked up the flower by accident, and the other that the latter had been deliberately placed there.

Rudge considered these for a moment; then he picked the flower out. The stem came out in a straight line from the little crevice in which it had been lodged; by no possible chance could it have got in there just like that as the boat brushed past the clump. The second inference was the correct one: somebody was trying to throw suspicion upon Sir Wilfrid Denny.

Rudge became very active. He knew perfectly well who had put that piece of valerian in the boat. He went up to the house. Constable Hempstead was there, cherishing busily as usual. Rudge asked one question of the company assembled in the kitchen, and it was Constable Hempstead who was able to answer it.

"Has that reporter from the *Evening Gazette* been up here to-day?"

"Yes, sir. I saw him from the other bank this morning. Near the boat-house, he was."

Rudge took his car, drove as fast as he dared to the nearest magistrate, and obtained a search-warrant. Then he headed for the Lord Marshall.

"Is that reporter from the *Evening Gazette* in?" he asked the porter.

"Mr. Graham? No, Mr. Rudge. He went out after dinner."

"What's the number of his room?"

"Seventeen."

"Thanks. No, don't come up. And say nothing about this to anyone."

The porter nodded importantly.

Rudge was busy for over half an hour, undisturbed. When he left, however, he had in his pocket nothing but a piece of paper on which he had laboriously typed a few sentences from a portable typewriter which stood on a table near the window.

As he passed unobtrusively out into the street he looked about him. On the other side of the road a man was lounging. Rudge nodded to him, and the other followed him round a corner.

"They're both in," he said in a low tone, as he reached the Inspector. "Had their dinner there, and haven't been out since." Since the discovery of the blood-stained frock, Mr. and Mrs. Holland had been placed by Superintendent Hawkesworth under close observation.

Rudge nodded. "Never mind about them. I want you to look after somebody else. That reporter chap from the *Evening Gazette*. Know him?"

"Him with the short hair and the spectacles?"

"Yes. Calls himself Graham."

"Isn't that his real name, then, Mr. Rudge?"

"It is not. His real name," said Rudge, "is Walter Fitzgerald."

9

"You should have rung me up last night, Rudge," said Major Twyfitt severely. "Or at least you should have got in touch with the Superintendent. The fellow might have got away."

"I had a man at the back of the Lord Marshall as well as the front all night, sir," pleaded Rudge.

The Superintendent said nothing, but his look was voluble.

"How long have you known this man Graham was Fitzgerald?"

"Not definitely till I identified that specimen of typing I took in his room as coming from the same machine that typed the Admiral's consent to Mrs. Holland's marriage. Of course, I suspected it before," said Rudge, with a side-glance at the Superintendent, "as soon as I heard about Hempstead finding those remains of a beard in the wash-basin trap at Rundel Croft; because I remembered that this reporter's face was a good deal lighter round the chin than on the forehead. I thought at first that he'd been dosing himself with some kind of sunburn application."

"And you say you rang up the *Evening Gazette* last night?"

"Yes, sir; and he's their man all right. *And* he had a beard when they saw him last. The editor told me he's not their real crime expert. He's ill as it happens, so when Fitzgerald rang them up on the morning after the murder to tell them he was on the spot and ask if he could cover it, they said he could, though I gather he wasn't on their salary-list before. Sort of free-lance contributor, but they liked his stuff. 'Graham' was the name he wrote under."

"Yes; that gave him an excuse to be on the spot and keep in touch with developments of course. Very handy, from his point of view. He doesn't know you suspect him? You're sure of that?"

"I've got no reason to think he does, sir."

"Well, let's hope he doesn't," said the Superintendent with energy. "Because if he's got wind of it and gets away —well, you'll be for it, Rudge."

"I didn't think there was enough evidence for an arrest," pleaded Rudge. "Not then."

"But you do now?"

"Well, that's for you and the Major to say," replied Rudge smugly. "But I haven't wasted the extra time, sir,

I can assure you." This was no less than the truth. Rudge had not got to bed at all the previous night.

"Tell us what you've done, then, man," said the Superintendent impatiently.

Rudge cleared his throat. "Perhaps I'd better run through the case as I saw it before last night, more or less. I don't mean the facts. We know those. I mean, the ideas that the facts gave me."

The silence of the other two encouraged him to do so.

"Well, first of all, of course, there was the question, *why* was the Admiral's body in a boat at all? So much easier, if you've got a boat handy, to have taken it out to sea and sunk it with a few weights. The only reason I could see was to create a misleading impression; and the only misleading impression I could see was that the body had floated down-stream instead of up—in other words, that the murder had been committed some way above Lingham. That gave me a pointer towards a theory that it had actually been committed in Whynmouth, or at any rate between Whynmouth and Lingham. Anyhow, I concentrated on that area."

"Even then," observed Major Twyfitt, "it seems a pretty poor reason for not sinking the body and hiding the fact of murder altogether."

"That also occurred to me, sir," Rudge replied, a trifle complacently. "I was sure there was another reason, and I believe I know now what it is. Old Ware put me on to it. I'm as certain as I am of anything that he knows more than he's let on; and I'm pretty certain he knows who killed the Admiral. Anyhow, he dropped me a hint. He said, how did I know it *was* murder?"

"What's that?" demanded the Superintendent.

"Not murder!" exclaimed the Major.

"I didn't say that, sir," Rudge replied quickly. "What

I do say is that old Ware doesn't think it was murder. Whether it was or not, of course we can't know yet, but I'll take my oath that's what Ware thinks."

"What's your evidence?" snapped the Superintendent.

"None, sir. An impression only. But I know Neddy Ware pretty well; and though he may not be above a bit of trout-poaching and so on, I'd bet all I've got that he wouldn't stand for murder. And my inference is that whatever the others wanted to do, he wouldn't stand for the body being sunk or any hanky-panky. I believe the boat was his idea altogether."

"You believe this and believe that," growled the Superintendent. "Let's have a bit of proof."

"There isn't any," Rudge returned, unabashed. "And in any case I only put it forward as my own idea. But I do suggest, sir, that there may be something in it; and if there is—why, it alters the case considerably."

"It is a possibility," Major Twyfitt agreed.

The Superintendent, seeing his murder slipping away from him, only looked sulky.

"Still, we must proceed as if there was no question of it being anything but murder," pointed out the Chief Constable.

"Of course, sir. So I'll get on with my reconstruction. Well, we had the Admiral being rowed down to Whynmouth by Neddy Ware, and this reporter fellow, the nephew, rowing the Vicarage boat after him about an hour later, with Mrs. Mount as his passenger."

"Eh?" said the startled Chief Constable, who did not remember having heard anything of the sort. "What's this?"

"I think it's obvious, sir. I mean," said Rudge, with a naughty glance at his Superintendent, "there's evidence to that effect. We know Mrs. Mount got to the Vicarage about eleven; we know the Vicar didn't see her till well past twelve; we know the Vicarage boat was taken out that night; we're pretty sure Fitzgerald had a hand in the business; we know Fitzgerald was Mrs. Mount's lover. What's the result? Why, that Fitzgerald, knowing she's coming down that night to see the Vicar about the divorce, intercepts her in the garden, takes her to the summer-house for a talk, decides they'd better go down to Whynmouth after the Admiral (it's more than possible there was some sort of appointment between the two men), takes the Vicar's hat to put on in case anyone sees them going off in the boat (nothing like a hat to establish identity), takes the Norwegian knife the boys left there, to cut the painter with—no!" said Rudge thoughtfully. "She ran back for the knife when they found they couldn't untie the knot."

"How the devil do you know that?"

"I don't know it, sir. But if she did it would explain a lot. It's always puzzled me that the Vicar was watering his garden so hard the next day in the blazing sun. Mr. Mount can't be such a bad gardener as all that. But suppose she'd left footprints on the beds when she ran back for the knife. A nice strong jet of water would destroy them, and so much less obvious than a fork or a trowel, the garden being under observation all the time by our men in the Admiral's boat-house. And he even gave the inside of the summer-house a bit of a splashing. Suppose she left powder scattered about there, like they do?"

"It's a possibility," the Chief Constable agreed with interest. "More than a possibility."

The Superintendent said nothing.

"Well, anyhow, as I said, we have Fitzgerald chasing after the Admiral. It would take him half an hour to forty minutes, I suppose, to get down to Whynmouth. Then there's a gap of, say, fifteen or twenty minutes, during which the Admiral is killed and arrangements made about the two boats. The body is dumped in the Vicarage one, the two painters tied together, and someone rows them up-stream. Who? Not Fitzgerald. He wouldn't have time; we've got him at Rundel Croft soon after twelve. Not Mrs. Mount; she's at the Vicarage at about the same time."

"Ware," nodded the Chief Constable. "Yes, that seems clear."

The Superintendent said nothing.

"Neddy Ware, sir, yes," said Rudge, who was now very much enjoying himself. "And cuts the two painters again when he arrives at Rundel Croft a couple of hours later, with his own knife which isn't so sharp as the Norwegian one."

"That doesn't sound like a naval man," demurred the Major, "to cut a painter instead of untying it."

"But supposing it wasn't a naval man who tied it, sir? Suppose it was a landsman, with a ridiculous knot, which the dragging in the water had made tighter still. Besides, it's my opinion that old Ware was in the sort of mood then when one does cut instead of untying, even a naval man."

"All right," assented the Chief Constable. "Go on."

The Superintendent said nothing.

"Fitzgerald must have come back by car, on the Whynmouth side of the river to drop Mrs. Mount at the Vicarage for her interview. And he parked the car while he was over at Rundel Croft. I made a bit of a bloomer over that, sir. I'd suspected he must have a car, but seeing he himself was at Rundel Croft I'd only had enquiries made that side of the river. As soon as Sergeant Appleton got back last night I sent him off to work the other side. He's found two witnesses who saw a car, with the lights out, standing just inside the Vicarage gate, behind the laurels, out of sight of the road, one at twelve-fifteen and one at twelve-forty."

"How could they have seen it if it was out of sight of the road?"

"How do people in the country see so much, sir? They'll have some plausible explanation you can be sure. But you know as well as I do that if it had been parked in the Vicar's cellar with a tarpaulin over it, someone would have seen it there. And very handy for us too."

Major Twyfitt laughed. "All right. How did Fitzgerald get across the river, then?"

"He must have swum it. No other way. I suggest he stripped quickly, rolled his clothes up in his coat, tossed the bundle across the stream (it's not more than forty feet wide there), and swum after it. And there he was, looking for File X as comfortable as you like, and his sister helping him, when along comes Holland and taps at the french windows. That must have given both of them a nasty shock. But he rose to it. Muttered to her to get rid of him at once, kept himself in the shadow and handed over the typed consent to their marriage. That was quite enough to send Holland half off his head with pleasure—far too much to have any room in his mind for noticing how young the Admiral was looking nowadays. Then Fitzgerald gets the papers, destroys them, goes upstairs and shaves off his beard, crosses the river again, picks up Mrs. Mount, and goes off with her in the car. I haven't been able to trace where they went, but I expect they made for London—as far away as they could."

"Then you think Holland was genuine in his identification of the Admiral that night?"

"I do, sir. Mind you, I think he knows the truth now all right; but he didn't then."

"That makes him an accessory after, too."

"Yes, sir. Though it seems likely that he's been told the same tale as Neddy Ware was—that it wasn't murder. And Mrs. Holland, too. That would explain why she didn't seem surprised, the first time I saw her, to hear that her uncle was dead, but she did jump when I said he'd been murdered."

"That fits very well, Rudge," commended Major Twy-fitt.

The Superintendent said at last: "Have you found the weapon?"

"No, sir," said Rudge.

"Ah," said the Superintendent.

"But I found this." Rudge produced from his breast-pocket a strip of brown paper. Unwrapping it, he brought to light a long slender Norwegian knife, rather rusty.

The Superintendent took it eagerly.

"Then you have found the weapon."

"No, sir."

"Where did you find it, Rudge?" interposed Major Twyfitt.

"In a clump of antirrhinums in the Vicar's garden, sir."

"Were you looking for it there?"

"Yes, sir. There was a nice bright moon last night."

"Why, Rudge," asked the Chief Constable patiently, "were you looking for this knife in a clump of antirrhinums last night in the Vicar's garden?"

"Well, sir, you see, I'd worked it out this way. Was the crime premeditated or was it not? Somehow, what with Ware's remarks and the rest, I didn't think it was. Anyhow, I could soon test it. If Fitzgerald had intended to murder the Admiral that night, he would have taken this knife along with him, because he'd have known as soon as he saw it that nothing would serve him better. If he hadn't the intention, I thought he might most probably have thrown it back into the garden as soon as he'd used it on the painter. So I had a look round Mr. Mount's ground last night within an easy throw of his mooring-post." Rudge by this time was so pleased with himself that he could not resist sending a highly unofficial beam at his superior officer.

Major Twyfitt smiled back. "Smart bit of work, Rudge."

"What I want," observed the Superintendent, unap-peased, "is the *weapon*."

"I found this too, sir."

Rudge produced another piece of brown paper from his pocket, and from it another knife, an ordinary jack-knife such as sailors and navvies use. "There are no prints on it," he said, as he laid it on the table.

"And where did you find that?"

"In a clump of valerian, sir, at the bottom of Sir Wilfrid Denny's garden, overhanging the river."

"Sir Wilfrid Denny's garden!"

"Yes, sir. It's like this." Rudge gave an account of his finding of the sprig of valerian stuck into the Admiral's boat, which had not been there when Sergeant Appleton overhauled it. "It's like those treasure-hunts," he added, "where you go from one clue to another. That valerian was a clue, so I followed it up, and that's what I found. It's a plant. There's not even any blood on the knife, only rust. Of course, the real weapon's at the bottom of the sea."

"You think so?"

"Rivers," said Rudge, "can be dragged."

"And you think that Fitzgerald planted these two clues?"

"I'm certain of it, sir."

"It's about time," remarked the Superintendent, "that we got our hooks on Master Fitzgerald."

Rudge glanced at the clock. "I'm expecting him at eleven-thirty. Another fifteen minutes to go. I told him I'd have an exclusive piece of information for him if he came along then."

"He'll come?" said the Chief Constable doubtfully. "You don't think you're taking a risk?"

"Sergeant Appleton's tailing him in any case, sir."

"If Fitzgerald gets away, Rudge," growled Superintendent Hawkesworth.

"He won't, sir. Is there anything else you want me to report on before he comes?"

"Have you traced that copy of the evening paper in his pocket?"

"No, sir. He must have picked it up in Whynmouth, perhaps at the Lord Marshall. I don't think there's much importance to be attached to it."

"You think now, then, that it was the Admiral who went to the Lord Marshall?" asked Major Twyfitt.

"I do, sir. I know the Superintendent thought differently, but we've proved he was in Whynmouth, so why shouldn't it have been him? It's my notion that he anticipated danger at the interview ahead of him, and wanted to take Holland along to stand by; but when the porter told him Holland was in bed he didn't bother to have him roused and just gave the first excuse that came into his head. Of course, he never intended to catch a train at all, but he had to say something."

"Humph!" said the Superintendent, not too pleased at having his bright idea snatched from him by a mere inspector.

"And the door-key in the Admiral's boat?" asked the Major.

"Why shouldn't the Admiral have dropped it there himself, sir? It seems a pity," said Rudge, "to bother to find complicated explanations when there's a simple one handy. I felt that," he added with a look of great innocence, "about the Admiral's visit to the Lord Marshall; though I know Mr. Hawkesworth didn't agree with me."

Mr. Hawkesworth's large face looked for a moment so suffused with honest emotion that the Chief Constable hurriedly led the conversation into quite a different track.

"And Mrs. Mount's death, Rudge? Have you got any further with your theory of murder there?"

"Not so far as evidence goes, sir," Rudge said slowly, "but I could put a case of murder for you, if you'd care to hear it; though I know well enough we could never put it before a jury as it stands."

"Let's hear it."

"If it was murder, sir, it was done this way. Mrs. Mount makes this appointment. She's lost her nerve, and she's going to give things away. The Hollands know a good deal already; she's going to tell them more. I don't know how much the Reverend knows, but he's going to know a good deal more by the time she's finished. Naturally, this doesn't suit a certain person's book. He gets wind of it, and goes there to stop her. He must have reached the house just before I got there myself. She lets him in, and they start arguing. Suddenly they see me coming up the drive. He snatches up the steel paper-knife from the desk, and threatens her with it if she utters a sound. She keeps quiet. They watch me hide in the laurels. Then an hour or so later along come the Hollands, and he does the same thing. They sit on the lawn, and the situation's saved for another few minutes. But he's getting badly rattled, and she's probably nearing hysteria. He doesn't trust her one inch. All the time, while the three of us are out there, he's got to keep the knife at her breast to make sure of her silence. And what does he do? He makes her hold it there herself, both hands on the hilt, and the point right on her heart; with one hand over hers he can control her more easily like that, and use his eyes elsewhere. She's half-dead with fright of him—sees he means murder—does whatever he tells her. Then the Hollands come up to the house again. From their conversation he learns that the front door, which he can't have shut properly, has blown ajar. They're coming in. He hears them go into the drawing-room, and then into the dining-room; he knows they're bound to come into the study. It's his life or hers now. What does he do? He's behind Mrs. Mount now, both his hands over hers on the hilt of the dagger. With a convulsive pull he forces the thing into her heart. She screams once. He drops her and darts behind the door, wiping his hands on his handkerchief. In come the Hollands; Mrs. runs out, Holland stays a moment, then follows her out of the house. I'm on my way across the lawn. The murderer's got a couple of seconds to get inside the lavatory just by the front door. He does it. But he can't leave the grounds in case he's seen. So then," concluded Rudge, somewhat breathlessly, "all he's got to do is to wait till the coast's clear, creep out of the house, hide round the angle of it, scuffle on the gravel, and walk in again. And that, sir, is just what I suggest he did do."

There was a silence after Rudge had finished.

Superintendent Hawkesworth broke it, by remarking quite mildly: "Can you prove he didn't come up the drive? What about those two on the lawn?"

"They couldn't see from where they were. The angle of the house is in the way."

"Besides, they wouldn't say."

There was another silence.

"Mr. Hawkesworth," said Rudge, a little diffidently, "who is to make the arrest, you or I?"

"You'd better. You've put in some very good work on this case," said the Superintendent, who after all was a fair man, "and I think you ought to have the credit of it. The one who makes the arrest always gets the credit. That is," he added rather perfunctorily, "if Major Twyfitt agrees."

"Certainly, certainly," said that gentleman. "I quite agree. Rudge has done very well. Saved us a lot of trouble, to say nothing of Scotland Yard."

"Thank you, sir," said Rudge modestly, and looked at the clock. The time was close on half-past eleven.

"Well, I suppose we can only wait," said the Chief Constable. All three were beginning to feel uneasy.

They did not have to wait long. Before the hands of the clock had reached the appointed time a constable put his head round the door to announce, in a stentorian whisper, that Mr. Graham was there, to see Mr. Rudge by appointment.

"Show him in," nodded the Major.

The cropped-headed reporter entered with no less than his usual assurance, greeting the three heartily and receiving three very curt nods in exchange. "What's this, Inspector?" he said. "Something rather special for me? That's very decent of you."

"Something very special," replied Rudge dryly. "I'm going to make an arrest."

"An arrest!" Fitzgerald stared at him. "Oh! For Admiral Penistone's death?"

"For Admiral Penistone's murder," returned Rudge grimly. "And something else."

"I see. Er—very good of you to let me in on it." The reporter's assurance was not so pronounced now. Without being asked he sat down in a chair as if his legs had suddenly gone weak. The three others eyed him in silence.

Again the constable put his head round the door. "Sir Wilfrid Denny, to see Mr. Rudge by appointment."

"Show him in, Gravestock," said Rudge. To his superiors he said briefly, as he rose from his chair: "I asked Sir Wilfrid to be good enough to come down here himself, so that we could ask him about—certain things."

The others nodded.

Rudge went to the door to meet Sir Wilfrid. Sir Wilfrid, however, was already in the doorway as Rudge reached it. Rudge was a large man, Sir Wilfrid a small one. It was Sir Wilfrid who sprawled on the floor. With every sign of embarrassment, and apologising heartily, Rudge helped him up and brushed him down.

"I'm sorry, sir. Most sorry. Very careless of me. Do you know Major Twyfitt? And Superintendent Hawkesworth? I'm so sorry to have brought you down here, sir, but there were just one or two questions we wanted to ask you, to clear up a doubtful point. It's about a sprig of valerian that was found wedged between two of the boards of Admiral Penistone's boat. Now, I've searched up and down the river, and the only clump of valerian growing close to the water is in your garden. We were wondering if you could account for the sprig in any way?"

Sir Wilfrid thrust his hands into his jacket pockets and stared at Rudge with perplexity. "No, I can't."

"Nor for this knife, found in the same clump of valerian, with traces of blood on it?"

Sir Wilfrid looked at Major Twyfitt, he looked at Superintendent Hawkesworth, he looked at Walter Fitzgerald. Then he coughed. "I never saw it before," he said.

"Thank you, sir. That's all I had to ask you. And now I have a very painful duty to perform."

Rudge paused, and looked hard at Sir Wilfrid. Sir Wilfrid coughed again, more rackingly.

"Sir Wilfrid Denny," said Rudge, "I arrest you for the murders of Hugh Lawrence Penistone and Celia Mount, and I warn you that anything you say may be used in evidence against you."

10

"Hardly, I think," replied Sir Wilfrid, dryly. "Well, I congratulate you, Inspector. How did you find out?" He sat, with an air of jauntiness, on the edge of the table.

"Look here, Denny," interposed Major Twyfitt awkwardly, as he and Superintendent Hawkesworth emerged slowly from the stupor into which they seemed to have fallen. "Look here, I don't know whether . . . I mean, better not say anything. Your solicitor . . ."

"I know perfectly well what I'm doing," returned Sir Wilfrid. "*He* gave me away, I suppose?" He nodded towards Fitzgerald, who had not moved from his chair.

"Am I to understand that you wish to make a statement, Sir Wilfrid?" put in Rudge suavely, though there seemed little ground for such an understanding.

"Yes, I'll make a statement, certainly. I killed both of them, I'll tell you that at once. I don't know whether it's any good adding it, but I didn't mean to kill the Admiral; at least, I suppose I did, but it was in self-defence. He went for me with a poker."

At the table the Superintendent had grabbed a piece of paper and was writing furiously.

"Then why did you kill Mrs. Mount, when you thought she was going to give you away?" asked Rudge.

"Really, Rudge," said the Chief Constable unhappily. "I don't think we should ask . . . Sir Wilfrid really should see his solicitor."

"Oh, I'll answer any questions. Why did I kill her? Because I didn't want to be arrested, of course. How could I have proved self-defence? When the circumstances came out, it would look as if I had every motive for murder."

"You mean your share in the Hong Kong business?"

"I see you know all about it. Yes. But I'm sorry about Mrs. Mount. I—I suppose I lost my head. Gave way to panic. Horrible thing to do—— I suppose," he added in a low voice to Walter Fitzgerald, "it's no good telling you that I'm ready to make amends with my own life?"

Fitzgerald got up without answering and, crossing to the mantelpiece, leaned his head on his hands.

"Better get this down quickly," said Sir Wilfrid to the Superintendent. "We haven't much time. The Admiral had suspected for some time my share in the Hong Kong business. Somehow or other I managed to stave him off. Then Ware ratted on me."

"Ware?"

"Yes. He'd known all along—though how the devil he found out I never discovered. That's why he settled here when he retired."

"He'd been blackmailing you?"

"Well, I suppose you'd call it that; but only a matter of a present of a pound or two now and then, and he never used any threats. He just *knew*, and I gave him a few pounds occasionally to keep his knowledge to himself. That's all. But the Admiral got hold of him; and whether he paid more, or appealed to 'duty' and 'honour' and the rest, I can't say, but Ware must have ratted. Then the Admiral came down to see me, breathing, as you may imagine, flames and death. He got me in a corner, till I couldn't persist in my denials any longer. Then he must have seen red, because he simply went for me, cold blind, with the poker. I snatched up the first thing I could (as a matter of fact it was a trench dagger one of my nephews once gave me as a War souvenir), dodged under the poker, and got in first. Then I went down to where Ware was waiting, with the Admiral's boat, and found that Fitzgerald and Mrs. Mount had just arrived in another boat."

"One minute, Sir Wilfrid," interrupted the Superintendent. "What time was that?"

"Oh, I suppose about twenty minutes to twelve. I told them what I'd done and that we must get rid of the body. I'm afraid I'd lost my head a bit, because I wouldn't listen to them when Ware and Fitzgerald both urged me to come out in the open and ring up the police. It was justifiable homicide, they said, and nothing could happen to me. But I knew that if I did, all that Hong Kong business would come out, and I should lose my pension in any case; and I thought it almost inevitable that I should have to face a charge of murder. In the end Fitzgerald agreed to stand by me, but we had a lot more trouble before we could persuade Ware. Finally he agreed that if he wasn't to be expected to tell any direct lies except to conceal the fact of his having been out with the Admiral that night at all, he wouldn't give me away; he would just know nothing. I was too upset to make any arrangements at all; as no doubt he's told you, Fitzgerald saw to our plans. Ware insisted that the body should not be concealed, everything was to be as plain and above board as it could be; so we went up to the house, had a stiff drink apiece, and put the body in the Vicar's boat, covered with a bit of tarpaulin. Ware undertook to tow it up-stream and set it adrift before returning the Admiral's boat to its boat-house. In the meantime Fitzgerald promised to go at once to Rundel Croft and look through the Admiral's papers, to destroy anything he might have in writing against me, which I understand he did. The next day, feeling unable to stay and face

it, I frankly took to my heels and escaped to Paris. Fitzgerald sent me word there that no suspicion seemed to be
directed against me, so I came back."

"And Mrs. Mount?"

In a low voice Sir Wilfrid gave the details. They turned
out to be almost exactly as Rudge had surmised, except
that he maintained that there again he had never really intended murder. Mrs. Mount, hearing the Hollands actually
in the next room, had made a desperate attempt to escape,
and in the struggle Sir Wilfrid had mechanically tightened
his grasp on her and so driven the knife in. There had been
no set plan in his subsequent movements. He had just run
in sheer panic from one hiding place to another as opportunity offered.

He had nothing else to say.

Major Twyfitt shook his head. "I shouldn't have let you
say anything, until you'd seen your solicitor."

"My dear fellow," returned Sir Wilfrid, almost happily,
"don't bother. I shall never face a judge. You heard me
cough just before your man arrested me? Under cover of
the second one I slipped something into my mouth which
I bought for just such an emergency in Paris. I've got
about ten minutes more to live, I reckon."

Major Twyfitt sprang forward in consternation, as did
the Superintendent. It is a bad thing for the police when
a prisoner succeeds in committing suicide under their noses.

Rudge, however, got there first. "Well," he said, "we'll
put you in safety for that ten minutes anyhow. Will you
come with me, please?" Taking the other by the arm he
led him from the room.

When he returned the Superintendent was telephoning
frantically for a doctor, who was out. "Put him in a cell,"
he said briefly. "Don't worry, sir. We don't need a doctor.
I knew what he'd got in his left-hand coat pocket. I ex-

pected it. So I made up another similar packet, and changed them during that collision. Here's his." Rudge produced a small twist of white paper.

"But how did you know what his packet looked like?" asked the Chief Constable.

"I did a bit of spying on Sir Wilfrid last night, sir, through the blinds of his sitting-room. I saw him making it up, and I guessed what it was, and I knew it was his left-hand pocket because he had his hand in it when he came in. Sir Wilfrid's just swallowed three tablets of bicarbonate of soda; that's all."

11

Major Twyfitt dropped back into his chair. Everyone seemed to have forgotten Walter Fitzgerald, who still stood by the mantelpiece in a dejected attitude.

"You knew last night it was Denny?"

"Not to say knew, sir. I'd suspected it for some time, ever since I interviewed him in his rose-garden. He seemed very eager to volunteer that he hardly knew the Admiral at all, and then, for a gentleman who lived right on the river, he seemed to know very little about the tides; I couldn't quite swallow that. Then there were those rumours about bad blood between him and the Admiral, and what with him having been in Hong Kong at the time I thought he might possibly be mixed up in that business on the wrong side; besides, he was a bit too strong against the Admiral having been an innocent party. And though he remembered that Mr. Fitzgerald was handsome, he couldn't remember whether he had a beard or not."

"Then you were pulling our legs this morning, when you told us all your suspicions were directed against— someone else?"

"Sir, I never told you. I didn't mention any name. I was quite sure in my own mind that it was Denny, but what was the good of saying so? I hadn't any real evidence. At first I thought of arresting—someone else in Sir Wilfrid's presence, with the idea that if he had done it he'd say so there and then. But that mightn't have come off. Then last night, when I saw him making up that packet, I knew for certain it was him; so I thought I'd take a chance and arrest him. If it came off, well and good. If it didn't . . ."

"You'd have been broken," said the Superintendent with severity.

"But it did, sir. I thought somehow it would," admitted Rudge, "if Sir Wilfrid thought he'd got the contents of that packet safe inside him."

"Very unofficial, Rudge," pronounced the Chief Constable. "Most unprofessional. But dam' smart."

"Thank you, sir."

"So now what about Mr. Fitzgerald here? I think we'd like to ask him a few questions."

"Fire away," said Walter, turning round. "I'll tell you anything you want to know. Thank God it's all over. It's been a nightmare, I can tell you. I knew you were after me."

"Now . . ." said Superintendent Hawkesworth, and began to put his questions.

Fitzgerald's tale of the night's happenings exactly bore out Rudge's reconstruction, except that he and Mrs. Mount had not returned to London that night. They had driven about forty miles and then turned the car into a wood and slept in it—so far as either of them could sleep. Mrs. Mount, as the days went by, had been more and more vehement that Denny should give himself up, and had even divulged some of the facts to her husband under the seal of confession; he had promised to join her in urging both Sir Wilfrid and Ware to go frankly to the police and tell them the truth.

Holland had been an innocent party all the time. Elma had known the truth, but Holland did not yet know who had killed the Admiral; he had, quite simply, taken Fitzgerald's word that he had not done so. The matter of the typewritten consent to the marriage had arisen in this way. Holland had met Fitzgerald in the East, seen that he was drifting, and liked him enough to try to pull him together. Walter, without telling him about the Hong Kong affair, had divulged that there was a charge hanging over him——

"The warrant out against you for forgery?" interposed the Superintendent.

"You know about that? Well, then, yes."

This charge prevented him from making himself known in England, and consequently from obtaining his inheritance. Holland promised to see what he could do. He interviewed the firm in Hong Kong, who undertook, in view of the time that had elapsed, to withdraw the charge if Walter repaid the money. This he could not do until he had received his inheritance, and he refused to allow Holland to lend him the money, a considerable sum. Holland had therefore undertaken to get in touch with the Admiral in England and try and bring about a reconciliation, so that the money could be advanced by the family; at the same time he promised to see Elma and assure her that everything was coming right at last.

While abroad Walter had always kept in touch with Elma, and when the Admiral tried to stop her communicating with him, Mrs. Mount had gone to the house as Elma's maid, both to keep a roof over her head and to act as a liaison.

The Admiral received Holland with suspicion, as a friend of Walter's, and at first would have nothing to do with him. Holland saw that it would take time to make him change his attitude, and settled down to play him as patiently as he could. In the meantime, having seen Elma, he promptly fell in love with her.

It was now Walter's turn to do Holland a favour. He had arrived in England, and taken lodgings in London. Mrs. Mount hurried up too, and he installed her near him, under the name of Arkwright. Walter was delighted to hear of Holland's feeling for Elma, for knowing himself, he had always feared that Elma, unless she became attached to somebody of strong character, might become a drifter too. He had strongly urged Elma, who was by no means in love herself, to accept Holland. Finally, seeing how much her brother wished it, Elma consented to do so. The Admiral, however, still proved an obstacle. He would not give his consent to Elma's marriage with any friend of Walter's. Holland had already improved his standing, but the Admiral was by no means won over.

In the meantime Elma too was trying to do something for Walter. He and Mrs. Mount had always wanted to get married, but the Vicar would not divorce her. Elma had fancied that Mr. Mount had shown signs of being interested in herself. She deliberately set about strengthening this interest in order to be able to use her influence with him to persuade him to agree to the divorce. It was for this reason that she always took particular trouble with her appearance whenever she was to meet him. Walter did not know of this at the time, but Holland observed with pain his fiancée's decided set at the Vicar, the reason for which she did not give him. He therefore told Walter that he had come to the end of his patience; he was going up to London to get a special licence, and he was going to use it, consent from the Admiral or no consent. He went.

Walter knew that this would put the Admiral's back up more than ever, and Elma would certainly lose the control of her money. He was aware, from his sister, of his uncle's obsession with regard to the Hong Kong incident, and resolved to use this in order to obtain consent to the marriage. He therefore typed out the form of consent and, taking his courage in his hands, went to see his uncle shortly after tea on the day of his death, lying in wait for him in the garden, so as to keep their meeting secret.

It was the first time he had seen the Admiral for many years, and at first the latter refused to have anything to do with him. When Walter said, however, that he could tell him the exact truth about the Hong Kong episode, the Admiral changed his tune. Walter then put his proposition: the truth in exchange for the consent. The Admiral did not hesitate; he signed on the spot. Thereupon Walter told him everything. He had to sacrifice Denny to do so, but after all Denny was a criminal; he had grossly tricked Walter; and Elma's marriage, to say nothing of Holland's happiness, could no longer be jeopardised to save Denny's face.

The Admiral was beside himself with rage. He raved, he swore, he thundered, he stamped. With the very greatest difficulty Walter calmed him down and made him promise to behave at the Vicar's as if nothing had happened at all. In the end, however, the Admiral had given this promise and had departed to dress, breathing fiery vengeance for the morrow.

Walter had intended to go across first thing the next morning to West End to warn Denny; it never occurred to him that the Admiral would do anything that night. Concealed, however, in the Vicar's garden, where he had an appointment with Mrs. Mount, he had seen the Admiral set out with Ware, whom doubtless he had intended to pump on the way, and was perturbed. He felt he must wait till Mrs. Mount came and then, talking it over, decided that they should both go down the river and put off the interview with the Vicar till they got back; this did not matter as there was no appointment, a surprise assault having been intended on the Vicar's conscience. The details of their departure had been exactly as Rudge had said.

The rest they had heard from Denny himself. When Walter got back to Rundel Croft he had broken the news to his sister that their uncle had been accidentally killed. She was shocked, but pulled herself together and helped him look for the papers.

"There was blood on her dress," said the Superintendent.

"So she told me afterwards. It must have come from my hand. Anything else?"

"The valerian?" asked Rudge.

Walter nodded. "I put it there. Whether my uncle's death was justifiable homicide or not (I believe it was) when it came to Celia . . . I wanted," said Walter simply, "to put you on the right track. I wanted Denny to hang."

"Then why didn't you come and tell us all you knew?" asked Rudge, reasonably enough.

"I could hardly give the fellow away," retorted Walter.

"Oh!" said Rudge. It was a distinction he could not appreciate.

"Look here," said the Superintendent suddenly. "What was behind that Hong Kong incident? It was you impersonating your uncle, I suppose?"

Walter flushed. "Yes. This is what happened. Denny had me to dinner one night and made me rather drunk. He suggested it would be a rag if I put on a naval uniform, which he happened to have handy, and went down to some dive and did a song-and-dance; somebody might mistake me for my uncle, and it would be a glorious joke. He knew my uncle hated me, and I hated him—at least, we didn't love each other. I was tickled to death, being a silly young ass, and agreed like a shot. Denny lent me the uniform and took me down there himself. I didn't have to act much; I was as drunk as a lord.

"The next day I was to go on a trek into the interior for my firm, miles away from newspapers or anything like that. Denny knew, and that's why that particular night was chosen. I didn't get back for some months, and by that time the whole thing was over. Denny put the wind up me. He said it was a fool thing to have done, that I had laid myself open to a criminal prosecution, and that he wouldn't back me up; the damage was done; I had better lie low and say nothing about it. I thought it was fishy, but I was frightened and agreed to keep quiet.

"I didn't come on the truth for years afterwards, and then only by chance. This was what lay behind it. There was a big ring of opium-smugglers operating in Hong Kong at that time. Denny was in charge of the customs, and he was in with the ring; they'd either blackmailed or bought him. My uncle had got wind of the ring and was getting close on their track. They had to get rid of him, or beat it; and they hit on that plan. My uncle was lured somehow into that street; a girl decoy, whom a Chinaman was pretending to maltreat, got him into the dive, he was sandbagged and then drugged, and his clothes saturated with whisky and opium. In the meantime I had fallen into it as well, like a child of two. I had a beard in those days too, and a little powder on it and a line or two on my face had made me so much like my uncle that nobody ever suspected that it might not be him—and even he himself had his doubts! Altogether, it was a very pretty little plot.

"Anything else?" He sauntered towards the door.

"We can't let him go," whispered the Superintendent urgently.

"But what can we hold him on?" Major Twyfitt whispered back.

"He's an accessory after."

"Not to a crime," smiled Walter, whose ears must have been particularly sharp. "You can't be an accessory after to justifiable homicide."

"That hasn't been proved yet," said the Superintendent sternly.

"No? Well, you can't detain me till it has been." With a quick movement Walter was through the door.

"We must hold him," muttered Hawkesworth, jumping up. "I don't know what on, but we must. Get him, Rudge, man! There's that Hong Kong warrant still out against him anyhow."

But Walter was already through the charge-room and at the street door. By the pavement stood a car, its engine ticking over. On seeing Walter, the driver thrust in the gear. The car jumped forward, and Walter leapt into the back.

"Walter Fitzgerald," enunciated the Superintendent, charging through the doorway, "I——"

"Don't want to lose you, but I think you ought to go," chanted Walter mockingly as the car gathered speed. "Good-bye, Superintendent. You can send any message through my sister."

Elma, sitting in front beside Holland, turned round and waved enthusiastic confirmation.

The Superintendent darted for the telephone. "I'll have that car stopped before it's gone three miles," he said grimly.

Major Twyfitt touched him on the shoulder. "Why

bother? We don't really want him, you know. We've got the right man. We'll let him go. It's my belief that he's in better hands than ours."

With an air of disgust the Superintendent relinquished the telephone. "As you say, sir, of course. But we ought to have held him. Yes, Gravestock?"

The burly constable looked scared. "Could you come to the cells, please, sir? I think there's something wrong with the prisoner Denny."

The three officers tramped there in silence.

"There's certainly something wrong with him," said the Superintendent a minute later. "He's dead. That's what's wrong with him. Rudge!"

In consternation Rudge drew from his pocket the wisp of paper and hurriedly opened it. "No," he said with relief, "these are his. He had my soda bics—nothing else."

"Then what did he die of?"

"He just died," said Major Twyfitt, looking down on the still figure. "He's old. He knew he was going to die—so he did die."

There was a moment's rather awed silence.

"And he never signed his confession," said the Superintendent disgustedly.

THE END

APPENDIX I

SOLUTIONS

CHAPTER I

By Canon Victor L. Whitechurch

No Solution

CHAPTER II

By G. D. H. and M. Cole

No Solution

CHAPTER III

By Henry Wade

IN 1919, soon after the War, Admiral Penistone (young, rapid promotion for brilliant active service exploits) becomes involved in a disreputable brawl in a house of illrepute in Hong Kong. Owing to his war services the Admiralty allow him to send in his papers, instead of court-martialling him. There were also involved in this brawl three other Englishmen: (1) Walter Fitzgerald, young and weak-charactered, struggling with drink and

drugs; (2) his friend, and partner in a trading concern,
Vanyke, an older man; (3) another trader, Holland. During the course of the brawl Fitzgerald is killed by Chinamen, but this is not known to the naval authorities when
they deal with Penistone.

Holland, learning of old Fitzgerald's will, blackmails
Penistone, his price being "the hand of your niece, Elma."
Elma, a woman of spasmodically passionate nature, does
for a time fall wildly in love with Holland, but cools off
and (when the story begins) is backing out of the engagement. This is the real cause of the Admiral's annoyance with his niece.

Elma is now setting her cap at the Vicar, a handsome
and vigorous man, though fifty. On the night in question
she persuades him to a romantic trip up the river after she
is supposed to have returned home. The Vicar's "shock"
at the news is largely due to his fear that this "adventure"
will "come out."

Penistone, after locking up the boat-house and finishing
his cigar out of doors, returns to his study, where he is
murdered by the butler, Emery. Emery is in fact Vanyke,
who believes Penistone to be morally, if not actually, responsible for the death of his "poor young friend, Walter."
"Emery" puts Penistone's overcoat back on to the body, to
suggest that he was killed out of doors. The newspaper
(the one delivered at the house at 9 p.m.) was splashed
with blood, so he thrust it in the pocket for the same reason. At 2.30 a.m. he carries the body to the boat-house,
unlocks it with the Admiral's key, rows across to the
Vicarage wharf, dumps the body in the boat (in which the
Vicar had left his hat on his romantic voyage) and cuts it
adrift. (This to suggest murder at the Vicarage—or at
least to lay a false trail.) As suggested by P.C. Hempstead,
the boat is stranded at slack tide and comes back on the

flow. Emery swabs out the Rundel Croft boat for fear of blood-stains.

Elma probably went to London to see her solicitors, and her dress and shoes may have been hidden by Emery, further to confuse the issue.

Probably Neddy Ware knew something about the Hong Kong incident.

CHAPTER IV

By Agatha Christie

THE real Elma Fitzgerald is dead and her brother Walter is masquerading as her, being unable to claim his inheritance under his own name as he is wanted by the police. Holland has been a friend of his in remote parts of the world. Walter finds it hard to get any definite statement as to money out of the Admiral and, to force his hand, pretends to be engaged to Holland. The Admiral will then be forced to hand over the money. Unknown to Walter, however, the Admiral has speculated with it and lost it.

Walter, who has been an actor at one time, has had no difficulty in deceiving the Admiral, who has not seen his niece since she was a child. He takes no great pains with Holland, but reserves his best effects of make-up when asked out in the neighbourhood, when he takes an artistic pleasure in playing the vamp.

The Admiral, however, has received an anonymous letter from "Célie," stating that "Elma" is a man. He slips this into his pocket unopened just before starting for the Vicarage and opens it when waiting for "Elma" to say good-bye to the Vicar.

He immediately taxes Walter with the truth as they go over in the boat, and says he will give him up to the police. Walter, who knows the Admiral's uncompromising character, stabs him as the boat glides into the boat-house.

He then goes up to the house and waits till all is quiet. Then he makes up as the Admiral, dons an overcoat, puts the newspaper in the pocket and shows himself at the Lord Marshall, which is badly lighted and where the Boots is a rustic who is nearly half-witted. He asks for Holland, then says he can't wait.

He returns. Later goes down to the boat-house, takes the boat across the river, puts the body in the other boat and cuts the painter. He thinks the boat will go out to sea, and as the Admiral's boat will be in the boat-house, the Admiral will be supposed to have left on foot and gone to town by train. The boat, however, drifts down and drifts into the bank, to be sent up-stream later.

The murder discovered, "Elma" hastens away with the white dress on which are blood-stains. He intends to return with a good excuse, secure in the *alibi* he has created.

The Vicar *did* take his boat out again. He met his former wife at Fernton Bridge. He was terribly anxious to have no "talk," hence his peculiar manner.

CHAPTER V

By John Rhode

THE so-called Admiral Penistone was an impostor. He was, I think, by profession a blackmailer (hence the files of newspaper cuttings) who had contrived to get several peo-

ple into his power, among them Sir Wilfrid Denny, who
had been impoverished by "Penistone's" constant demands.

Denny decides to commit the murder. He learns that
"Penistone" has arranged to meet Holland on the night of
the ninth, and lies in wait for him at Fernton Bridge. As
he passes, Denny hails him, saying that he has urgent business to discuss—perhaps that he has money which "Penistone" had demanded. He gets back into the boat, sitting
in the stern with "Penistone" facing him as he rows. When
they reach the railway bridge (see Map) he suddenly rises
and plunges the dagger into "Penistone" as he leans forward to take a stroke.

He leaves the boat under the bridge, among the piles,
where it is safe from observation in the dark. He then calls
at an hotel in Whynmouth, in order to establish his presence there at a particular hour (11 p.m.). He slips out
from here, and goes to the Lord Marshall, where he imper-
sonates "Penistone," not a very difficult matter owing to
the darkness of the hall, with the object of suggesting that
"Penistone" was then alive. Then he returned to the first
hotel, where he remains till after midnight. He had thus
established as good an alibi as he could.

The body, being under cover of the bridge, remains dry.
As soon as the tide slackens, he rows up the river, trans-
fers the body to the Vicar's boat, swings the stern in to
shore, and lands. Seeing the Vicar's hat, he puts that in the
boat, by way of confusing the trail. Then he proceeds according to Ware's speculation.

He replaces the Admiral's boat in the Rundel Croft
boat-house, making the mistake of doing so bow first. This
done, he walks home to West End. His sudden departure
for London is concerned with the will of John Martin Fitzgerald, a subject at present somewhat obscure.

CHAPTER VI

By Milward Kennedy

1. FOUR men are engaged in the supply of arms to Chinese armies: they are Mr. X (main financial element), Admiral Penistone (Gunnery Expert: acquainted with China: retired under a cloud from the Navy: the Admiral has a smaller financial interest), Sir Wilfrid Denny (formerly of the Chinese Customs Service) and Holland (who does the "transactions on the spot"). Holland is naturally unready to discuss his business with the police.

2. The Admiral wants to increase his financial holding—in other words to oust Mr. X. He is in negotiation with Sir Wilfrid and Holland to that end.

3. Sir Wilfrid is reluctant; he refuses to move openly and warns Mr. X secretly.

4. Mr. X, already suspicious of the Admiral and wishing to keep an eye on his doings, has persuaded his mistress to go as French maid to Elma Fitzgerald.

5. When the Admiral moves to Rundel Croft: (a) Sir Wilfrid is afraid Mr. X will think he too is letting him down; (b) the "French maid" discovers that just across the river lives the husband whom she deserted ten years ago. She clears out, and tells Mr. X why.

6. Sir Wilfrid reports to Mr. X that the Admiral is trying to arrange a meeting of the three partners. Holland apparently has agreed. Sir Wilfrid is told to agree also and to get the meeting held at some "neutral" place, say near (not on) Fernton Bridge. He is told, moreover, not to let it be known that he has any dealings with Holland and the Admiral.

7. The Admiral will not give his assent to Elma marrying Holland unless Holland falls in with his "commercial" plans, and further agrees to put into the new concern which he hopes to form some of the capital which Elma will acquire. Perhaps he also wants to help in "manipulating" her brother's money. Her brother, always a rolling stone, has disappeared, but has been heard of too recently for his death to be "presumed."

8. Mr. X, informed by Sir Wilfrid of the time and place fixed for the "secret meeting," drives down dressed as a chauffeur and wearing gauntlets. He insists that the "French maid" is to go to the Vicarage and so arrange matters with the Vicar that she can resume her place at Rundel Croft if necessary. He hopes, himself, whilst she is with the Vicar, to get into Rundel Croft (with which he is perfectly familiar, thanks to the "French maid's" account of it) and to extract various documents relating to "Chinese Contracts."

9. While the "French maid" is with the Vicar Mr. X walks down through the garden, intending to cross the river in the Vicar's boat. He meets the Admiral, who has just returned in his boat.

10. The Admiral hustles away after dinner at the Vicarage, because he wants to get Elma home, and then go to his "secret meeting." He tidies up his boat as usual, but finds he has left his pipe at the Vicarage and his cigar-case is empty. He goes and gets his coat, meaning to *walk* to the bridge; but it is practically as quick to cross to the Vicarage, get his pipe and walk on from there. (According to the Map, the distances are practically identical.)

11. Mr. X and the Admiral talk. Mr. X produces the evening paper with its Chinese news. The Admiral, conscious of the "secret meeting," is somewhat uncomfortable. They retire to the summer-house. There, there is not only the

Vicar's hat but also the knife. The talk ends in a quarrel
and Mr. X stabs the Admiral. The time is about 11 p.m.

12. Mr. X reflects that his arrangements hold good for a
murder as much as for anything else. He has even told Sir
Wilfrid, as it happens, to use the Admiral's name when he
asks for Holland at his hotel—which may make it appear
that the Admiral was alive and in Whynmouth at 11 p.m.

13. He finds the key of the french window, crosses in
the Admiral's boat (leaving the body in the summer-
house), collects the papers from the study, locks up again
and re-crosses in the Admiral's boat—by mistake dropping
the key. He assumes that he has dropped it in the river, he
dares not strike a light to make sure.

14. He waits in the car. When the "French maid" re-
appears (and he is, of course, quite satisfied that neither
she nor the Vicar will talk about the meeting) he tells her
to drive gently on alone to Fernton Bridge and thence
towards Rundel Croft. When he is sure that the Vicarage
is asleep, he carries the dead body down to the Vicar's
boat, leaving the knife with (not in) the body and adding
the Vicar's hat to the cargo. His original intention is to set
the boat adrift, but then he realises that the river is
probably tidal and that the boat might not drift out to
sea. So he decides to leave things as they are. (The body
therefore has been "under cover" until nearly one o'clock;
and the blood has ceased to flow before the body is put in
the boat.) Mr. X crosses again in the Admiral's boat
(which he fastens up wrongly), makes his way through the
grounds of Rundel Croft to the car, and so departs with
the "French maid."

15. The non-appearance of the Admiral perturbs both
Holland and Sir Wilfrid. They wait a considerable time,
and then Sir Wilfrid goes home (next morning, when Mr.
X telephones to "enquire" about the meeting, he hurries

up to London). Holland decides to have it out with the
Admiral then and there. He starts to walk to Rundel Croft,
sees a car standing near the entrance and decides to go
round *via* the Vicarage. For the whole business is somewhat fishy and he has no wish to be seen. His anxiety not
to attract notice retards his progress. To his horror he finds
the body in the Vicar's boat; it is by now about two
o'clock. He realises his danger—he has no alibi; the Admiral may have said he was going to see him by the bridge;
there is the question of the will and the marriage. He
thinks things out deliberately. The tide will turn, he supposes, fairly soon and start to run up the river—"away
from the bridge," as it were. He must wait for the turn.
The waiting is anxious work; he gets more and more
jumpy, and more and more anxious to clear off. At about
three o'clock the tide is slackening. He cuts the painter—
not because he cannot reach to untie the knot, but because
to cut it suits his state of mind—it *seems* quicker than untying a knot. Then he thinks of finger-prints and throws
the knife into the river.

16. Holland's plan is now to try and make it appear that
he spent the night at his hotel. He must see Elma as soon
as he can reasonably appear at Rundel Croft. He is there
before the Inspector. Emery has to be "drilled" a bit; also
Jennie Merton. The delay when the Inspector calls is thus
explained. Elma and Holland agree that there is no evidence but theirs that the Admiral hesitated to consent to
their marriage; Holland was accepted as her fiancé. So the
"will" motive will not be so serious; anyhow it can be
argued that Elma is likely soon to inherit her brother's
money. If they get married she cannot be made to give evidence against her husband—and only she can say what the
Admiral meant to do after dinner at the Vicarage. They
have already got a licence—for the circumstances (the

gun-running, the Admiral's "negotiation," etc.) have suggested the need to be ready to marry at short notice. They go off to London.

17. The "favourite frock" was never hidden. But it was a favourite, and therefore suitable for the occasion in London: and for the same reason Elma hesitated to let her new and untried maid pack it for her in the suit-case. She folded it herself, put it on a shelf and packed it on top after seeing the Inspector. As to her regard for her appearance—she (like some others) took more trouble before strangers than before intimates (she had no time in the Inspector's case, of course). Her "acting" during the interview was what one would expect—partly good and partly bad.

18. As for the Vicar: when first the police come, the thing uppermost in his mind is that nothing must come out about his wife's visit. He has his sons to think of, above all (almost his first thought). His hat can have nothing to do with it; he will stick to his story; he knows nothing about the murder and cannot be connected with it—and if the visit of the "French maid" comes out, there might be an added complication. And then, after he has maintained the "all quiet after ten-fifteen" story, comes the loss of the knife, and his discovery of ominous stains in his summer-house. He will water the garden, and if he misdirects the hose-pipe, it will merely be a sign of his worldly incompetence.

Chapter VII

By Dorothy L. Sayers

JOHN MARTIN FITZGERALD of Winchester, solicitor, married, in 1888, Mary Penistone, and had by her two surviving children, Walter, born in 1889 and Elma, born in 1898.

In 1909, Walter, aged twenty, got into some kind of trouble with his father and left the country. He went to China and got a job as a clerk with a tobacco company in Hong Kong, where, being idle and vicious, though handsome and attractive, he got into the opium-smuggling business.

The assistant-commissioner in the Chinese customs was a man called Wilfrid Denny, who had got into difficulties through having an extravagant wife, and was heavily in debt to a big Chinese money-lender. Denny soon found that the price of this "accommodation" was to be the turning of a blind eye to the passage of opium through the customs. This brought him into contact with Walter, who soon saw himself in a position to blackmail the weak and foolish Denny. Denny was then about forty years of age.

In 1911, the Captain in command of the cruiser *Huntingdonshire*, stationed at Hong Kong, was Captain Penistone, young Fitzgerald's uncle, and to get the opium through meant getting it past Penistone. The previous Captain had been fairly easy to diddle, but Penistone was alert and incorruptible. He was then forty-three, a vigorous, jovial man, well liked by his crew, and a smart officer. As it was impossible to square him, it was necessary to get rid of him. Walter, in collusion with Denny, used his knowledge of his uncle's character to involve him in some discreditable affair (e.g., with a woman, or in connection with the ill-treatment of natives). Penistone, though really innocent, is made to appear at the very least extremely indiscreet, and is advised to send in his papers.

Penistone never knew who was at the bottom of his trouble—and did not even know that Walter was in Hong Kong, but he became a changed and soured man. During the War he is permitted to rejoin and retires finally with the rank of Admiral in recognition of his services, but he still broods on what he might have done but for "the trouble," and when the War is over he determines to get to the bottom of the business. He energetically collects information about everything and everybody who might possibly have been concerned in the plot against him—a job made more difficult by the post-war confusion in China. The thing has become almost a monomania.

Meanwhile, Walter continues his illicit activities, and in 1914 commits himself to a forgery. The War breaks out just in time to rescue him from arrest. He manages to get away and joins up. But the warrant is still out against him, and if he survives it seems likely that he will be haled up and sent to a long term of penal servitude. He therefore makes arrangements to disappear. He sends home a letter of the "Dear Father-I-have-neglected-you-all-but-hope-I-am-now-forgiven-and-have-turned-over-a-new-leaf - and-am-doing-my-duty" type, enclosing, in case of accident, a will drawn in favour of Elma.

After the Loos show in September, 1915, Walter deserts and disappears. He is "missing, supposed killed." Old Fitzgerald, who has long repented of his harshness to "dear Walter, poor boy," is now getting very doddery and ill. Having come into money, he redrafts his will, but retains the dispositions made some years previously in favour of Walter and Elma, for Walter has turned up once and he may turn up again. (See Chapter VII.)

Meanwhile, Walter has contrived to turn up somewhere else with somebody else's papers. He keeps secretly in touch with Elma, to whom he is still the wonderful and beloved "big brother"—a radiant memory of childhood. If Walter is in trouble, it must be the fault of some wicked person who got him into it. Walter takes Elma into his confidence. The idea is to prove his death, when Elma will come into

his share of the money and hand it over to him in his new
name.

Old Fitzgerald dies in 1916. Nothing much can be done
till 1918–19, when the British prisoners of war are re-
leased and the "presumption" of the death of missing com-
batants is recognised by the courts.

Everything is put in trim for "presuming" the death of
Walter, when an inconvenient person turns up who knew
Walter when he first joined the Army and states positively
that he saw him alive in Buda-Pesth in 1918. He does not
know the name under which Walter was then passing, but
insists that he cannot be mistaken in the man. Under the
circumstances, the court refuses to presume death. Note:
It is only *now* that it becomes necessary for Elma to marry
in order to provide Walter with money. See Chapter VII
as regards her present opportunities. This is when the forgery business comes to light (see Chapter VII).

Time goes on. Walter, now known as Mr. X, is living
rapidly and expensively abroad—chiefly on his wits and by
exploiting his charm of manner. In 1920 he seduces a Mrs.
Mount, who is staying at Monte Carlo with some friends,
and has some money of her own. Walter is at a low ebb, or
he would not be bothered with the parson's wife. Having
sucked her dry, he abandons her to get on as best she can.
She takes a post as a maid in Paris.

Life becomes increasingly sordid and difficult for Walter. Then one day he hears that Denny has retired to England with a knighthood and a pension. Splendid idea! He
will blackmail Denny! He does so—knowing that Denny
dare not expose him for fear that the old Chinese story
will come out, when pop goes Denny's pension.

Walter's line is: pay me, and I keep quiet. Stop the payments and I blow the gaff. I am so damned hard up that I
don't really care a curse whether I go to prison or not, but

you will be for it, my lad! The miserable Denny pays up: all his savings go—the proceeds of the smuggling business, and he has to go on paying Walter out of his modest pension.

Meanwhile the Admiral (now living in Cornwall), in the course of his energetic enquiries, has at last got upon the track of the old Hong Kong business. A man called Arthur Holland, who, under cover of a vague export business, does a certain amount of secret enquiry in China (he is probably .mixed up with Chinese post-war politics), gives him some useful information. The Admiral is beginning to suspect that (*a*) Walter is alive, (*b*) Walter was concerned in his disgrace, (*c*) Denny had something to do with it also.

Walter is now becoming bolder. He has grown a beard and changed his appearance, and one day he turns up on Denny's doorstep. Denny must now keep him and establish him firmly in his new personality as Mr. X. If not—up goes the monkey!

Denny is harried from pillar to post. He *knows* (from what Walter has told him in moments of expansiveness), however, that there is one person in England whom "Mr. X" does not want to meet, and that is Mr. Mount. Mr. Mount knows enough about "Mr. X" *as* Mr. X to make any place too hot to hold him. Denny consults Crockford, discovers that Mount has taken a living at Lingham and takes a house in the same neighbourhood. Walter, returning from a trip abroad, finds that Denny has fled to sanctuary. He tries to dislodge Denny, but Denny sits tight.

But now a new source of trouble begins. Denny writes in agitation to Walter. He has heard from the Admiral. The Admiral—after all these years!—is most tiresomely starting to ask questions about that dead-and-buried business in Hong Kong. He looks as though he really suspected something. Denny is doing his best to be amiable and non-committal, but it is all dreadfully difficult.

Walter feels that a little spying ought to be done. He hunts up his former mistress, Mrs. Mount, over whom he still exerts great influence, and makes her go as French maid to his sister, under the name of Célie Blanc. She is to find out what she can about who comes to the house and what the Admiral is doing, and to act as liaison between Walter and Elma. For the Admiral, suspecting that Elma knows where Walter is, is beginning to keep her under strict control and supervise her correspondence.

To Elma, of course, Walter is the poor, wronged boy who never gets a chance. She is anxious to get him his money, by fair means or foul. As the scheme to prove the death was a failure, she now wants to make over her own share of the money to him. Fortunately, Holland has fallen desperately in love with her sulky beauty. Though temperamentally disinclined to marriage, she is keen to marry Holland to get the money. The Admiral has a pretty shrewd idea of this, and therefore tries to oppose the marriage. Elma, of course, does not confide in Holland—he is a tool of the Admiral's. Everybody is in a conspiracy to keep dear Walter out of his own. She therefore breaks off open correspondence with Walter, and treats the Admiral with the contempt he deserves.

Holland has been told by the Admiral that if he marries Elma, she will probably send all her money to this scamp of a brother. But Holland, being in love, says he wants Elma, not her money. The Admiral says: "You won't get my consent." Holland replies: "I don't care." But Elma *does* care. The control of the money is what she is marrying him for. The situation drags on. Elma alternates between encouraging Holland and rebuffing him. If she seems too affectionate he will urge marriage without the Admiral's consent; if she appears too mercenary he may get put off altogether. As he is the only man whom she has much opportunity of meeting nowadays, and no other suitor seems forthcoming, she must keep him on the lead if possible.

Mrs. Mount is a weak sort of woman, still infatuated by Walter. I think she knows him to be Fitzgerald all right, but supposes, like Elma, that he has been deeply wronged. Walter is quite cocksure that she is completely under his thumb, and, as a bait, has promised to marry her if she succeeds in helping him to get the money.

Very well, then. The Admiral comes to the conclusion that the one person who really can help him to find Walter and disentangle the Chinese business is Denny. Making one of his lightning decisions, he takes Rundel Croft, and carries the whole family off there, bag and baggage.

This is dreadfully disconcerting to Walter, and Mrs. Mount is appalled when she finds herself—not only in the same village as, but actually next door to, her former husband. (I don't think Walter mentioned to Mrs. Mount where her husband was living—why should he?—and by the time Mrs. Mount has been able to tell Walter where they are going, the move has taken place. Or it is just possible that Mrs. Mount *did* know, but deliberately didn't tell Walter at first, because she was bitten with the idea of getting a sight of her two boys. Perhaps this latter idea makes the thing more credible and more suitable to Mrs. Mount's weakly emotional character.)

The Vicar, of course, sees and recognises his wife, and is greatly shocked. He has an interview with her in private, in which he regains a good deal of his old influence over her, as a priest, at least, if not as a man. He asks her kindly about Walter (whom he, of course, knows only as X)—is she still living with him? She has never asked for a divorce and he, the Vicar, would never think of divorcing her on his own account, as it is against his principles. To him, she is always his wife; if she *asks* for divorce, he will not let his religious convictions stand in her way. She is touched by his real consideration for her, and admits that X has behaved badly to her, but that she now has hopes that he may marry her after all, if his "affairs" can be put right. Mrs. Mount (always readily accessible to the latest influence) becomes very much troubled after this interview. Moreover, from what she hears at the Admiral's, she begins to fear that she is being mixed up in something much more wicked and dangerous than the restitution of a persecuted man to his "rights." After all, she can by this time have few illusions as to Walter's personal character. She works herself up to going to the Vicar again, and telling him what she knows of the story, under the seal of confession.

The Vicar is stern with her. It is absurd to suppose that he can give her absolution. She is not repentant—she is merely frightened. She is deceiving her employer and engaging in a conspiracy to defeat the ends of justice. Her duty is to break with Walter and make a clean breast of everything to the Admiral.

Mrs. Mount characteristically does neither one thing nor the other. She won't go on with it and she daren't tell the Admiral—she simply leaves Rundel Croft, merely telling Walter that her husband has recognised her and that the situation is impossible. Walter is annoyed, but recognises that she is no longer to be trusted. He tells her not to be a fool. Why shouldn't Elma marry Holland? Nothing more is contemplated. He gets out of her an exact description of the Admiral's house and the Vicarage, etc.

Two weeks later, Walter hears from Denny. The Admiral is getting dangerously near to the truth. "Old friends"

have been visiting him: something has been discovered.
The Admiral must be silenced.

Walter agrees. His plan is to:

(*a*) Kill the Admiral.
(*b*) Manufacture proof of his (Walter's) death at
    some period *subsequent* to old Fitzgerald's death.
(*c*) Let Elma inherit *Walter's* share of the money
    under *Walter's* will of 1915.

He and Denny will then be safe, and *all* the money will
be, to all intents and purposes, in Walter's hands. If Denny
is good, he shall get a share of it. Walter then gets Denny
to convey a letter to Elma. He says he has found means to
obtain a hold over the Admiral and force him into giving
consent to Elma's marriage with Holland. She is to say
nothing of this to Holland (who might high-mindedly
object to these methods), but she is to tell Holland that
she is ready to marry him, Admiral or no Admiral. Holland is to get a special licence, and she will come up to
town to marry him on the morning of August 10th.

The plan is then laid to murder the Admiral, steal the
compromising papers, and thus leave everything happy and
comfortable all round.

The Murder

1. Holland comes down unexpectedly by the eight-fifty
to see the Admiral. He is worried by the idea that he will
injure Elma's prospects by marrying her, and wants to give
the Admiral a final chance of consenting before it is too
late. He rings up from the Lord Marshall and is answered
by Mrs. Emery. He hears that Elma and the Admiral are
out to dinner and will probably not be back till pretty late.

This is tiresome, but he must do what he can. He will stay the night and make one more effort to see the Admiral but, if not, he will simply go up to town next morning and carry out his plan. He dines at the Lord Marshall and then goes out for a walk; while doing so he is seen by Denny.

2. Denny has told the Admiral that he has found out something the Admiral would like to know about Walter and the Chinese business. He has got hold of a man who knows something. This man is "in trouble" and cannot appear openly, but if the Admiral will come down after dinner to an old deserted boat-house near Fernton Bridge, Denny and "the man" will meet him there. The rendezvous is fixed for 11.15 sharp. The Admiral swallows the bait eagerly. Walter (through Denny) has told Elma about all this, though to her, of course, "the man" is the mysterious person who has got "the hold" over the Admiral and is going to squeeze the consent to the marriage out of him. The Admiral, equally of course, thinks Elma is quite in the dark about it all.

3. The plan for the murder is this: Denny is to go on foot to the old boat-house, meet the Admiral at 11.15 and hold him in talk. Meantime, Walter goes to the Lord Marshall, arriving about 11.15. There, with his beard and family resemblance to his uncle the Admiral, he will easily be mistaken for him in the dim light. He is to leave some sort of message. (When Walter hears from Denny that Holland is in Whynmouth, they seize on this circumstance. Walter is to ask for *him*, suggesting that Holland may be involved in the business if anything goes wrong with their plans.) Thus they will establish the fact that the Admiral intended to travel by the 11.25 train. Walter will then take Denny's car to Fernton Bridge (about three minutes by car) and, while Denny holds up the Admiral, Walter will bash him savagely about the head with a blunt instru-

ment. The body is then to be taken to the level crossing,
which is the kind worked by a lever from the signal-box.
All this should not take more than about seven minutes
(say, one minute for the bashing, three minutes from boat-
house to car, three minutes to level crossing—this allows
him to drive at only thirty-five miles an hour over one
and a quarter of a mile or thereabouts—he could really go
much faster for that brief distance). At about 11.22 they
will carry the body on to the *down* line, through the side
wickets, trusting to the darkness. At 11.24 the down express is due to pass through, not stopping at Whynmouth.
With any luck it will smash up the Admiral and the conclusion will be drawn that he met his death by accident,
through passing the level crossing through the wickets as
a short cut from the Lord Marshall to the UP platform
(see Map).

Walter will then go on to Rundel Croft to see Elma,
who is expecting him. He will explain that the meeting has
taken place, and that, in consequence of what has transpired, the Admiral has gone up to town, but that, before
going, he has given consent to the marriage. Walter will
then hand Elma the typewritten consent, which he has
forged for the purpose. Elma is to carry on and marry
Holland at once, since Walter needs money desperately
and there is no time to be lost.

4. This beautiful plan goes wrong. What actually happens is this. Mrs. Mount, who, what with the Vicar and
one thing and another, has begun to suspect Walter of
worse things than she ever thought him capable of, has
started to do a little detecting on her own account. I think
she probably intercepts some communication from Denny
referring to the date and time of the meeting of the Admiral. She is living in London either with Walter or in
some place selected by him. She discovers (*a*) that Walter

has no genuine intention of ever marrying her, having made other arrangements, and (*b*) that there is a plan to do away with the Admiral that same night. She determines to warn the Admiral. There is no train she can catch (the 8.50 has gone and the express doesn't stop at Whynmouth), so she hires a car and starts out for Lingham.

She does not go straight to Rundel Croft, preferring not to face Walter, who may be there (she does not know *details* of the plot). She will try to get hold of the Vicar and warn *him*. In the village she directs the chauffeur to stop at the Vicarage gate and wait for her. She will not be many minutes. She reaches the Vicarage at 10.40. (N.B.— This is earlier than the constable said in Chapter VI, but he only said *about* 10.45.) She does not like to ring the bell (the boys! the servants!)—perhaps the Vicar is down the garden having his bed-time pipe (she remembers his habits). She creeps down to the summer-house. Nobody there —only the Vicar's hat and Peter's knife on the table. She wonders what to do. Shall she throw stones at the Vicar's bedroom window? (But which is it?) Or shall she take the boat and go boldly across to Rundel Croft? She is playing with the open knife, and it occurs to her that if she has to face Walter on her own it may be a useful weapon. Suddenly she hears the unmistakable noise of oars in the rowlocks. She hurries down to the boat-house and in the summer dusk sees the Admiral starting off down the river. He must be going to the fatal rendezvous! In the summer-house she has snatched up what she thinks is her black calfskin bag, but is really the Vicar's hat. She pulls the Vicar's boat in by the rope at the stern, but, owing to the strong stream and the stiffness of the new painter, has some difficulty in unhitching the painter from the mooring-post. She therefore cuts the painter with Peter's knife, and I think that at this point she drops the knife into the river, to be subsequently found. She gets the rowlocks into place and starts off in pursuit of the Admiral, who by this time is well away down the river. (She may try to hail him, but the Admiral will probably pay no attention—or she may be afraid of causing a disturbance. The boys! the servants!)

5. *The Coat.* The Admiral has decided to go by river to the meeting. To get the car out means making a racket, and he does not walk because he has a game leg as a result of the War. (This will make it O.K. about his not being supposed capable of walking to Whynmouth in the time, by the way.) He waits in the boat-house till Elma is well out of the way and reflects that he had better take a coat with him, since he will get hot rowing and the interview in the old boat-house may be a long one. He goes up to the house and fetches the coat, and returning re-locks the french window. He then gets the boat out. He reckons that with the tide setting strongly down the river, he will make Fernton Bridge well within the half-hour, being a vigorous old boy at the oars.

6. Mrs. Mount is not able to make such good time down the river as he does. She used to boat in the old days with the Vicar, but she is out of practice. Actually, the Admiral makes Fernton Bridge in twenty-five minutes, arriving at 11.10, to find Denny waiting for him. Mrs. Mount arrives five minutes later. She sees the boat but no Admiral. She moors at the rotten old raft and creeping round the boat-house, which is derelict and water-logged, sees Denny and the Admiral behind it. Now, Denny has the grimmest doubts about Walter. He thinks it quite likely that Walter may do *him* in, as well as the Admiral. He has therefore come armed with a knife—a relic of Chinese days, no doubt. Mrs. Mount calls out to the Admiral: "Take care, Admiral! They mean to murder you." The Admiral (who

has the grimmest doubts about Denny!) turns menacingly on Denny. Denny loses his silly head, whips out the knife and stabs the Admiral. Mrs. Mount shrieks and collapses.

7. At this distressing moment, enter Walter, having carried out his part of the programme. He is aghast to find the Admiral dead, with a wound in him which by no stretch of imagination could be inflicted by a railway engine—and Mrs. Mount having hysterics in the background! He is furious with both Mrs. Mount and Denny. They wrangle in angry whispers. Denny says he couldn't help it. Walter says he is a blasted idiot. Denny says, couldn't they go on and carry out the plan—perhaps the dagger-wound won't be noticed in the general mess-up. While they waste time in recriminations and in subduing Mrs. Mount—who is showing every disposition to scream and attract people on the road—a distant roar and rumble is heard, and the 11.24 thunders over the railway bridge. It is too late. The only other train that night is the 11.25 and there is no time to do anything about that.

8. Now what are they to do? Here they are with two boats, a car, a woman and a corpse. The easiest thing would be to let the Admiral float peacefully out to sea, but, with the tide running as it is, he would be down at the harbour in half an hour. Somebody would find him—and then there would be enquiries at Rundel Croft, and it is urgently necessary that Walter should go up there and collect the papers. Then, too, the search would at once be made up-river; blood and footprints would be discovered at Fernton Bridge. Much better to suggest that the crime was committed elsewhere. The Vicar's boat—the Vicar's hat— why not take the whole caboodle back to Rundel Croft and leave the Vicar to explain things as best he can? Walter will take the car to the house and get the papers and leave the forged permit-to-marry. Mrs. Mount and the

miserable Denny must get the boats back as best they can, stream or no stream.

9. "By the way," says Walter, "how did Mrs. Mount get here?" After a certain amount of harrying and bullying he gets the story out of her. Damn it! That chauffeur must be got rid of! Here they are—it is already twelve o'clock (for there has been a good deal of argument). No time to lose. Walter returns to the car and drives along to the Vicarage. The car has gone! This is puzzling and tiresome, but it is all the more imperative to make haste. He returns over Fernton Bridge and drives to Rundel Croft, concealing the car somewhere off the road. Here he gets in through the french window with Elma's key, goes into the study and starts hunting for the papers.

10. *The Car.* Meanwhile the hired chauffeur has been getting impatient. His fare said she would only be a few minutes and here it is getting on for an hour. Nobody seems to have opened the door to her. The Vicarage is as dark as a tomb. He gets a strong impression that he has been bilked. He hoots violently several times and then walks up to the side-door, which is the first he comes to, and hammers on it. The Vicar, who sleeps over the side-door (servants and boys on the river side of house) looks out. What is the matter? Some parishioner dying? The chauffeur's reply is unintelligible—to him—but he thinks he had better come down and see what it is all about. Chauffeur says, Will the lady be long, because he has got to get back to his garage, he has, for another job? Vicar says, What lady?—Lady what came in here. Describes lady. Is he going to get his money? Because, if not—shows every intention of making a disturbance. The Vicar, who with extreme uneasiness has recognised the description of the lady, does some quick thinking. At all costs a disturbance

must be prevented. He makes some sort of explanation
and pays the man off, after taking his name and the address of the garage. Then he returns and ponders. Where
did his wife go? Why did she come? Perhaps she is over at
Rundel Croft. He goes down to the boat-house. His boat
is out. She must have gone across in it. He shakes his head
over this. Obviously the poor woman is still under that
scoundrel's thumb. What will she do when she returns and
finds the car gone? Obviously he must wait and explain
what has happened. He will drive her himself if necessary.
He returns and dresses; then sits in his bedroom to watch
the road. (Why does not he watch the boat-house? Because, if Walter returns with her there may be trouble and
possibly a noise—and then, the boys! the servants!—In
any case she *must* return to where she left the car, so he
will wait at the high-road side of the house.)

11. Denny and Mrs. Mount are now left to bring the
boats back. They swab up the blood behind the old boat-
house as best they can. Mrs. Mount, threatened by Denny
whom she has just seen kill a man, helps without protest.
Denny puts the Admiral's coat on him—(or he put it on
himself when he arrived)—and stuffs in the pocket the
evening paper which Walter or Denny brought to the
meeting. (It was purchased in Whynmouth that night or
Walter brought it from town.) At about one o'clock they
start with the slack of the tide. They put the body in the
Vicar's boat, unshipping the rowlocks, and putting Denny's
coat over it to hide the face. This explains why the body
is not wet with the dew. The Vicar's boat with the body in
it is tied by the painter to the stern of the Admiral's boat
and towed along. The incompetent Denny naturally ties
it in one of those landsman's knots which nothing but a
marlin-spike will ever undo, especially as the painter has
got wet and the new rope has swollen with the water. With

a boat to tow and two incompetent oarsmen, they do not
make very good time, and the ghastly dawn is breaking
before they get up to Rundel Croft. Walter is there, chaf-
ing at the delay. He has locked the window and brought
the key, but in helping the idiotic Denny alongside he
drops the key. It falls, as he thinks, into the mud, but
actually into the Admiral's boat and is kicked under the
boards by Denny. Anyway, they can't search now. It is
getting light. Damn Denny and his inextricable knot!
They hew the rope off with Denny's knife and push the
boat with the body adrift. It dawdles out into the river
and fetches up against the opposite bank. Later, the tide
frees it and carries it on up the river. They hack and tear
away the remains of the rope from the Admiral's boat,
having taken it into the boat-house wrong end first. Then
they return to Whynmouth in Denny's car, dropping
Walter and Mrs. Mount. Walter retrieves his own car from
wherever he left it when he came from London and takes
Mrs. Mount away in it—and if that poor woman comes
out of this business alive I shall be very much surprised.
(N.B.—Or Walter's car can be used throughout. Or Walter and Mrs. Mount may return to town by the milk-train.
In any case these movements of cars should be trace-
able.)

12. *Holland*. What has he been doing? He *may*, of
course, have been innocently in bed and asleep, but I think
it would be more fun if he wasn't. I think that, after putting out his boots to be cleaned, he thought he would have
another shot at the Admiral. He went out, unseen by the
Boots, sometime between ten and eleven (not too early, or
the family will not have returned from the Vicarage). He
strolls two and a half miles leisurely in his rubber-soled
canvas shoes. He reaches Rundel Croft say at 11.15 (Admiral at boat-house, Elma upstairs). House dark. They are

not in yet. He goes down to the boat-house. No boat. They
are still at the Vicarage. Good. He goes for a stroll down
the road, keeping an eye on the house. No lights yet. Very
odd. He muses on love and marriage and recites the Ode
to the Nightingale to fill up time. House still dark. Can he
have missed them? He goes down to the boat-house again.
Boat still out. No lights anywhere. Past midnight. Well, he
can hardly knock them up at this time of night. Hullo!
Somebody has gone in by the drawing-room window!
Light in the study. He distinctly sees the Admiral's bearded
profile (really Walter's, of course, with the family resemblance) in the study. Curiouser and curiouser. Where is
the boat? He goes up to the house. The curtains have now
been drawn in the study, but there is a light in the
drawing-room now. He taps. Elma opens the window. She
seems very much startled at seeing him. Can he see the
Admiral? No—Oh, no—but there is no need. The Admiral
has consented to the marriage. Look! Here is the written
consent. Then, says Holland, there is no need to go to London to-morrow. Oh, yes—let them do it now, as it is all
settled. In fact, the Admiral has only given his consent on
the understanding that she never darkens his french windows again. Has he, by Jove! He'll tell the blighter what
he thinks of him. Please, *no!* that will only make things
worse. *Please* do as she tells him. Of course, darling—and
she does love him, doesn't she?—Oh, of course, but please
go now. Very well—but she is looking so beautiful to-
night. Very well. Good night, sweetheart.

Exit Holland to ramble round in a dream of ecstasy till
he is ashamed to knock up the Lord Marshall. Instead, he
drifts round the harbour (where he may be seen if necessary) till six, when he goes in, unseen by Boots who is occupied in the bar. (Observe that Holland will now be

ready to swear that he saw the Admiral alive after midnight.)

When the news of the Admiral's death comes along, he
is worried. He must see Elma. He goes to Rundel Croft,
thinking that, as things are, she won't want to go through
with the marriage. He is delayed by Inspector Rudge, and
when he gets free learns that Elma has gone to town as per
schedule. He hastens after her, and, feeling that there is
going to be a lot of trouble about this business, marries her.
As his wife he can protect her. He sees, naturally, that it is
impossible for them to stay in town as she suggests—they
will have to go back for the inquest and funeral—but she
is upset, and for the moment he humours her. (Note: He
says nothing to Rudge about his midnight excursion, fear-
ing to be detained. He will get hold of Elma first. Indeed,
he may possibly at this point suspect Elma himself.)

13. *Elma.* The emphasis laid on the time spent in calling
Elma and in dressing seems to me a little exaggerated.
When she hears of the death, she is horrified. She can hardly
help suspecting Walter of some guilty knowledge, but
hopes, naturally, that the crime was committed by the
other unknown man after Walter left them. She feels faint
and sick—but will Emery bring her a cup of tea and she
will try to pull herself together. Emery does so. Yes—she is
better now—tell the Inspector she will be down in a quarter of an hour. She thinks over what she had better say.
Nobody knows about Walter. Holland evidently thinks it
was the Admiral who came in at midnight. She had better
say nothing. She hopes Holland will say nothing without
consulting her—in fact, he is probably already in town.
She must tell Jennie to pack. Her white frock will do to
be married in—she looks at it! Heavens! A smear of blood
on the waist. Walter's hand or coat must have made the
mark when he greeted her.

Then Walter——! Horrible. She hastily hides the dress, gets into her clothes and comes down.

Time to break news	.	.	.	.	.	5 minutes
Time to prepare tea	.	.	.	.	5	"
Time to drink tea	.	.	.	.	5	"
Time to examine dress and prepare story	.	.	.	.	.	5	"
Time to dress	.	.	.	.	5	"
					25	"

Elma will, of course, leave Holland to suppose that it *was* the Admiral he saw in the study, since otherwise she will have to explain about Walter. But she will have difficulty in explaining why she let Rudge suppose that she last saw the Admiral at ten o'clock.

14. *The Vicar.* Goes out early in the morning. No one has come to the car. What has happened? Finds his wife's bag in summer-house and marks of high heels on path leading from house to summer-house, also on flower-bed near summer-house. (Note: It is the path between the summer-house and boat-house that is of brick. The other garden paths will be of gravel.) Anxious to avoid scandal, he takes a rake and fork and digs these over.

The weather has been hot and dry, but there has been rain on and off for a week or so before. (Note: There has been no *prolonged* drought, or Neddy Ware would have had something to say about its effect on the height of the river, which appears to be at least normal.) Therefore the earth, when turned up, looks suspiciously black and moist. After hearing of the murder the Vicar cannot help suspecting his wife of complicity or guilty knowledge at least. He learns the difference between preaching and practising the religious man's duty to the State. He conceals the bag and waters the dug-up patches.

He *must* now find his wife. He *must* know whether she is guilty or not (his boys' mother hanged for murder!!!). He hopes that she is not guilty and that by proving to her that he is aware of her presence that night in his summer-house, he may induce her to reveal what she knows about Walter. He cannot, of course, supply this information himself, since it is impossible for him to reveal what he heard in confession. He knows the address of the garage from which she hired the car. As soon as he possibly can, without arousing the suspicions of the police, he must get upon her track.

15. The Admiral's pipe was left on the Vicar's table during his visit. It has no significance in the plot except that, when coupled with Holland's story of having seen the Admiral at Rundel Croft after midnight, it may serve to throw fresh suspicion on the Vicar.

CHAPTER VIII

By Ronald A. Knox

CHAPTER I. The salient feature of the situation—none of the later contributors have dealt with it—seems to me the fact that the body is in a boat at all. A murder in a boat is very unlikely; but why put a body into a boat, when it would be simpler to throw it into the stream? Unless, indeed, a very elaborate frame-up is intended, the position of the boat on the river having been artificially engineered so as to cast suspicion of murder upon some innocent person.

If Canon Whitechurch has any murderer in view at all,

Ware should be the man—we must assume that Canon Whitechurch respects the honour of the cloth. *Ceteris paribus,* in a modern detective story the first person named is likely to be the criminal.

In favour of Ware's guilt, it must be observed that he claims not to recognise Penistone's corpse, though he had met him long before on the China station. It does not seem probable that Ware would not know Penistone by sight after even a month's residence, in the height of the summer, since Ware was always fishing, and Penistone kept a boat. Against Ware's guilt, the fact that Penistone has come to settle next door to him forms an improbable coincidence, if we are to suppose that Ware harboured an old grudge against him.

I once laid it down that no Chinaman should appear in a detective story. I feel inclined to extend the rule so as to apply to residents in China. It appears that Admiral Penistone, Sir W. Denny, Walter Fitzgerald, Ware, and Holland are all intimate with China, which seems overdoing it.

Chapter 2. I imagine that the Coles meant to incriminate Elma, though they may have had their eye on Denny.

Chapter 3. Wade seems to suspect Elma; the packing up or concealing of her evening things points this way. (Why *did* she dress up to meet the Vicar? This must be considered.) The words "And if it was . . ." on p. 49 seem more designed to incriminate Ware; so does Appleton's theory of the murder having taken place up-stream.

Does dew form on boats floating in rivers? The encyclopædia gives me no help.

Chapter 4. Mrs. Christie seems suspicious of Denny; he is hard up, Penistone's change of residence is attributed to a desire to be near him, and, according to Mrs. Davis, Denny was none too pleased over it. On the ordinary principles of a mystery story, this should mean that Penistone is blackmailing Denny. I cannot find out what is the importance, if any, of the Vicar's runaway wife. She left her husband in 1920, well after the War, so it seems difficult to identify her with Elma, who was with her uncle at that time. How far is Whynmouth from London?

Chapter 5. Rhode seems to be fixing it on Holland. Penistone might have gone to Whynmouth to interview Holland, who met and murdered him, and conveyed him up-stream; afterwards transferring the corpse into the Vicar's boat, and running the other boat in head first. But of course Denny is under suspicion, from the position of his house. And again, Ware's insistence that the murder was committed down-stream might be an effort to exculpate the real criminal, himself. How far up was the river tidal?

Chapter 6. Kennedy seems to point to the Vicar. If not, why was the weapon taken from the Vicarage summer-house? (Unless caught up at random.) And why does the Vicar water the garden so thoroughly, if he is not obliterating footprints? (I take it we are not to fix a juvenile crime on the sons.) I do not understand the woman in the car. If she was Elma, I do not see how she got there. If anybody else, she is a new character, not mentioned in the first five chapters, and therefore on my own principles not the criminal. She might be the Vicar's runaway wife; but it seems a coincidence that she should have happened to pay a call on a night so *accidentée* already.

Chapter 7. I suppose Miss Sayers thinks the Vicar knew something about it all. The length of the rope ought to indicate that the Vicarage boat was twice moored that night, and loosed each time by a cutting of the painter from a position of disadvantage; hence the missing two feet of rope, which should be hanging up somewhere, unless deliberately removed since the murder. The double loosing

of the boat suggests either that there were two separate
plots afoot, or else that there has been a very elaborate
frame-up.

The return of the Hollands, with their story of having
seen Penistone alive after midnight, seems to put a wholly
new complexion on the story; I wish I could discover what.
If the permission to marry was genuine, their motive for
murder ceases, and their motive for hurry is difficult to see.
If they were the murderers, why throw suspicion on themselves by their haste to marry? It all beats me, and I wish
she had not left me to conduct the interview.

Anyhow, this is my solution:

Walter Fitzgerald took strongly after his mother and
could, with make-up, pass as the Admiral, his uncle. It was
probably thus that he managed to shift a peccadillo of his
own in Shanghai on to his uncle's shoulders. The Admiral
suspected this; which is why he collected papers in his desk
calculated to blast Walter's reputation if he reappeared in
Europe. Almost more important, the Admiral held and was
suppressing papers which would have proved Walter's innocence in the matter of forgery, and would have made it
possible for him to reappear in Society. Walter survived the
War, and ran away with Celia Mount, the Vicar's wife, in
1920. Celia, to further his interests, went to act as (French)
maid to Elma, the sister. Elma knew that her brother
meant to recover the papers, but not that he intended to
murder, and thus silence, his uncle. The Admiral came to
Lingham so as to be near Denny, whom he was blackmailing. Celia, finding her husband so close, went to see
him and urged him to divorce her. He refused on conscien-
tious grounds. She left, having taken a wax impression of
the key of the Admiral's desk.

Holland had somehow become an enemy of Walter's in
China. Walter therefore decided to saddle him with what-

ever suspicion attached to the murder. Elma was not in love with Holland, but wanted to marry him so as to get the full control of her own money. Penistone refused his consent, because he suspected Holland, whom he had met in Sir Wilfrid's house, of acting in Sir Wilfrid's interests.

Walter and Celia, on the fatal night, motored down to Lingham. They knew from Elma the plans of the Rundel Croft household. Celia was put down at the Vicarage, where she found the Vicar in the garden, and persuaded him to ferry her across in his boat and detain the Admiral in conversation, while she went into the study and secured the papers "needed to save an innocent man." The Vicar had to cut his painter, owing to the state of the tide. Celia secured the papers, about 10.30; and sent a telephone message as from Elma (who was upstairs, ignorant of her presence) asking Holland to come round at midnight. Meanwhile (the Vicar still talking to the Admiral) Walter has gone to the inn and posed as Penistone, hoping thus to implicate Holland. (It would be found that he had not taken the train, and that Holland had gone out at night; it would be assumed that the murder had taken place, and the body set adrift, at or near Whynmouth. Perhaps the plotters made a mistake about the tides.) Then Walter returned to Rundel Croft, where he either murdered Penistone, or found him murdered by Celia (caught in her act of theft). The Vicar, who was scheduled to keep the Admiral in talk till (say) eleven, was waiting at the boat-house, and ferried Celia across; she told him to go to bed, the chauffeur would pick her up. Actually she returned, stumbling over flower-beds, to the river, cut the painter a second time (she was much shorter than Mount) and re-joined Walter. He, meanwhile, had put Penistone's body into its greatcoat, and thrust a paper into the pocket to suggest that Penistone had really gone to Whynmouth.

He meant to put the body into the Admiral's boat, but imagined that this would be the one moored by its bows; hence actually he put the body in the Vicar's boat (where the hat had been left by accident) and, using the Admiral's boat, towed boat and body out to midstream; then cut adrift. Celia pointed out the mistake when he landed, but it was too late to do anything; Holland's steps were heard on the gravel. Walter rushed into the study and personated the Admiral, showing Holland the forged consent. He left this in an envelope for Elma (who knew it was a forgery); Holland went home, letting himself in by a door he had left unlocked; Walter and Celia got off in their car.

On the discovery of the body, Elma hastened to marry Holland, thinking that Walter was the murderer and she would lose another chance of marrying; Holland hastened to marry Elma, chivalrously, because he thought she would be under suspicion. Denny, hearing (from Emery) that documents had been taken from the desk, dashed up to London to know what was being done with those which compromised him. Mount found the extra coil hanging to the mooring-post, did not understand it, but destroyed it to screen his wife, which was also why he obliterated her footmarks on the bed. The white dress (which had been worn by Elma because she wanted to attract the Vicar, hoping to persuade him to divorce Celia) was taken up to London because it was the nearest thing she had got to a wedding-dress.

The precise time of the murder and the precise distance to which the corpse was towed by Walter are to be settled by the tide experts. Walter wanted to make it look as if the boat had been drifted up with the tide all, or most of, the way from Whynmouth. The key was left in the Admiral's boat by Celia. This was meant to suggest that Peniston had left all locked when he (supposedly) went to Whynmouth; and would have done so but for Walter's confusion of the two boats. Celia had a false key to the french window, as well as to the desk.

The plotters assumed that Holland's story would be disbelieved, and that he would be thought to have murdered Penistone at or near Whynmouth round about eleven o'clock.

CHAPTER IX

By Freeman Wills Crofts

ON THE afternoon before the crime, Walter calls on Celia, whom he has fixed up at the Judd Street hotel. After he leaves, she somehow suspects what is going to be done that night. She is horror-struck and resolves at all costs to save Penistone. She will enlist Mount's help, who, through her confession, knows the circumstances. The five-thirty train has gone, so she travels by the seven to Drychester and motors to the Vicarage. The house seems shut up and before knocking she goes to see if Mount is in the summer-house. While making up her mind to knock, she sees Penistone starting. She grasps the knife and what she thinks is her bag and rushes to the river, shouting as loud as she can. But the Admiral doesn't hear her. She thinks it may be too late if she goes for Mount, so she follows Penistone herself. If desirable, she can have seen (or felt?) the knife in the summer-house. She cannot untie the painter, so runs back for the knife.

She comes on Penistone's boat about half a mile down the river. (If it was at the bridge, there would not be time for Walter to get back to personate Penistone.) There she finds Walter and Denny, and the Admiral already murdered. Denny seems almost out of his mind with fear. She is horrified. She fears Walter is guilty, but she doesn't *know*. They tell her Penistone committed suicide. She doesn't believe it, but she doesn't *know*. Weakly, she takes no step. Walter sends her to his car, which is hidden close by. He and Denny row the boats back and shove both into the Rundel Croft boat-house. Denny waits while Walter goes up and steals the papers—which clear Penistone's character, incidentally revealing the trick Walter and Denny have played on him in China. Walter tells Elma what has happened. She is aghast, but cannot do anything without destroying Walter, of whom she is so fond. She decides to know nothing about what has happened.

Walter has prepared the consent, and this he gives to Holland. When Holland goes, Walter and Denny put the body into the Vicar's boat, as the best thing they can think of, and send the boat adrift. They had intended to throw it into the river, but the Vicar's boat seems a better idea. This putting the boats into the boat-house accounts for the boat's tidal movements, as also the clothing on the body being dry.

Denny then walks home, letting himself in unseen. Walter takes Celia to London, but because he is afraid of her giving the show away he takes her on to Paris till the storm blows over.

It should be explained that Celia took the Vicar's hat by mistake, and therefore left her bag behind. In this bag Mount found the Drychester and London addresses.

Chronology

The dates appear to be as follows:

Monday, 8th August.—New moon.

Tuesday, 9th August.—Penistone dines with Mount. The murder in the evening.

Wednesday, 10th August.—Discovery of body. Rudge investigates up to end of 39 Articles.

Thursday, 11th August.—Rudge reports to his superiors and investigates lives of Rundel Croft household.

Friday, 12th August.—The inquest. Rudge goes to Drychester and London.

Saturday, 13th August.—Rudge finds Judd Street hotel.

Monday, 15th August.—Rudge goes to Drychester and reports to Super.

CHAPTER X

By Edgar Jepson

WALTER is the murderer. He has a beard and strongly resembles his uncle the Admiral, whom he impersonated at the Lord Marshall. After the crime he returns to Rundel Croft, sees his sister, whose help he enlists by means of some explanation that does not give the real facts, is mistaken by Holland for the Admiral, while he is searching for File X, which contains the truth about the Hong Kong incident and Walter's share in it, and then goes upstairs to shave off his dangerous beard in the bathroom. By this means he is able to go unrecognised, and keep in touch with the situation, by posing as the reporter for the *Evening Gazette*.

CHAPTER XI

By Clemence Dane

HERE, roughly, are the points I have made. Célie, the French maid, and the Vicar's wife are one person. She has been living with Walter, the murderer, or at any rate, there is a tie of some sort between them, and she knows enough to make her dangerous. He knows that she has gone down to consult her former husband (or for any purpose anybody likes to invent) and desires to divert suspicion from himself, and on to the Vicar by a second murder; or, alternately thinks that she intends to give him away. Anyway, he follows her down.

She has gone to the Vicarage, found her husband is out, and the maids also. (A genuine accident this: they had been given a day's holiday by the Vicar. He and they have gone to a local flower-show at some distance, or a village outing of some sort.) She has also written to the Hollands to meet her there, for purposes of consultation.

Célie, not knowing that the Vicar's absence is more than temporary, wanders into the garden, and there picks the greengages, then comes back to the house and encounters Walter. There is some sort of an argument. At any rate he murders her, arranging it to look like suicide, and leaves only a few minutes before the Inspector arrives. Walter thinks himself unseen, but later it must transpire that one of the villagers has seen him. He has a perfectly good excuse: he has called to see the Vicar in pursuit of his reporter's duties, and, like everyone else, has found the house empty. The Inspector, however, knows that Célie has been in the garden within ten minutes of his own arrival—the wet greengage stones and the handkerchief—and that therefore she must have encountered Walter, who would have just had time to murder her and leave without running into Rudge.

If more time is needed, the handkerchief and greengage stones can be found lying in the shade and would thus take longer to dry. The other importance of the greengage clue is Rudge's deduction from it, before Walter's recognition by a villager happens, that a woman who strolls cheerfully into a garden and eats greengages is not likely to commit suicide three minutes later. The funeral card is a false clue: it is really written by one of the servants or by the Vicar himself, and is a genuine message to any possible caller. Or it might be a fake message written in the Vicar's handwriting by Walter in order to avoid the discovery of the murder for several hours. I don't know how to explain Elma and Holland's share or non-share in the business. It's quite inexplicable to me. So I have gone on the ground that they are two perfectly innocent people, and that all the evidence that points to them is purely accidental. I am, frankly, in a complete muddle as to what has happened, and have tried to write a chapter that anybody can use to prove anything they like.

APPENDIX II

NOTES ON MOORING OF BOAT

(Extract from letter from John Rhode)

I, TOO, wanted it to be necessary to get into the boat in order to cast it off or make it fast again. Now, as it happens, in a river with a considerable rise and fall of tide (as this river must have had, to account for the swiftness of the ebb and flow of the tidal stream), this is nearly always necessary, if it is desired to keep the boat afloat at all states of the tide. One method of mooring a boat under these circumstances is as I visualised it.

The mooring-post is driven into the bed of the stream, beyond low-water mark, in water deep enough to float the boat at all times. A hard, made of a few loads of stone, is run from the bank to low-water mark, to save ploughing through the mud. A ring-bolt is fixed at the shore end of this hard.

Now, having been out in the boat, you want to come ashore. Right. Make fast the painter to the mooring-post. Pole the boat round till her stern touches the hard. Jump ashore, taking with you the end of a light line, made fast at the other end to the ring in the stern of the boat. Then push the boat off again, and make fast your end of the line to the ring-bolt on shore, adjusting the length of the line so that the boat lies parallel, during the ebb, with the bank.

Having had your drink, you want to put off again. Cast off the line, and haul the stern of the boat in till it touches the hard. Jump in with the line up in the stern. Go forward, haul in on painter till you are near enough to the post, then cast off.

I gather that you want someone to get into the boat and cast off the painter. As you will see, unless the boat is approached by water, this is necessary in any case. In describing the incident, remember how the boat swings. During the ebb the boat lies as described. But during the flood the stern will swing in of itself, and will remain touching the shore throughout the flood. This, of course, does not matter since the water is rising.

Remember, too, that any particular point in the tidal phase occurs (near enough for this purpose) about three-quarters of an hour later on successive days. Don't make it high-water at 10 a.m. one day and low-water at 11 a.m. the next. Also, in a river like this, the tide ebbs longer than it flows. I laid down rules for this particular river, though I don't remember them exactly now, for the guidance of those who followed.

As for the distance of the pole from high-water mark, you can, within limits, make this to suit yourself. If you allow twelve feet or more, measuring horizontally, between H.W.O.S.T. and L.W.O.S.T., and six feet or more between L.W.O.S.T. and the post, you won't be far wrong. These distances can be increased almost indefinitely, but I shouldn't decrease them much, or you will make your bank awkwardly steep.

COUNSEL'S OPINION
ON FITZGERALD'S WILL

HAVE looked up your point in the library this afternoon and the result of my researches, for what they are worth, is that it certainly has been held again and again, where a certain person's consent to marriage was required and that person had died by act of God, or at least by no fault of the beneficiary, the condition requiring a particular consent is void.

None of the cases run the thing so fine that there is only twenty-four hours between the death of the person whose consent is required and the wedding of the beneficiary who wants an absolute title to the property, and I think it would be necessary, where the death is within twenty-four hours of the ceremony, for the beneficiary, in order to get her absolute right, if there were any contest, to show:

Either (1) That she intended to ask the necessary consent before the marriage ceremony;

(2) That she was prevented by the death, and would have had time to ask consent but for the death;

and (3) If suggested that the death was any fault of hers, to defend herself against the allegation;

or else That the ceremony was not arranged until after death had made it impossible to obtain the necessary consent. Provided this last is true, it matters not how soon after the death the beneficiary claims to treat the condition as void.

As to the last possibility, I am no authority on marriage licences, but from the books it appears that provided one party has resided *fifteen* days *in the locality in which it is intended the marriage should take place,* notice may be given to the registrar by that party and a marriage licence obtained from the registrar after the lapse of one full week-day—in law language in forty-two to forty-eight hours, provided Sunday does not intervene.

This procedure is applicable to marriages in any other place than the established church, i.e., registrar's office, or Nonconformist place of worship licensed for marriages.

Without the fifteen days of previous residence the business takes longer.

Once obtained a marriage licence is available for quite a long time: three months I think, but you might verify this. It is possible that one of your parties had got a licence and was waiting for a favourable opportunity for the beneficiary to ask the necessary consent. This sort of licence is only granted for marriage in a particular place. See Whitaker.

In the case of conditions, subsequent, if the condition is impossible through the act of God, the gift remains, tho' there may be a gift over on non-performance of the condition. *For instance, if the person whose consent to a marriage is required dies before the marriage.*

Collett v Collett. 35. B. 312.

In this case the widowed mother's consent to marriage was required. The mother died in 1856.

In July, 1865, her daughter Helena married.

Master of the Rolls held "that the gift over (i.e., to remainder man in case of life tenancy only) will not take effect, if the performance of the condition has become impossible thro' the act of God, and *no default of the person who had to perform it.*

"Here it is reasonably certain that the mother, if she had lived, would have given her consent to this marriage, one eligible in all respects."

The principle is the presumption of the testator not requiring the performance of impossibilities, and that his intention will be substantially carried into effect by permitting it to be executed as far as can be done.

"The condition having become impossible by act of God, her estate for life is become absolute." *Aislabie v. Rice.* 3 Mad. 25 C.

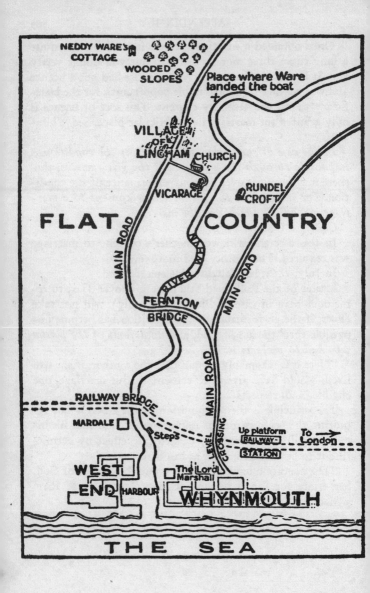